'OF MANY HEROES'

'OF MANY HEROES'

An Indian Essay in Literary Historiography

G.N. DEVY

Orient BlackSwan

'OF MANY HEROES': AN INDIAN ESSAY IN LITERARY HISTORIOGRAPHY

Orient Blackswan Private Limited

Registered Office
3-6-752 Himayatnagar, Hyderabad 500 029, Telangana, India

Other Offices
Bengaluru, Bhopal, Chennai, Guwahati,
Hyderabad, Jaipur, Kolkata, Lucknow,
Mumbai, New Delhi, Noida, Patna, Vijayawada

First Edition 1998
This paperback edition 2017

025723
30062017

ISBN 978-93-86689-17-7

Typeset at
Techastra Solutions Pvt. Ltd, Hyderabad 500 033

Printed in India at
B. B. Press, Noida

Published by
Orient Blackswan Private Limited
3-6-752 Himayatnagar,
Hyderabad 500 029, Telangana, India
e-mail: info@orientblackswan.com

For Sujit Mukherjee and Meenakshi Mukherjee
path-finders

We are unaware of the beginning and the end of the world:
The first and last pages of this old book have fallen away...

From the *Shahjahan-nama* by Abu Talib Kalim,
seventeenth century historian and poet

Contents

Acknowledgements *ix*

Introduction to the Paperback Edition *xi*

1. Some Indian Questions 1
2. History and Literary History 5
3. Time and Territory 11
4. Two Paradigms of History 17
5. Bhartrihari's Metaphors 21
6. The Conventions of Literary History 29
7. Jnanadeva's Agenda 46
8. Pre-Colonial Historiography 56
9. Warton's Imaginative Savages 66
10. Jones and the 'Gentoos' 75
11. Formation and Transformation of a Canon 84
12. Some Western Approaches to Literary History 98
13. Post-Colonial Indian Approaches 108
14. Para-Literature 134
15. *Swa* and *Para*: Self and the Other 143
16. Tradition and Transactions 148
17. Translation as Origin 152
18. The Course and the Discourse of History 157
19. Nation in Narration 161
20. The Garden and the Forest 166

Notes and References *169*

Annotated Bibliography *186*

Index *210*

Acknowledgements

I would like to thank the following individuals and institutions:

The Forbes Gujarat Sabha of Bombay and Dr. Prabodh Parikh for inviting me to lecture in June 1988 on 'Literary History'; The Gujarat Sahitya Parishad, Ahmedabad and Dr. Chandrakant Topiwala for asking me to give the Gujarat University Lecture for 1989 on 'Literary History'; The Commonwealth Centre for Literary and Cultural Change at The University of Virginia and Prof. Ralph Cohen for inviting me to lecture on 'Indian Literary History: Colonialism and Amnesia';

The Department of English at the Maharaja Sayajirao University of Baroda for allowing me to teach courses in Comparative Literature and Literary History and students in these courses for shaping my approach to Comparative Literature;

Prof. Dieter Riemenschneider of Goethe University, Frankfurt, Prof. Sisir Kumar Das of Delhi University, Prof. Vilas Sarang of Bombay University, Prof. Wolfgang Zach of the University at Graz, Prof. Manavendra Bandopadhya of Jadavpur University for inviting me to seminars on literary history, comparative literature, literary translation, para-literature, and related topics;

New Quest, Etad, Bombay Literary Review, Critical Practice, Litcrit for publishing sections of this book in previous versions; Mrs. Niyati Derasari-Pandya and Dr. Shirish Panchal for translating some sections into Gujarati;

The British Council for a grant-in-aid to consult library resources in Britain in summer 1988, and the Association of Commonwealth Universities at London for the THB Symons Fellowship award, 1991.

The School of English at the University of Leeds, and its Head, Prof. Inga-Stina Ewbank, and the Department of English, Media and

Theater Studies at the University of Ulster at Coleraine, and its Head, Prof. Robert Welch for providing excellent academic facilities;

The Staff at the Brotherton Library in Leeds, the University Library at Coleraine and the Sterling Library at Yale;

Mr. S.K. Rana and Ms. Deepa Hari for helping me in preparing the final draft and Ms. Alphy J. Plakkoottam for preparing the press copy.

Though this book has been long in preparation, a substantial part of it was composed during my affiliation with the University of Ulster at Coleraine in August–September 1991. During my entire stay Prof. Robert Welch and Mrs. Angela Welch looked after me with utmost generosity and affection. I do not know how to thank them.

The draft I prepared at the University of Ulster at Coleraine was revised and extended during my tenure as a Fulbright Fellow at the University of Yale, New Haven. I have had the benefit of several discussions with Prof. Geoffrey Hartman during my stay there between April and October 1992. I am also thankful to him for introducing me to Prof. Rene Wellek, the most important scholar of literary historiography in our time.

The main inspiration for this book comes from the historiographical work by Dr. Sujit Mukherjee. As a modest token of the acknowledgement of that debt, I dedicate this book to him and to Prof. Meenakshi Mukherjee, whose scholarship I have admired over the last three decades.

G.N. Devy
Baroda/Leeds/Coleraine/New Haven
1991–97

Introduction to the Paperback Edition

Quarter of a century ago, when I fancied the lines from Abu Talib Kalim's seventeenth-century *Shahjahan-nama* for the epigraph of this 'essay', I was not aware that one day they would literally apply to this book, in which form my essay was published. Indeed by now, the first and the last few pages of my personal copy of '*Of Many Heroes*' have come off. I imagine this would also be the case with its copies in various libraries. If for nothing else but this purely material reason, I am happy that the book is being re-issued as a paperback, and that it will be available at a more affordable price to students. As it was conceived and written in an era which the present generation of students may consider 'a long time back', a brief introduction to the book may be in order.

Prior to writing '*Of Many Heroes*', I had written another essay under the title *After Amnesia*, in which I had discussed the state of literary criticism in the *bhashas*. It had some elaborate discussion on the clash of cultures that the colonial experience brought to our lot, and the strange effects of that clash on our cultural memory. Two of these effects highlighted in that essay were a) our undue reverence for Western forms of knowledge, and b) our inordinate glorification of the ancient Indian past. In *After Amnesia*, I was pitching for revisiting the present in terms of its own complexities and a turning away from the intellectually distant past (*purva*) and from the culturally distant West (*paschim*). When I was writing the essay, I was not clear whether it would be published, if published whether it would be read, and if read whether it would be well-received. Therefore, for two or three years after I completed writing it, I kept away the typed pages of the manuscript in a state of uncertain existence. It was Dr Sujit Mukherjee who encouraged me to send it to

Orient Longman, as the publishing house was called at that time. As the publishers decided to take it up, I thought of adding more material to the manuscript in order to give the essay more substance. However, in those years, I was occupied in various social activities, which made it impossible for me to write more than just a few pages. I appended those pages to the essay as an epilogue. The concluding sentence of the epilogue to *After Amnesia* read, 'We need to get over the sense of guilt through an open-eyed approach to history in order to build a modern Indian critical discourse.'

When I could free myself from my social commitments, I decided to return to this question of 'an open-eyed approach to history'. '*Of Many Heroes*' was the result. Therefore, the two essays form a single argument, and if read together should make better sense. And therefore too, I did not think it necessary to write an introduction to '*Of Many Heroes*'. The best introduction to it was—I thought—the preceding essay: *After Amnesia*.

As I was writing different sections of this book, I had the essay structure in mind. In order to ensure that it is not misunderstood as a book written in chapters, I took an extra care of stating so in the subtitle of the book: 'An Indian Essay in Literary Historiography'. The opening and concluding lines of every section were clearly phrased to mark the continuities. Thus, the first 13 sections formed a continuous single narrative, and the last seven sections were provided to underscore the theoretical underpinnings of the argument. However, when the print copy of my typescript was being prepared, the typesetter perhaps felt that placing the sections as self-contained segments—as short essays—might make the text look less ponderous and more palatable for the readers. I was aware that this would reduce the gravity of my argument. Yet—I do not recall exactly why—I did not try to argue with the typesetter. The result was the first edition of '*Of Many Heroes*', which appeared under the imprint of Orient Longman in 1998. Since books have their life and sanctity, I did not wish to suggest to the publishers, now Orient BlackSwan, to reconfigure the text and make it look like a single essay. I am happy to leave it as it is.

'*Of Many Heroes*' is kind of a 'history' of literary history in India. It begins with the rejection of the nineteenth-century European idea of history as a continuous narrative, and tries to explore if any alternate ways of re-telling the past would make any better sense of 'things as they were'. Towards this end, I tried to re-visit several 'takes' on literary past available in the past eras of Indian literature. I was curious to know how a Kalidasa, an Akkama or a Kabir would have looked at their 'traditions', how various theorists would have construed their idea of 'the past'. This search was the reason for my naming the essay 'An Indian Essay in Historiography', rather than calling it 'An Essay on Indian Historiography'. In other words, I was trying to see if it would be possible to 'think Indian' while dealing with the history of Indian literature. However, my aim was not to promote one or the other ways of looking at the literary past available in various Indian traditions of philosophy or knowledge. The aim was rather to establish that there are many possible ways of doing so.

After locating these possibilities and discussing their main features, I, in this essay, turn to take stock of the theoretical positions in literary historiography in the West, as they developed from the eighteenth century onward. One could have gone back to the ancient past and discussed some of those fascinating philosophical positions in Greek and Latin. However, as my focus was India, I thought it would be proper to examine only the texts available during the centuries when the stock of Indian knowledge and philosophical assumptions started getting impacted by Western schools of thought. Hence, I begin with Warton's *History*, and then move to the times of William Jones and the rise of what we call the 'modern history' in India. This brings me to the question of the *plurality* of the Western literary historiography accessible to modern Indian historians of literature. Finally, I describe the multiplicity of approaches to literary history which prevailed in India during the twentieth century. All in all, this is an essay that demonstrates and celebrates the 'many-ness' of approaches to literary history.

One may ask: do I have any specific theoretical approach? Keeping that probable question in view, I have discussed in the last seven sections of the essay the issues and assumptions involved in formulating a theory of history and historiography. My conclusion is that, given the nature of history as a phenomenon, more specifically that of 'literary' history—an existence with a constantly shifting semantic address—it would be most realistic to accept many histories as being equally unreliable or reliable as re-presentations of the past. Accepting diversity would be our way out of any one-track adherence to the past or the West.

When I was working on this essay, in 1990–91, I was not so acutely aware as I am now that the question of history may assume such disproportionately high centrality to the political discourse in

India during the coming three decades. As I look back in retrospect to arguments and debates during the last quarter century, the replacement of old myths by new myths, of old deification by new deification, the new environ of folklore about history, I notice that 'history'—constructed rightly or wrongly—is now replacing 'argument'. It seems that the great creativity that the Indian intellectuals showed during the times of the freedom struggle—the colonial era, to be precise—or even the great originality that the poets and thinkers of the bhasha period—the medieval ages, as it is popularly known—brought to bear upon the social discourse, seem to have hit a parched course. The recent, and entirely unproductive, emphasis on restructuring history has brought us to a situation where speaking in metaphors and even euphemisms alone allows one the space for intellectual interrogation. Yet, I shall venture into briefly stating my observations.

The struggle for independence in India was also to some extent a struggle for decolonising our minds. M. K. Gandhi's *Hind Swaraj* (1909) is the most classic of the statements in that direction. The struggle for independence was also at the same time our struggle to create a new nation with a humane society that would be ready to uphold the ideas of equality and dignity of every individual. B.R. Ambedkar's *Annihilation of Caste* (1936) is the most passionate plea to bring about this transformation in India. In some sense, the two founding fathers of India had indicated, between the two of them, how it would be necessary to reject the entire baggage that the West brings to us in the name of modernity, or the past brings to us in the name of nativity. During the post-Gandhi-Ambedkar era in India, their ideas were gradually turned into a ritualistic memory and were subverted. The rejection of the oppressive West came to be seen as an unquestioning adherence to the past, and the freedom from the oppressive past came to be seen as alienation from the past, together with an unmatched enthusiasm for imbibing the West. This has reduced the India of today to a society without any great central idea, an idea that will free us further and move us forward in history. We are caught between the tyranny of reductive nationalism and reductive secularism. I believe that acceptance of diversity may help us in going beyond the present reactionary era. Diversity can be an ideal useful for deepening our democracy, securing our biodiversity, our cultural diversity and for setting right our perspectives on life, culture and history. I would like to hope that, from that perspective, '*Of Many Heroes*' is probably still a relevant work. I hope the young scholars of today will read it in that perspective, without reducing it to being a book of denials. I hope the critical affirmation of the diversity in '*Of Many Heroes*' will not be easily overlooked.

G.N. Devy
Dharwad
1 December 2016

1

Some Indian Questions

Indian literature is a historian's despair. The three thousand years of its past, within which there is an amazing recurrence of trends, styles and themes, makes a mockery of periodization. The profound interdependence between religion, philosophy and literature in India defies assessment in terms of the aesthetic categories evolved in the modern West; and the healthy acceptance of certain kinds of re-renderings (particularly those originating in the epics) as 'original' works raises important philosophical questions about the nature of literature as a form of creativity. The multiplicity of cultures, sects and languages in India poses an incredibly difficult challenge to literary comparatism. All modern literary languages in India, of the Dravidian family as well as of the Indo-Aryan family, have had intimate literary exchanges with the ancient Sanskrit, Pali and Prakrit languages, the medieval Apabhramsa languages as well as Persian and Arabic, and modern European languages (primarily English but also, in some cases, Portuguese and French). Besides, there have been similar exchanges between the Dravidian languages and the modern Indo-Aryan languages, and, inevitably, within the Dravidian and Indo-Aryan languages. Altogether, the cultural history of literatures in Indian languages is far more complex than one imagines.

The oldest among the living literary languages in India, Tamil, has a continuous history of three thousand years. The youngest among the literary languages in India, English, has a history, within the Indian context, of not more than two hundred years. Histories of other literatures stretch in between these two outer limits. Kannada has a literary history of fifteen hundred years, Marathi about eight hundred years, and Oriya five hundred years. Obviously, a single historiographic formula cannot prove adequate to describe each and every literature in India. The appropriateness of a common approach is further called to question by the fact that there is a vast variation of sociology, culture and political history from language to language. Some languages such as Sanskrit, Persian and English have been the languages of political domination; other languages have been for most part of their history the dominated languages. Some languages have had the sociology of trade, industry and a general economic prosperity. Others have had a sociology of combative survival. These variations are naturally reflected in the respective literatures. In addition to these native differences in the contexts of Indian literature, there were differences added to them by a large variety of interactions with the two experiences of prolonged political domination by foreign cultures. Of these the Islamic domination affected the northern languages and literatures more profoundly, and gave India a new literary language, Urdu. The British colonial domination affected the upper layers of Indian society, mainly in the urban areas, giving another literary language to India, the Indo-English. A literary historiography not sensitive to the range and complexity of differences in Indian literary traditions stands the risk of distorting its subject.

Literary history as practised in India in the twentieth century has been greatly interested in devising critical labels for periods, genres, styles and schools of literary writing. It has certainly made impressive achievements in locating documentary sources and textual evidences towards constructing narratives of literary practices in India. The beginning of this difficult task of constructing historical narratives about India was made by European Indologists during the nineteenth century; and, in the course of time, when they left, Indian scholars took over. Thus the sense of history institutionalised in modern literary historiography in India is mainly of Western origin. Since the context for this development was that of colonialism, the Western sense of history came to be considered in India as the universally valid sense of history. This practice has two damaging consequences for the field of literary study in India: one, the question whether India ever had any sense of literary history of its own before the contact with the modern. West became a permanently sealed question; and two, there exists an inevitable gap between the nature of histories of various Indian literatures and the master-narrative employed to construct these histories. In recent years there has been a movement towards re-defining the goals of literary historiography in India. This movement comes mainly from the advocates of comparative literary study; but much of its brilliance and energy are devoted to postulating a non-existent pan-Indian field of literary study, an 'Indian Literature' though it is composed in several dozen languages.

Since the question of alterity is implicit in colonialism, the cognitive exchanges between the confronting cultures take place necessarily in terms of closed concepts. The rituals of cultural exchange cautiously guarded by the rules of domination render an equal exchange impossible. During the colonial period a static image of India was circulated in the West, and a static image of the West was circulated in India. The Western sense of literature, and the Western sense of history of literature, which in fact have been fields of cultural thought full of cross-currents and radical disagreements, are seen by Indian literary scholars as relatively stable structures of unified thought which can be transplanted in India. It would be interesting to enquire whether the discourse of literary history, which was in the making precisely during the period of high colonialism, was not in any way influenced by Europe's colonial encounter with the rest of the world, and what, if any, is the relationship of 'knowledge' to 'power' in that discourse. One of the aims of this essay is to discuss, in relation to the major issues briefly outlined above, the gap between Indian literature and the current practices in literary historiography.

An attempt is made here to reconstruct the conventions of literary history in India prior to India's colonial encounter with the modern West. The area of traditional historiography in India is indeed very vast, and within the scope of the present essay no more than a bare outline can be offered. My attempt is not to prove that the discipline of historiography existed in ancient and medieval India in the form acceptable to contemporary fashions in literary study. I have merely tried to point out that a certain amount of textual evidence is available in Sanskrit, the bhashas and Persian to indicate the nature of historiographical consciousness in ancient and medieval India. I have further tried to explore the dependence of Western literary historiography on the experience of colonizing other cultures. That exploration, it is hoped, will provide the proper context to understand the shift in Indian literary historiography from the pre-colonial conventions of history to post-colonial approaches to literary history. A brief account of some major twentieth century theories of literary history in the West is presented in order to indicate how the contemporary Indian approaches are substantially different in orientation. Since the history of literature in Indian languages is governed by their specific cultural features, it becomes, necessary to bring in a discussion of these features. The concluding sections of this essay, therefore, move in the direction of a theoretical discussion of issues pertaining to some unique aspects of Indian literary culture.

The primary aim of this essay is not to refute Western literary historiography. The aim is also not to substitute in place of the current historiographical practices some new or more appropriate practice. This essay is not an attempt at fresh theorizing. Its simple aim is to understand and review the conventions of literary historiography in ancient, medieval, colonial and contemporary India. If, in the process, my explorations are found to have any theoretical substance, it should be seen as an entirely unintended effect.

2

History and Literary History

History did not emerge as a discipline until it became the basis for ideological rhetoric. Whether it was initiated by the revolutionary intellectual or Napoleon Bonaparte himself, the striking worker in the British factories or the white colonizers, every procedure of power-acquisition commenced in the West with the claim of being on the right side of History. Similarly, the emergence of literary history as a 'subject' is intimately linked with the rise of literature as a means of social domination.[1] As is the case in Europe, so too in India. When literature gets institutionalized, it gets into classrooms and, in turn, becomes an instrument of class-division. That is when a given literature generates the rhetoric of its history.

Literary history is basically an apparatus of canon formation, which is a process of drawing and re-drawing the boundaries of fields of literary production in terms of what is socially acceptable or unacceptable. Literary history reflects the values of the society in which the historian lives, or for which he writes. A history of literature without these values and the judgements implicit in them is as impossible as a state without power-structures. Justification of the authority wielding power is in fact the main purpose of canons.

Panini, the ancient Indian linguist, had a good insight into the procedures of canon formation. Commenting on canonical language, the *updishtha*, he says, it is the community of the learned, the *shishtha*, that decides what is good in language.[2] And it is their language ability that decides who are learned. So the learned decide what is learning, which decides who is learned. But when it was pointed out to him that this is a circuitous argument, he confessed that it is the social consent that ultimately puts the stamp of recognition on the learned, vesting in them the authority and the function of legitimizing language. Canon formation is thus the process of translating the rules of social domination to the field of aesthetic creation.

What the exact relationship between the growth of colonialism and the development of literary historiography has been in Europe has not been studied so far. However, it is worth noting that the earliest literary history in English, Thomas Warton's *History of English Poetry* (1774),[3] came about the same time as the earliest translations of Oriental literary texts by European scholars. The earliest historians and historiographers of literature in Germany were themselves scholars of Oriental languages. Wilhelm von Humboldt published *On the Task of the Historian* (1821), which influenced the *History of the Poetic National Literature of the Germans* (1835-42) of Gervinus, who also authored *Fundamentals of the Theory of Historiography.*[4] All through the nineteenth century history, historiography and literary history developed rapidly in the world of European scholarship. Colonialism and nationalism provided the appropriate background for this development.

Primarily, canon and nation were the two goals of European literary historiography.[5] However, histories have also been written keeping in view forms of literature, genres and sub-genres, style-epochs; single author, influence and reception; gender, class and race; philosophic, political and social contexts; and periods of literature. At the same time literary history has received attention from philosophers and literary theorists. Thus during the last two centuries literary history has been a dynamic field of literary study.

Though the expression 'literary history' does not accurately reflect the major themes and concerns of this field, the designation has acquired stability. The main problem that the expression poses is that if a narrative is literary, it ceases to be history. On the other hand, if it is historical, it ceases to be literary. One would have liked to replace the expression with a more suitable one. However, critical expressions come to acquire their privileges through long historical processes which are better left uncontested. What is more important here is to note that, whether it is the organic vision of history or the analytical vision of history within which a historian works, literary history has to negotiate a highly problematic relationship between the objective and the subjective. It is so for the obvious reason that 'literary history' at once refers to two different, if interdependent, systems of signs: (*a*) the past of a literary tradition as it *was*, the system of signs that literary texts form, and (*b*) a narration *about* the past of a literary tradition, the system of signs that represents the past.

Whatever be one's vision of history, literary history cannot escape the fate of being a narrative, a kind of fiction which represents an order of signs in past existence. The narrative gets further complicated because literary signs are no less complex than events in human existence, whereas the degree of freedom with which a historian can narrate them is relatively restricted. The discourse of literary history is required to operate within the conditions imposed upon it by the nature of language, logic and reality that literary history deals with.[6]

Historical narratives not only order events to be represented, but also select them: and quite often these events are invented by historians. The process of exclusion and inclusion of events in historical narratives is tacitly guided by the general principles of inclusion and exclusion sanctioned by the community for which, and within which, the narrative is being constructed. It is these principles, which remain almost entirely unarticulated, that constitute a community's sense of self. In fact, the same sense of self, in relation to the associated sense of the other, becomes the community's sense of tradition when projected onto a vaster temporal scale. Literary history, like other forms of historical narrative, can but represent through symbolic selection of texts this unconscious sense of tradition formed collectively and unconsciously by a community of readers. Yet, the sense of self itself is considerably influenced by works of literature in its oral and written forms. The historiographical community is not a community tightly sealed off from literary practice and participation. If literary history is moulded by a community's sense of the self-other relationship, this sense itself originates, to some extent, in literature and language. Literature and the historical consciousness of literature in fact form a continuity, which literary history intercepts temporarily, and, thus, creates a fiction.

As in other forms of narration, in literary history too the narrator does not have unconditional and uncontroverted space to construct the narrative. The historian has to be involved in the narration not as a disinterested analyst but as a politically preconstituted subject. The narration is conditioned, therefore, by the conscious or the unconscious ideology of race, class and gender within which the historian's intellectual sympathies are engaged. It can be said that every historical narrative was written in the ideological space within the consciousness of the historian much before it was written in language.

Histories may be fiction; yet, the temporal sequencing in history does not have the same degree of freedom as the temporal sequencing in fiction. For instance, one cannot begin a historical narrative in the present and lead it backward in time. This binding is accepted by history because the discourse of history is required to have consistency with the dominant concepts of space and time that the community of its readers puts into circulation as meaningful concepts. Fiction has the verbal space and a fictional time to allow it a greater freedom of temporal movement. The concept of time and the temporal scale employed by literary history have to have a sanction from what the community of its users believes to be rational.

Literary events differ from other historical events in that literary events do not affect the material world in the same way as the 'real' historical events affect it. Literary events are 'virtual' events. On the other hand, literary events, such as plays or poems, have the capacity to survive over long periods of time; and every time they are encountered, they may take on a fresh life. Clearly, literary events belong to a different order of events. Besides, history deals clearly with past events, whereas literary history has to deal with events which seem to belong to the past but also belong to the present. History mediates between the readers of the narrative and the past that is narrated; but in the case of literary history this mediation is superfluous because the readers of literary history have direct personal access to the past literary events.

If the superfluity of literary history stems from its being language about indestructible language, it also faces a limitation on account of being a narrative about a discourse of language, a tradition or convention of literature. Literary history may be a narrative; but the exact form it will or should take depends on the nature of the events to be narrated. Not all narratives are good enough for each and every kind of literary tradition. In fact, it is always the literary events themselves that guide the discourse and mode of literary history.

At the same time, like fiction, history of literature depends on a prior existence of conventions of historical writings for its own survival and growth. History and so also literary history are not inventions that can be suddenly made by a genius of great imagination in any given period. Both disciplines acquire identity and visibility through slow progressions during which these disciplines acquire the ability to represent happenings. In other words, literary history initially has to develop its system of symbolic representation—in which gradation, classification, designation become symbolic modes—simultaneously as it orders and selects literary events. All subsequent developments in the field try to systematize the symbolic system of representation.

If literary history, like other forms of history, is indeed a form of fiction, it cannot take birth unless a community has invented fiction as a medium of encountering life and the universe. The development of history in any given society will correspond to the development of fiction and its status as a mode of organizing perceptions in that society. The forms of history too will correspond to the forms of fiction. Besides, since literary history is expected to account for the aesthetic fluctuations within a literary tradition, it has to employ standards of excellence, criteria of assessment, categories of description and other apparatus developed by literary criticism, theory and aesthetics. Hence any historical narrative depends for its cognitive ability on the status of criticism and theory backing it up.[7] In turn, criticism and theory depend on developments in other disciplines such as philosophy, linguistics, anthropology, political thought and psychology. On the other hand, literary criticism itself depends on developments in literature, and, therefore, on the cognitive store of literary history. Thus, literary history is an involved interdisciplinary enterprise.

Conceding that the discourse of literary history is severely restricted, does it have any space of its own to form an interpretative discipline, with what R.S. Crane calls, 'the critical and historical principles' of its own? The answer to this polemical question is in pointing out not the theoretical viability but the historical necessity of its existence. The answer is that it *is* there, that it has come to stay in modern intellectual pursuits.

In fact, literary history has been at the very heart of academic study and research of literature all over the world during the last two centuries, and, even if in a different form, much longer in India. What is taught as literature in schools and universities all over the world is some form of historical representation of literature rather than the process of literary creativity itself. Institutionalized study of literature turns literary history into the means of raising powerful and persuasive myths about literature, privileging some areas of creativity and repressing or concealing others. No literature, recognised as literature, escapes the fate of being represented by literary historiographers.

3

Time and Territory

Structures of historical narratives invariably depend on the sense of time shared by the community for which the narratives are produced. Concepts of time, in turn, are interlocked with other cultural constructs. Western discourses of knowledge about non-Western societies assume that the concept of time operative in traditional societies is 'cyclical'. This other sense of time is opposed to the 'linear' sense of time in Western societies. Often, the imitative scholarship in non-Western nations tends to accept this facile distinction as a valid philosophic observation.

'Cyclical' and 'linear' are in fact only historiographical notions and not attributes either of time or of the perceiving human consciousness. The distinction, whatever its source, accurately reflects the unequal power positions of the cultures having a 'linear' sense of time (the colonizing cultures) and those with a 'cyclical' sense of time (the cultures that were colonized). Similarly, it is claimed that the communities that have not mastered their immediate natural environment live in some kind of 'mythical' or 'magical' time. In mythologies all over the world one comes across the notion of a supernatural keeper of time. Similarly, most schools of metaphysics accept the idea of eternity, time beyond human grasp, as an objective fact. The origin of a community's sense of time can be traced to its perception of the geographical space which it inhabits.

Ancient Indian iconography recognised the interdependence between notions of Time and Space by depicting Time as a coiled serpent, the *Ananta*, who forms the seat or bed of Vishnu, the supporter of Space. Heinrich Zimmer comments on the representation of the *sheshashayi* posture of Vishnu:

> Vishnu sleeps. Like a spider that has climbed up the thread that once issued from its own organism, drawing

> it back into itself, the god has consumed again the web of the universe. Alone upon the immortal substance of the ocean, a giant figure, submerged partly, partly afloat, he takes delight in slumber. There is no one to behold him, no one to comprehend him; there is no knowledge of him, except within himself.
> This giant, "Lord of Maya", and the cosmic ocean on which he is recumbent, are dual manifestations of a single essence; for the ocean, as well as the human form, is Vishnu. Furthermore, since in Hindu mythology the symbol for water is the serpent (*naga*), Vishnu is presented, normally, as reposing on the coils of a prodigious snake, his favourite symbolic animal, the serpent Ananta, "Endless". So that, not only the gigantic anthropomorphic form and the boundless element, but the reptile too is Vishnu. It is on a serpent ocean of his own immortal substance that the Cosmic Man passes the universal night.[1]

The interdependence of the notions of space and the notions of time, their essential unity, is depicted in Hindu myth as much as in Hindu art. Ananta, the symbol for time, is endless and yet potentially a figure that moves forward, one of its motions is cyclical and the other linear. In Hindu iconography Vishnu is the mythological figure in whose person Time and Space unite.

Myths compress vast temporal spans within the brief moment of narration probably because they are created in communities which imagine themselves to be living at the centre of the vast space engulfing them. Myth is thus the earliest science that reduces space to humanly perceptible measures.

The quest for creating historical narratives originates in communities that have acquired the intellectual means of arriving at complex spatial abstractions, or alternately have political control of vast territories. The great Indian epic *Mahabharata* was called in its earlier and simpler form *Jaya*, which was *itihasa*, history of a king's triumph in a war. Thus, the intimate relationship between territorial conquest and creation of historical narrative is owned in the initial title of the *Mahabharata.* The Homeric epics in the Greek language show a comparable intimacy between the sense of time and the sense of territorial possession. Virgil's *Aeneid* can be cited as the third great illustration of this correspondence.

At an abstract level the modern discipline of Psychology provides a fascinating story of history replacing myth in correspondence with the associated sense of mental space. In Greek mythology, Psyche was believed to be a beautiful young princess, so beautiful that she caused much jealousy among other princesses. Not only were her two older sisters jealous of her, but also the goddess Aphrodite. The jealous goddess ordered Cupid, or Eros, to inspire Psyche with love for the vilest among men; but, as it always happens in myths, Cupid himself fell in love with her and started visiting her secretly every night. The jealous sisters of Psyche told her that the person she embraced in the darkness every night was a hideous monster. So, Psyche lighted her lamp while Cupid slept, and she saw the most beautiful of the gods. However, as she stared at him, a drop of hot oil fell on his shoulder. It woke him up, and he fled. She then wandered in search of him, till, at last, she found him; and the two entered into an immortal union.[2] This myth, contained most of the central concerns of Freudian psychoanalysis: jealousy, desire, sex, fear, guilt, nostalgia, quest for pleasure, and the revolt of the youngest sister (the Ego) against the two older sisters (the Super Ego and the Reality Principle). The atmosphere in the traditional story full of darkness, desire and deception is in consonance with Freud's conception of the working of the mind. Freud's achievement was that he turned this myth into a historical narrative by introducing temporality in terms of a sequence of the stages through which the mind is formed: the subconscious associated with childhood or the primitive followed by the more accessible parts of the consciousness associated with the adult and the civilized aspects of life. Thus the mapping of the territory of consciousness resulted in the case of Freudian psychoanalysis in turning a myth into a neat historical narrative. When the initial mapping of the inner space acquired more empirical evidence, the history of human consciousness was further extended beyond the province of the individual's psyche into the collective unconscious and racial memory.

Communities confined to relatively small geographical areas are content with the local folklore for their history and mythology. On the other hand, communities poised for vast territorial explorations or occupation tend to project aggressive historical images. The *Ramayana* describes the entire genealogy of Rama, giving this character an immense historical proportion; on the other hand the vanquished Ravana is given a relatively compressed historical representation. When spatially dispossessed societies involve themselves in attempts to regain their territorial autonomy, they often tend to create fresh and alluring images of their past. The Celtic Revival in Ireland at the beginning of the twentieth century, or the so called Indian Renaissance with its revival of tradition, are some important examples of this tendency.

If, as conjectured so far, the human attitude to time is so closely intertwined with the human attitude to space, perhaps then, the rise of History as an academic and political project towards the end of the eighteenth century in Europe, its subsequent growth during the nineteenth century, and the attendant development of historiography during the last two hundred years may have had a corresponding sequence of attitudes towards territorial control. Of course, such interdependence cannot be proved through any mechanical and uniform formula. Nor can one expect this initial correspondence to guide the disciplines of history and historiography beyond the most elementary stages of their birth and spread. Nevertheless, it will not be amiss to assume that the European colonial aspiration of establishing political and administrative order over unimaginably vast geographical areas directly affected Europe's desire to create an intellectual order within its own history. There is another dimension to this hypothesis, one of greater importance to us in India.

If colonization gives a boost to historiography in the colonizing cultures, it also creates serious historiographical inversions for the colonized cultures. Colonization adds to the history of the colonizers; it also takes away some history of the colonized. As examples of this process of dehistoriation one can think of the disciplines of Anthropology and Orientalism. Anthropology, a science of the study of primitive[1] cultures, a science created in Europe, places its subject out of the flow of history first, before analysing it. Orientalism, another science thus created for the study of the 'once civilized' cultures, freezes parts of the historical flow to which its subject belongs. In it, the ancient Orient is given precedence over the contemporary Orient. Repression or reversal of history of other societies is an attribute of colonialism because it seeks to make comparable territorial ingression.

As the structuralist view goes, history is never controlled in isolation and exclusively by some master devices: it is being made and unmade by every single relationship among the constituents of the whole process. To go by this argument, colonialism has had an extremely important role to play in shaping the discourse of history in Europe. E.H. Carr, eminent British historian, admits as much in his comments on recent changes in history:

> What I have called the expansion of reason in our twentieth century revolution has particular consequences for the historian; for the expansion of reason means, in essence, the emergence into history of groups and classes, of people and continents, that hitherto lay outside it... Modern history begins when more and more people emerge into social and political consciousness, become aware of their respective groups as historical entities having a past and a future, and enter fully into history.[3]

Certainly, the history of History (and of literary history) in Europe cannot at all be thought of in isolation from the history of colonization. If one were to try, one could perhaps identify in the story of colonialism the shadows of Ranke, Hegel, Marx, Nietzsche, Collingwood and others.

Given that history as an academic discipline does not dwell on neutral ground, it becomes necessary to re-examine two popular assertions about Indian history; the first is that the Indian sense of time is cyclical, the second that consciousness about history is a unique gift of the West to India, and that such a sense did not exist in India to the same degree as it did in Europe. Any Indian intellectual interested in history is invariably faced with the following two posers: Was there a native historiography in India? And what, if any, is the Indian sense of time? Both these are very large questions. And in the context of general history and historiography some contemporary Indian scholars have tried to face at least one of the two questions. Thanks to their efforts we know much about history in ancient and medieval India. However, literary scholars have not made much progress in understanding the native traditions of literary historiography in India. Sujit Mukherjee makes a tentative beginning towards founding a truly Indian literary historiography, but does not go far enough as he considers literary history to be a discipline entirely of European origin.[4] Probably, the most significant work on literary historiography published in India in recent times is Ram Vilas Sharma's *Bharatiya Sahitya Itihasa ke Samasyaen*. He analyses the linguistic complexity of Indian literature.[5] Similarly, the question of Indian philosophies of time has not attracted adequate scholarly attention within India so far. Anindita Niyogi Balslev's study of time in Indian philosophy points to an area of scholarship that Indian scholars will do well to develop.[6] The recent work by Romila Thapar, *Time as a Metaphor of History: Early India* provides a fascinating example of how explorations in this direction can enrich our understanding not only of history but also of culture and creativity.[7]

The result of not exploring the native conventions of literary history is the failure to understand the native processes of canon-formation and, therefore, the aesthetics of literature. Indian tradition is rich in literary theory. Most of these theories are available to modern Indian scholars as texts to which they cannot relate intellectually. Nor do they understand why the theories disappeared suddenly and mysteriously. These problems come from the general failure to internalize tradition, and from not knowing the means to do so. Again, contemporary histories of literature may generally leave Indian readers unsatisfied; not all that one values in literature is included in these histories.

During the twentieth century, Indian literary scholars have paid much attention to criticism and theory. In comparison, literary history and historiography have remained perilously neglected. If in modern India there *seems* to have occurred a radical break with the Indian literary past, it has nevertheless occurred without a continuous intellectual battling with that past. The break shows no signs of being a historiographical rebellion; it is just a case of simple amnesia that colonization inevitably causes. In order that the intellectual energy expended in the sphere of abstract criticism by modern literary scholars in India should bear the desired fruits it is first necessary to re-examine Indian literary historiography on its own terms.

4

Two Paradigms of History

"History is of two types," writes Rajashekhara, "of a single hero, and of many heroes."[1] The terms employed by the tenth century poet-critic to represent the two types are *parakriya* and *purakalpa,* and his respective illustrations for them, the *Ramayana* and the *Mahabharata.* Rajashekhara, the first Indian critic to propose sociology of literature as a distinct field of study, is so completely forgotten now that this remark of his is likely to be brushed aside as a stray intellectual accident by modern literary scholars. However, it is neither stray nor accidental, for it is integrated with the typology of knowledge as presented in his *Kavyamimansa.* Anticipating the modern term 'humanities', Rajashekhara calls the fields of knowledge described by him *paurusheya vidya,* human sciences. According to him, history is one of the fourteen human sciences. And he does not forget to caution his readers against the popular confusion between *purana* and *itihasa,* myth and history, while pointing out that they have distinct narrative styles.

The semantic range covered by the four terms put to service by Rajashekhara—*purana, itihasa, purakalpa* and *parakriya*— is vast. According to V.V. Apte's dictionary,[2] *pura* means 'in former times', 'up to the present time', 'the east', 'a castle'; *purakalpa* means 'a former creation', 'a story of the past', 'a former age'; and *itihasa* means 'legend' as well as 'tradition recognised as a proof'. The awareness that history is a narrative about the past as well as the past itself, brings Rajashekhara to modern historiographical concerns. Yet, 'tradition recognised as a proof', the acceptance of tradition as the source of legitimation of new experiences, is an aspect of his historiography which sets him off from post-colonial historians of literature.

The typology of knowledge presented by Rajashekhara, and the conceptualizing of history within it, enable us to locate a paradigm of history handed down the generations in Indian intellectual tradition. If this vision of history as a source of intellectual authority and legitimation can at all be placed in opposition to another view of history, perhaps, the terms 'organic' and 'analytical' should be used to designate the two visions. The most crucial difference between the two visions would be that the relationship between the past and the perceiving consciousness is more of mutual accommodation in the organic vision of history, while it is more of mutual appropriation in the analytical vision.

Where does one find an expression of the analytical mode? One is not only tempted to turn immediately to Western discourses of history, but, indeed, the temptation is enhanced by the etymology of 'history' in English. Initially, the Greek *histor* meant 'judge' both a noun and a verb, before it gave rise to *historein*, 'to narrate'. When it was accepted by Latin, it became *historia* and acquired the meaning of 'enquiry'. The English term 'history' combines all these meanings: 'to judge, to narrate, to enquire' as well as 'judgement, narration, enquiry in the past'. Besides, English has given 'history', as have the other modern European languages derived from Latin, the dignity of being a human science. The judgemental tone of historical inquiries in the West points to the analytical vision implicit in them.

Tempting though it is to contrast Rajashekhara's view of history with the views of Western philosophers of history, such a juxtaposition is not really necessary. It is possible to seek the historiographical counter-point to the *Kavyamimansa* within the Indian intellectual tradition itself. Rajashekhara's criticism was written in times of great political turbulence in the subcontinent. In his century, the tenth, institutions of political authority had been declining rapidly; and with them the concept of authority in religious and metaphysical practices. It was this radical shift in the sense of authority that triggered off the philosophic clash between the Acharyas and the Bhaktas during the next four centuries. Rajashekhara himself was acutely aware of the changes taking place in his times, as his play *Karpuramanjiri*[3], written in the Shataka style, shows. The play was written in the Maharashtri Apabhramsa dialect and not in Sanskrit, indicating that Sanskrit as the language of literature was soon to be a thing of the past. The play depicts moral chaos as the ruling passion of his times. Other changes too were taking place, in linguistics and semantics, in the theory of *sphota* in particular, and in the sense of Time proposed by the Sankhya eschatology. It was inevitable then that the community of scholars and critics for whom the *Kavyamimansa* was composed received Rajashekhara's historiography in relation to the profound changes that distinguished their century. As a result, we find that the organic model of history is quietly dropped by Bhoja of the next generation. *Atitartha pradhanyad itihasa:* history must produce meaning, it must have a logical sequence, was the pronouncement of Bhoja.[4]

The *Shringaraprakasha* of Bhoja is a compendium of critical concepts, with information about their historical evolution and the debates surrounding the more important concepts. This work amply displays the love for hair-splitting classification that Sanskrit scholarship valued. Bhoja's classification of literary plots provides an instance of his analytical zeal. Narrative plots had been classified into two broad types by Bharata,[5] who preceded Bhoja by seven or eight centuries. The two types were, plots based on already known stories and those invented by poets. Dhananjaya, a commentator of Bharata who preceded Bhoja by a century, had added one more type, the cross-breed of Bharata's two types.[6] Bhoja, on the other hand, speaks of five types of narratives. Two of those should interest us here: one is purely history, *itihasa*, the other history-based, *itihasashraya*.[7] He does not accept the view that the *Mahabharata* and the *Ramayana* are the best examples of history. For him history-plays must depict historically known personalities and not mythological persons. Historical narratives must be organized within rational temporal schemes. He opines that poetry can improve upon history by combining fact with imagination so as to produce well-structured narratives. He calls this class of story the history-based plot, illustrated by the play *Kumarasambhava,* On the other hand, the plots using history in its 'pure' form should have a *prabandhasharira*, a structural order. The narrative structure which the history writer employs to construct his story is described by Bhoja by using the concept of *pratisamskara.* It is his comprehensive term for the analytical and imaginative investment by the narrator in his narrative. *Pratisamskara* corresponds to 'representation'. Clearly, then, Bhoja's view of history is substantially different from the view Rajashekhara had taken. In one view the present judges the past; in another view the past valorizes the present.

It must immediately be stated that neither Rajashekhara nor Bhoja were greatly original when it came to literary classification. They both allude to a number of predecessors and contemporaries from whom they borrowed ideas freely. One imagines therefore that they represent the general trends in philosophic and critical thinking prevalent during their times. The versions of history presented by Rajashekhara and Bhoja had been shaped through philosophical and cultural movements during the initial phases of the classical period, A large variety of theories of Time, theories of Meaning and theories of cognition had gone into the making of the discourses of history current in classical India, from the third century to the tenth century. An awareness of some of the more important of those theories can be useful in reconstructing traditional literary historiography in India.

5

Bhartrihari's Metaphors

Though historiography was not his primary concern, Bhartrihari was interested in the dialectical relation between Time and human consciousness. His enquiry into the philosophical status of Time, and into the linguistic devices employed to represent abstractions of time, forms the subject of *Kalasamuddesha,*[1] a section of hundred and fourteen verses (*karikas*) in his *Vakyapadiya,* Because he was primarily a poet, it is easier to get into the spirit of his argument through Bhartrihari's metaphors.

The metaphors in the *Kalasamuddesha* are pastoral, and they reflect a metaphysics affected by the ease and quietude of agrarian life. One of the metaphors for Time used in the early part of Bhartrhari's thesis is that of a bird-catcher who uses captive birds to allure other birds. As he describes it, the birds captured are tied to an invisible string which the bird-catcher releases to let the birds fly, only to pull it back to get the flying birds home, and with them more birds.[2] Time is the bird catcher, and all human actions are like birds tied to it by an invisible string. Thus, for Bhartrihari, Time is one of the permanent limits of human existence. On the other hand, Time cannot be perceived independent of human actions. Time is eternity, but it is also duration. If human existence is entrapped within eternity, duration is entrapped within human action. To bring out this mutual confinement, Bhartrihari likens Time to the air entering the human body.[3] Air by itself has no 'before' and 'after', no temporal sequence; but once inside the body, it performs all the actions that the body performs and, thereby, acquires a temporal sequence. In the philosopher's view, duration and temporal sequence are caused by the cognition. Time is eternal and transcends durations created by the human consciousness, for durations vanish but Time does not vanish.

According to Bhartrihari, Time is like a road on which durations walk. He asserts, "There is no difference in the length of the road because of the difference of wayfarers and their goings."[4] The image of the solid steady road is likely to create the impression that in Bhartrihari's abstraction Time is static, even if it is imperishable. However, this philosopher-linguist was not interested merely in conceptualizing an abstract time. His interest was to study the cognition of Time in relation to its impersonal pre-cognition form. Hence, in another metaphor, which he uses repeatedly, he speaks of Time as a current or a stream. Occasionally he also speaks of it as a fountain. Given a current of water, says Bhartrihari, and two openings of different width filtering the current, we may have two different speeds for the outflowing currents.[5] The speeds are caused by the recipients of the current which has its own speed. Durations, sequence and temporality are caused by the perceiving consciousness.

Hydraulic imagery is used by Bhartrihari once again in explaining the etymology of the Sanskrit word for Time, *kala*; and it must be understood in the context of the ancient Indian concept of *dravya*, indestructible substances which constitute the universe. He writes:

> *Jalayantrabramaveshasadrishibhih pravrittibhih*
> *Sa kalahkalayan sarvah kalakhyam labhate vibhuh.*[6]

In the words of his translator, "With motions similar to the turnings and agitations of a water wheel, it (that is, time) all-pervading, driving all parts (*kala*, of the material world), obtains the name 'time' (*kala*)."[7]

At the beginning of his discourse on Time, Bhartrihari refers to the dispute existing among other schools of philosophy regarding whether *kala* is *shakti, atman* or *devta*— a force, spirit or godhead. He then states that whatever *kala* may be, it turns the metaphorical water wheel driving the individual containers of water in an endless cycle. It is this image of the water wheel, or windmill, taken quite literally and out of its philosophic context that gives rise to the vulgar idea that the sense of Time in India is 'cyclical'. We should not overlook Bhartrihari's image of a road — a linear image — for Time. Besides, the purpose in using the water wheel or windmill image is not to show the circularity of Time but to show the origin of temporality and durations caused by the cognitive process of fragmentary perceptions. Sequentiality, whether of events taking place in durations or of phonemes culminating in words, was of abiding interest to Bhartrihari. If Time is eternal, transcendent and essentially indivisible, what is it in human perception that causes the cognition of temporal sequentiality of events? This is the major philosophic anxiety in Bhartrihari's thesis on Time. To explain the duality of Time (and time), he postulates the principle of "suspension and permission": *pratibandhabhyanujnabbyam.* "It (that is, time) is called the operator (literally, string holder) of this mechanical contrivance 'world'. It ... divides the universe by suspension and permission".[8] In this particular formulation, Time is the puppeteer bringing about events which have beginnings and endings. Events are 'permitted' by Time to take place, then they are 'suspended' from the game of existence. Here, once again, we are in danger of overlooking the fact that Bhartrihari is employing a metaphor with which he seeks to reconcile the duality of Time. It is not a metaphor commenting on human destiny as such. It is indeed necessary to be patient with Bhartrihari. His primary interest in *Kalasamuddesha* is not the human life but the inevitable fragmentation of Time in human cognition. So, immediately after employing the metaphor of a puppeteer,[9] he hastens to add: "Its (that is time's) self is manifoldly divided by differences resting on alien activities. For, there exists no elementary substance that could be either divided or undivided."[10]

If Bhartrihari was interested in the philosophy of Time and its cognition, it is in his linguistics that the interest originated. Appropriately, the *Kalasamuddesha* is a constituent of the *Vakyapadiya* and not an independent treatise. All his metaphors for time, therefore, finally point to the behaviour of language in relation to time. Having asserted that Time is single and indivisible in essence, and having explained the apparent divisions of Time through the principle of suspension and permission, he goes on to comment:

> (Time), having activity as its superimposition, becomes past, future and present, (which are) divided by eleven forms. Amongst these, past (time) is of five kinds; future (time) is of four kinds; present (time) is of two kinds; thus (altogether) there are eleven fabrications....[11]

The five forms of the past tense, or the five varieties of cognition related to the past that Bhartrihari mentions, are drawn from

Panini’s grammar — the general past (*samanya*), the past related to the current day (*adyatan*), that related not to the current day (*anadyatan*), that which combines the *adyatan* and the *anadyatan*, and finally the unknown past (the *paroksha*). These are cognitive possibilities that language opens up in the context of human relation to the past.

In order to get closer to the spirit of Bhartrihari’s philosophic speculations on Time it is useful to refer to the semantic theory of *sphota.* Bhartrihari himself was the leading figure among the grammarian-philosophers of his time who subscribed to one variety of the *sphota* theory in opposition to another variety of the theory propounded by the Vaisesika school of philosophers. The doctrine of *sphota* in the grammarians’ version argued that words are not merely a collection or sequence of phonemes. They are signs which help us identify meaning. However, meaning has a pre-phonetic existence; and thus, meaning is at once identical with the sequence of phonemes and, at the same time, transcends the phonetic representation. *Sphota* is the term used by the grammarians, the *vaiyakaranas*, to denote meaning which exists in pre-verbal and, therefore, eternal form. We can now see how close Bhartrihari’s concept of *kala* is to his concept of *sphota.* In his thesis, they both appear fragmented in language, and are seemingly dependent on duration and sequence, but have in their essential form a non-fragmented and, therefore, eternal, existence. Just as meaning in the human cognition has its source in *sphota,* time and tense in the human cognition have their origin in *kala.* And, again, just as *sphota* endows cognitive structures to material episodes of verbal articulation, *kala* endows cognitive structures to the temporal fragments perceived in the sequential events of human life. Clearly then Time is completely analogous to Meaning for Bhartrihari; and to that extent, the *Vakyapadiya* is as much a philosophy of language as it is of history. Once we get to see the analogy between semantics and the philosophy of Time in ancient India, we are no longer surprised to find that the thinkers who opposed Bhartrihari’s semantics are also those who opposed his view of Time.

The most significant critiques of Bhartrihari’s theory of cognition and semantics were presented by the Buddhist thinker Dignaga and the *mimansaka* Kumarila Bhatta, both of whom were Bhartrihari’s near contemporaries. The entire debate between Bhartrihari and Kumarila is splendidly summed up in Mandana

Misra's *Sphotasiddhi*, an illuminating treatise on the history of the *sphota* theory.[12] Mandana Misra was a senior contemporary of Sankara in the ninth century. It is important to take into account these details, because Sankara put Bhartrihari's *sphota* theory to the most central use in propounding his theory of the *brahman*, turning the theory of linguistic cognition into the theory of Knowledge of the Self.[13] But to catch up with Kumarila we must travel four centuries back in time.

The Mimansaka view of meaning was that the phonetic sequence and structure of words have absolute ontological status. Sequences of phonemes do indeed reveal the meaning of words, but the sequentiality by itself is no proof to say that meaning, or *sphota*, transcends and precedes the phonemic expression. Kumarila Bhatta, who is the chief spokesman of this view, maintains in his *Slokavarttika* that even if meaning is not entirely contingent as a linguistic category, there is no need to postulate an independent entity of *sphota* over and above the phonetic expression of meaning. "The word, whether it be the sentence or the individual word, is nothing more than a collection or group of phonemes and it is with this collection that meaning is associated."[14] And, in this thesis on cognition, as in Bhartrihari's, meaning is seen as being completely analogous to Time. In fact, at the height of his polemics, Kumarila almost starts speaking of Time instead of meaning. For instance, he writes:

> The reaching of the preceding point of space become the cause of the reaching of the next point of space... (because) Moments of the act of going succeed in bringing one to the desired place...[15]

If Kumarila provides the critique of Bhartrihari's theory of meaning, Dignaga provides the critique of the theory of cognition. Dignaga's major philosophical work, *Pramanasamuccaya*, comes to us filtered through the *Pramanavarttika* of Dharmakirti, who was the main commentator on Dignaga.[16] However, recent scholarly interest in his work has led to remarkable achievements in recovering his thought. His objection to Bhartrihari's semantics was that meaning does not exist outside the carriers of meaning. Reviving the debate about the place of names in language initially started by Katyayana, Dignaga says that "names are given to things on the basis of a quality which properly belongs to them."[17]

That is, Dignaga denies the need to posit a transcendental sphere of *sphota* for language to be able to transact meaning. Dignaga further extends his logic to assert that language ís not eternal, "nor is it an independent source of truth."[18] His view of language is that it functions by virtue of being logically structured, by sharing structures with *anumana*. Inference is, therefore, the primary mode of cognition in Dignaga's theory.

Kumarila's linguistics and Dignaga's theory of inference have a corresponding philosophy of Time. There is a lively debate among the philosophers of their time about whether time is perceived or whether it is inferred. Several philosophers from the Mimansa school and the Nyaya-Vaisesika school join the debate, carried out through texts, such as the *Sastadipika* of Parthasarathi Misra, *Manameyodaya* of Narayana Bhatta, the *Kalaprakaranam* section in *Nyaya-Kandali* of Sridhara, and the *Nyaya-Manjart* of Jayanta Bhatta.[19] These are, perhaps, textual records of scholarly debates that took place among assemblies of scholars. In this debate we find these two points of view contending with each other: 'Time is perception' and 'Time is inference'.

Apart from this debate there were other philosophical positions on the question of time and change in other schools of Indian thought. Among the Brahminical schools, the Sankhya and Yoga schools of philosophy had valuable things to say about the philosophy of Time. The non-Brahminical schools, namely, Buddhism and Jainism had even more important things to say about the issue, and they said them in even more sophisticated ways. In the *Yogasutra* Patanjali had argued that "just as the atom is the minimal limit of matter, so the moment is the minimal duration taken by an atom to change its position."[20] The Yoga school considers the minimal duration, the moment, as absolute reality. Change is inherent in the nature of things; and, therefore, the universe will not be alike at any two given moments. In other words no two moments are alike. Thus this school distinguishes the present from the past. The Sankhya school has a different method of approaching the problem of change. K.C. Bhattacharya presents a contrasting picture of the two approaches:

> Neither system admits time as a separate *tattva:* time is to both concrete becoming or *parinama,* which is not conceived as an event in time. *Parinama* may be understood as the cause turning up its own limitation or as

> the limited effect having got manifested. In the former conception, the real objective fact is the act of cause, its act of turning up or the reproduction, the succession of cause and effect being only a retrospective construction as in the Bergsonian view. In the latter conception, the real fact is the antecedence of the cause to the effect, the prior becoming of the effect, but the causal act as the initial moment of this becoming is but an abstraction. Hence to Yoga, which represents the former conception, time is real as the causal act, the initiation or the initial moment of becoming (*kshana*) ... To the latter or Sankhya conception of becoming, the effect being pre-existent in the cause is never turned up, so that the time-relation of sequence alone—the prior process of manifestation constitutive of the manifestness of the effect—is real time.[21]

Indeed, the Yoga concept of Time is at the very heart of its philosophy of salvation, through concentration or *ekagrata* on a single point of time, the present. The concepts of Time in Jainism and Buddhism made radical departures from the concepts in the Brahminical school of thought. The Jain philosophers—and a large multitude of them wrote on Time—propose that Time exists as atoms. Time was considered as one of the basic substances constituting the universe. The definition of Time offered by Kundakunda, about a century before Bhartrihari, sums up the Jaina view:

> The quality of space is to give room, of *dharma* to cause motion, of *adharma* to cause rest. The quality of time is to roll on, of the self, awareness. You should know, in short, that all these qualities are formless. Souls, aggregates of matter, *dharma*, *adharma*, and the space contain innumerable dimensional points. Space is both in the universe and in that which is beyond it. *Dharma* and *adharma* extend throughout the universe only; likewise time, because it depends on the other two substances, these other substances being soul and matter. As the dimensional points of space, so are the dimensional points of other substances, except time. The atom has no dimensional point, but hence is ex-

> plained the development of dimensional points. But a moment has no dimensional point. It occurs when a substance with a single dimension crosses a dimensional point of space.[22]

The Jaina thinkers made a broad distinction between Time as it *exists,* and Time as it *is measured,* between the ontological and the epistemological abstractions about time. Time exists by itself in the form of the *kalanus,* atoms of Time, whereas Time as measured by human intelligence is seen as *vyavahara kala.* The Jaina view lists nearly twenty-five such measures beginning with *samaya,* the minutest, to *Samvatsara,* a year's measure.[23]

The depth and the variety of the philosophy of time in India cannot be brought out in a sketchy account such as the present one. There is no reason to believe that once a certain view was propounded it remained unmodified throughout the centuries of Indian tradition. There was a continuous exchange and confrontation between different views, each of which was enriched further by continuous cross-fertilization with views originating in other schools of philosophy and theology.

In her study of cognitions of time in ancient India, Romila Thapar observes:

> the characterizing of societies as using either cyclic or linear time is an inadequate explanation for the centrality or otherwise of history .... It seems more appropriate to enquire into how a society uses a particular category and what is being intended by that use.[24]

Therefore, it will be profitable to examine the ways in which various theories of time in classical India were put to use by literary scholars while reconstructing literary traditions.

6

The Conventions of Literary History

Was there any literary history in India prior to India's contact with the modern West? And if there was, what was the nature of that consciousness of history? In attempting to answer these large questions, one must first move from the singular 'history' to the plural 'histories'. Plurality of relations with the literary past was a distinguishing mark of ancient Indian literature. The nature of each of the several relations with the past depended on the type of literature in question and its social function. In order to understand the polyvalence of literary historiography in ancient India it is necessary to step out of the concepts of genre and period. Literary works apparently belonging together by virtue of a common genre were often accorded greatly dissimilar status in Indian literary canon; and vastly different aesthetic expectations were brought to bear on stylistically comparable works belonging to one given period. This was so because in ancient India literature was classified in terms of several canons existing simultaneously. To a student of Sanskrit literature in the tenth century it was acceptable to classify literature into the following five categories: (1) *Suta*-literature, (2) *Mantra*-literature, (3) *Shastra*, (4) *Akshara*-literature, and (5) Prakrit. And if this student knew Tamil, there would be the sixth category of *Sangam* literature.

Suta-Literature

The distinction between suta literature and mantra literature was proposed by S.V. Ketkar, and was approvingly accepted by scholars like Iravati Karve and V.S. Sukhtankar.[1] According to Ketkar, suta (or sauta) literature is "literature belonging to the sutas, preserved and sung by the sutas and perhaps largely composed by the sutas. This literature embodied the secular political tradition of Sanskrit literature..."[2] According to Iravati Karve,

> A class of people called *sutas*, representing the illegitimate progeny of the *Kshatriyas*, performed various functions at the court. They were counsellors and friends of kings, charioteers, and also bards. Some of these moved from place to place, wherever they knew that people were likely to assemble, and told their stories which consisted mainly of exploits of love and adventure of ancient and ruling kings and princes. A book in many respects like the *Mahabharata* was the *Ramayana*, a narrative sung from place to place. Out of these grew a later type of literature called the *Puranas*...[3]

Thus, *suta* literature was largely an oral tradition of literature, though it was not a non-lexical tradition. Almost every work in this tradition of Indian literature was initially a written work, which was handed down to subsequent generations in the form of public recitation. In the process of oral transmission the text was changed, enlarged, and to it was also added the history of recitations. Since the *suta*-texts were treated as essential parts of collective memory and collective inheritance, the particulars about their specific historical moments of origin and individual authorships were not considered important in the *suta* literary canon.

The *Mahabharata*, which is easily the most complex of the *suta* literary works, offers us glimpses into the history of its making and transmission. Vyasa, to whom the initial authorship of the poem is ascribed and who was an eyewitness to the war described in it, composed it, perhaps under the title *Jaya* or *Itihasa*. At that stage it is believed to have been much shorter in length. The original had perhaps not more than 24,000 verses. Vyasa seems to have taught the epic to five of his pupils who made their own recensions. One of the pupils was Vaishampayana. He recited the epic on the occasion of the serpent-sacrifice ritual performed by King Janmejaya. Lomharshana, who was present on this occasion, heard it, and recited it again in the hermitage of the sage Saunaka in the Naimisha forest. By this time, probably, the 24,000 verses of *Jaya* had already turned into the 60,000 verses of the *Mahabharata*.[4] But even after this, generations of poets kept adding verses to it. The result is the present version comprising 100,000 verses.

The *Ramayana* is another important *suta* text; and *the puranas* too are *suta* texts. Not only scholars, but even common people knew that the *Mahabharata* was composed first, the *Ramayana* later, and the *Puranas* the last; but the cultural centrality of these texts was such that they were or are rarely thought of as merely linguistic compositions. As a result, they were never allowed to belong to the past, or to have an existence that was detached from the collective consciousness. Hence, their historical status as texts was of marginal interest to scholars involved in their transmission.

In India people are rarely self-conscious about the intimate intertextuality of the *suta* texts and life as it is lived. This phenomenon strikes an outsider as uniquely Indian. Milton Singer, for instance, comments:

> Before I went to India, I knew these stories as occurring in printed books called the *Ramayana*, the *Mahabharata* and the *Bhagvatapurana*, parts of which I had read in translation. This knowledge gave me a welcome sense of recognition when I heard some of the stories, but it did not prepare me for the rich variety of ways in which they are told and retold. Seldom did I come across an Indian who had read these stories as I did, simply in a book. This is not how they learn them and it is not how they think of them. There is a sense of intimate familiarity with the characters and incidents in references made to Harishchandra, Rama and Sita, Krishna, Arjuna, and Prahlada as if the world of the stories were also the everyday world. The cultural and physical landscapes are literally and imaginatively printed with them.[5]

Thus, the Indian attitude to the *suta* texts involves the sense of 'the presence of the past' but not of 'the pastness of the past'. The principle subject of *suta* literature was history itself. Even the *puranas*, which have a greatly rambling style of narration, were basically 'historical' records providing information about dynasties and genealogies, and also contain within themselves some historical information about their composition and transmission; but to think of them as 'books' will not be appropriate to their purpose and history. It is only during the last hundred years or so that *suta* texts have been subjected to textual research and scholarship; the first critical edition of the *Mahabharata* was published by the Bhandarkar Oriental Institute in Pune;[6] the first critical edition of the *Ramayana* was published by the Oriental Institute in Baroda;[7] and in Varanasi, V. Raghavan started issuing editions of various *Puranas* through the Kashiraj Trust. Traditionally, however, *suta* texts were seen as constituting the continuous collective memory and were not considered as literary events. That is why Naimisharanya, the location of every recitation of the *Mahabharata* and the *Puranas*, became an essential part of people's unconscious personality, and Vyasa, the original author of these texts, came to be considered a *Chiranjiva*, an ever-living mortal.

It is, however, necessary to first distinguish the *suta* literary tradition from other traditions of folk literature or oral literature. The linguistic structures, narrative strategies and aesthetic devices such as characterization and plot-structure in *suta* literature are as sophisticated and imaginatively varied as in any tradition of 'written' literature. Besides, this tradition continues to survive even in the age of printing and electronic mass communication. An interesting example of a *suta* text in contemporary use on a wide scale is the *Satya Narayan Katha*. This *katha* has a definite textual source; and in fact the story itself is about a certain text and its several recitations. Thus it is a text about a text; and the person who recites it usually reads it out from a printed text. Yet, no one who knows the story has ever read it as a book. It is to be heard by people, as it is recited by a Brahmin. The practice has nothing to do whatsoever with literacy and education.

The *suta* narratology, whether in the epics, the *puranas* or the *kathas,* has some recurring features. One of them is the opening which seeks to combine myth and history. Ludo Rocher comments, "The *Mahabharata* begins like most *puranas*, with the arrival of the *suta* in the Naimisha forest.... And the seers ask Ugrashravas: Tell us that ancient Lore...."[8] The fictional time created in the narrative, time which seeks to combine myth and history, conceptually corresponds to the cognitive possibility recognized in the grammar of Panini and Bhartrihari when they describe the past tense which combines the *adyatan* and the *anadyatan.* The historiographical attitude to *suta* literature in Indian tradition allowed for the recitation's simultaneous existence in the *adyatan* past and the *anadyatan* past. Traditionally,

Indian audiences were brought up to believe that the recitation by a known *suta* within their hearing was essentially no different from one that was heard in Saunaka's hermitage in the Naimisha forest from Lomaharshana or Romaharshana in some remote and unspecified past.

Mantra Literature

The historiographical attitude towards the *mantra* literature—the Vedic hymns, the *brahmanas, Upanishads,* and in extreme cases some *vedangas*—corresponded to the cognitive possibility offered by the grammatical category of *paroksha* past tense. Once Panini, Katyayana and Patanjali had constructed the enormous *vyakarana*—machinery to prohibit 'vulgarization' of the *bhasha*, the Vedic verses began to be treated as if they were divinely and not humanly, composed. Vedic literature forms an excellent instance of linguistic creativity fully integrated with the life of the community surrounding it; it is an eloquent commentary on the history of the people who wrote it. Yet scholars in the post-Panini period were encouraged to believe that the *Vedas* were gospel, literally heard by the rishis from a divine source. The *Vedas* became *shruti*, the *Upanishads, smriti.* And both were removed from the historical sphere altogether.

During the nineteenth century many European scholars took an interest in ancient Indian literature. Some of them determined 1500 BC as the possible date for the earliest of the Vedic compositions. On the other hand, Indian scholars, more particularly B.G. Tilak and his followers, argued that the Vedas were composed much earlier — around 4500 BC.[9] It is claimed however, by every scholar of Vedic literature that it is the most ancient body of literary expression anywhere in the world. The history of transmission of this literature through a period of four thousand years, or perhaps more, shows that unparalleled scholarly care and editorial precision have been lavished on it by the generations involved in the process of its transmission. Indeed, the historiographical attitude claimed and enjoyed by the Vedic literary tradition has been simply unique. The transmission of Vedic literature cannot be compared, to the transmission by the *sutas* of the epics and the *puranas.* The *sutas* were free to make marginal changes in the metres, accents and, occasionally, whole sections of verses. They were at liberty to add new verses to the body of poetry they handed down to the next generations. The transmission of Vedic literature permitted not the slightest linguistic freedom to the individual involved in the process. Max Muller has observed that, unlike the Homeric epics, the *Vedas* make no reference to the art of writing.[10] But no written text, reproduced by different scholiasts and reprinted in different lexical styles, would have succeeded in preserving the original poetic speech in the exact original form to the last and the finest phonetic detail. The mind-boggling achievement in continuous memorization of the Vedic verses for four thousand years can only be imagined when we have some idea of the stylistic features of Vedic texts.

The Vedic metre depends on the number of syllables, but not on the length of the syllable. The Gayatri metre has twenty-four syllables. Ushnik has twenty-eight syllables. Anushtup has thirty-two syllables. And, in this manner of change in the metre with the addition of every four syllables, the Vedic metres range from the Gayatri with twenty-four syllables to the Atidhriti with seventy-six syllables, adding up to fourteen metres. The total number of *Riks* or verses in the *Rigveda* is 10580 ¼, divided into ten chapters or *mandalas*.[11] These are composed by twenty-three different *rishis*, and over an extended period of several centuries. Thus the style of composition, the level of semantic complexity, registers of poetic diction and thematic concerns vary considerably from one *mandala* to another. To commit to memory all the verses without the slightest variation of accent and change even of a syllable must have required long years of disciplined training. That this training formed an essential part of school education in ancient India is evident from the fact that specialist text books, companion volumes and classified indexes were prepared to assist this training. Katyayana, for instance had prepared a Vedic *sarvanukramani*, a general index giving the names of the *rishis* credited with having contributed to *Rigveda*, the exact number of verses composed by each, the chapter and section division of the verses, the metres and also the names of gods in whose praise the verses were composed.[12] In terms of historical scholarship in literature, such *anukramanis* — and there were many — are of pioneering importance. However, the aim of these scholarly exercises was not to enable other scholars to place the *shrutis* in a historical context and to see them critically. The aim was the exact opposite; it was to abstract the *shrutis* from the flow of time altogether so that they became timeless and ahistorical. What happened to the *Vedas*, happened also to the *Upanishads* and the associated Vedic texts. And, though Indians made impressive progress in certain sciences, agriculture, philosophy and linguistics continuously for a thousand years after the *Vedas* were composed, the ancient literary scholarship persisted in its belief that the *Vedas* held literally all knowledge in them, and that no knowledge could surpass that contained in the *Vedas*. Traces of this historical fallacy survive in India even today. The logical result of making Vedic literature the ultimate authority in the sphere of knowledge was the emergence of a rhetoric of knowledge which made *authority* a fundamental source of knowledge. This view then was institutionalized through the Nyaya school of philosophy.

The profound impact of this faith in Authority as knowledge on historiography can be seen in works like Kshemaraja's Pratyabhijnahrdayam.[13] An eleventh century Kashmir philosopher and a disciple of Abhinavagupta, Kshemaraja draws an imaginary topography of spiritual fulfilment by describing the descent of the divine into the human world, which in his opinion is necessarily followed by a corresponding human ascent. This doctrine of 'recognition' postulates perception as recollection of what was always known: the greater the capacity to 'remember', the higher the human consciousness can ascend in the realm of the spirit. His argument that all new knowledge has always been present in the human consciousness, even if momentarily clouded, derived support from the notion of authority vested with sovereignty in the Vedas. And, hence, even if the Vedic texts are supremely historical as documents, and even if the very history of these texts is eloquently inscribed in them, these texts were removed from the sphere of history by a jealously guarded tradition of scholarship. If the attitude to the suta literature was non-historical, the attitude to the mantra literature was trans-historical. It did belong to the past, but that past was beyond the grasp of students of literature.

Shastra Literature

As against the two traditions of literary transmission discussed above, the *shastra* tradition and the *akshara* literary traditions were given greater historiographical attention in ancient India. The *shastras* were numerous; and the ancient Indian scholars were prolific writers. Though generally speaking a *shastra* text was a text dealing with any subject systematically, *shastra* and imaginative literature were not thought of as mutually exclusive categories. Rather, *shastra* was the ethical and cognitive aspect of a text. An illuminating example of actual usage of the term *shastra* by ancient Indian writers is to be found in Anandavardhana's *Dhvanyaloka.* In chapter four (*Uddyota IV*), he is discussing the aesthetic complexity of the *Mahabharata* in terms of the *Rasa* aesthetics, when he writes:

> And so... it is revealed that everything different from the blessed one is ephemeral, and thereby it is well established that looking at the *Mahabharata* as a *shastra*, the highest goal of man, namely *moksha,* is alone intended as the most important of the goals of life, and looking at it as poetry, *shantarasa,* which is characterised by the nourishing of the happiness that succeeds the destruction of desire, is intended as the most important of all the *rasas.*[14]

The fact that the canonical status of texts did not depend on the genre in which they were composed but rather on the function they were expected to perform in the sphere of their reception needs to be stressed again and again when we consider the history of ancient Indian literature. Both the *shastras* and the *akshara* texts were composed in verse, prose, or a combination of the two. Both were seen as products of known human authorship. And, as against the *suta* literature and the *mantra* literature which remained in 'fashion' for ever, the *shastras* and the *akshara*-literature were freely subjected to the vagaries of literary taste, shifts in critical views and the climate of philosophical opinion. Philosophical debate and literary disagreement were the common features of the scholarly community that developed these two branches of ancient Indian literature. In other words, these two types had the benefit of belonging to critical traditions with clear historical perspectives.

Linguistics and poetics were considered *shastras.* Between the fourth century BC and the seventeenth century AD — a period of about two thousand years — every linguist in India knew about all linguistics scholarship preceding him. He knew the major *sutras* or theoretical formulations as well as the *bhashyas* or the related commentaries. Between Bhamah and Dandin, critics of the sixth and seventh centuries, and Bhoja, who belonged to the eleventh century, there was a gap of half a millennium; and yet, Bhoja knew their exact critical positions in relation to narrative poetry, *sargabandha*, or poetic styles, *riti*. Between Bharata and Abhinavagupta the gap was of more than six centuries; but Abhinavagupta knew Bharata's formulations on aesthetic emotion to the last letter.

It was not just the relationship with his predecessors within the same *shastra* about which a given thinker was aware; invariably, he was also aware of the relationship between his intellectual or philosophical position and the other related sciences. It is very clear from the text of Abhinava's comments on the *shantarasa* that he was fully aware that his theoretical position related in various ways to the literary criticism of Ashvagosha, Bharata, Anandavardhana, Bhattatauta, Bhattanayaka, as well as the philosophic positions in *Vedanta*, *Vijnanabhairava*, *Yogavasishtha* and Kashmir Saivism. On the other hand, Abhinavagupta, in *Gitarthasangraha,* his commentary on the *Gita,*[15] leaves us in no doubt regarding the line of philosophers and critics to whom he alludes, and who included Katyayana, Saushuka, Bhutiraja, Bhattenduraja, Kallata, Mukula, Somananda, Utpaldeva, Lakshamanagupta and many other scholars.

In the ancient Indian style of philosophic or critical commentary textual evidence was considered of very great importance. Even when critics made some very original point or observation, they tried to establish its validity by quoting a multitude of verses in support from the available literature, written by predecessors as well as their contemporaries. Modern scholarship of Sanskrit texts has often found that whereas the verses quoted were accurate there was usually no mention of the name of the author quoted. In any text on poetics, for instance, one finds citations from other poets running into hundreds; but the acknowledgment of authorship is rare. This was so not because the writers and critics were plagiarists but because the verses quoted, and their sources, formed a vast collective fund of literature to which the community of readers had an active access. It would have been superfluous, therefore, for an ancient Indian critic to mention the names of each and every author and text to which he alluded. The *shastras* were generally taught in schools and universities. Scholars were required to defend their philosophical positions in assemblies of scholars; and, therefore, exacting knowledge of the *shastras* was essential for every aspiring scholar. Similarly, a knowledge of poetry and drama was considered a social asset. The ability to talk about literature was considered the mark of intellectual and social nobility. There was thus a sense of community among the people who wrote and those for whom they wrote.

Akshara Literature

The *akshara* literature, composed primarily for aesthetic pleasure, used a variety of genres and forms. It included works written in verse, prose and narrative or dramatic forms. The *akshara* canon was fairly well defined during the later centuries of classical Indian literature. It included works by Sudraka, Harsha, Kalidasa, Vishakhadatta, Bhattanayaka, Bhavabhuti, Bhartrihari, Bharavi, Bhatti, Kumaradasa, Magha, Dandin, Subandhu and Banabhatta. After the eighth century, the volume of compositions expanded. They became stylistically more rigid and thematically less complex. The community of literates declined, giving rise to excessive and often pointless advancement in theoretical literature. And the canon lost its purpose as well as real social importance. But, till such a time as there was a relatively unified literary community—perhaps till the end of the eighth century—the *akshara* literature was preserved very systematically; and its historicity was never overlooked.

Between the fifth century BC and the tenth century AD literary and philosophical works were preserved by reproducing manuscript copies from time to time. These copies were made by teachers in schools and universities, more particularly those living in residential institutions.[16] Rajashekhara describes a normal day in the life of an *acharya*-poet. In this description, Rajashekhara records that poets wrote every day for a certain number of hours.[17] Poetry, or linguistic compositions in other forms, were perceived during the post-Vedic period of Sanskrit (as well as Prakrit) literature as essentially written forms. The manuscript copies at schools and centres of learning were used by scholars being trained in the *shastras* and *kavyas*. Often scholars from other centres visited these institutions as part of their nationwide pilgrimage and brought information with them about new compositions or older, lesser known works. Thus through the networks of places of pilgrimage and the residential schools literary manuscripts were replicated and preserved. This method was in use till the beginning of the thirteenth century when paper replaced the traditional materials used for writing manuscripts.

The major difference between the *shastras* and the *akshara* literature, however, was that the *shastras*, which required explanation and comment from learned teachers, formed a part of the school syllabus. The *akshara* literature, on the other hand, was self-explanatory. Initially, the *shastras* made no claim to authority. But their place in the education system inevitably brought an association of authority with them in the course of time. When we compare the texts of philosophic treatises from the time of Panini with those in the age of Sankara, periods separated by about eleven centuries, we find that the later texts have no hesitation in claiming direct lineage from the *Vedas*. The later *shastras* share with the *Vedas* their authority, a consequence of the institutionalized teaching of the *shastras*. On the other hand, the works of *akshara* literature, the plays, stories and poems, were perceived and experienced with a sense of immediacy. The readers were expected to be *sahridaya*, on the same mental plane as the author himself. And, even if a certain mythological characterization was associated with poetry in the figure of *Kavyapurusha*, its metaphoric nature was never entirely overlooked.[18] This variation in attitudes, towards the *shastras* and the *akshara* literature as reflected in the historiographical status of the two types, corresponded roughly to the cognitive difference between the two categories of the '*anadyatan*' past and the *adyatan* past.

Bharata, the earliest literary critic gives us the impression that he comes at the end of a long line of theorists, and that he is presenting a mere summary of their work, but there appears to be no textual evidence to support his statement. That is exactly what happens with Panini's grammar. That is also the case with Chanakya's *Arthashastra*. As a matter of historical fact, there is no major literary or philosophical 'lost' period between the composition of the Vedic anthologies (*samhitas*) and a settled text of the *Mahabharata*, on the one hand, and Panini, Patanjali and Bharata, on the other hand. One has to conclude, therefore, that the cultural practice of assigning an older date of origin to the *shastra* texts than their actual date of composition was aimed at enhancing their authority.[19] This was possible because the organizing criterion for the *shastras* was not 'period' but 'school of thought.' Every text was given a very definite place in terms of the school of philosophy or thought it postulated or explained. The chronological placement of a text was given secondary importance, and it was subsumed within the category of 'school'. In contrast, the *akskara* literature was accorded the status of 'undiminishing youth'. The mythological *Kavyapurusha* was but a youthful child. There are numerous references to the capacity of poetry to remain 'ever-charming' in discussions of *alamhara* and *vakrokti*, poetic language. *Akshara* meant undiminishing, just as it meant 'letters'. When Bhavabhuti hoped that perhaps his poetry would be appreciated by the right kind of readers a thousand years later,[20] he was voicing the received notions of the everlasting immediacy of *akshara* literature. For ancient Indian readers, all *akshara* literature belonged to the *adyatan* past.

Prakrit Literature

Perhaps the only area of literature in ancient India which received the kind of historiographical care that would find modern approval was the area of Prakrit literature. It needs to be added at once that it is not a body of literature in a single language or a single language variety. Traditionally, Prakrit literature would include the works in Pali; the Buddhist canonical works; dramatic literature in regional deviations of Sanskrit such as Sauraseni, Magadhi, and Maharashtri which had dramatic as well as lyrical literature; and finally, the Jaina canonical works in Maharashtri and Sauraseni. Prakrit is perhaps a negative description, being a comprehensive term applied to languages and literature without social support and cultural sanction. In other words, Prakrit literature includes all para-literatures in ancient India. And, precisely for this reason, Prakrit languages and styles have been more experimental. This experimental nature of Prakrit styles is reflected in the reactions of the Sanskrit writers to them. Practically every Sanskrit writer or thinker has had to come to terms with the changes taking place in Sanskrit in the course of its history. Bharata makes a mention of dramatic literature in Prakrit. Some writers like Kalidasa, Bhavabhuti, Vishakhadutta and Bana made use of Prakrit registers of diction to make their characters life-like. Dandin even went to the extent of building a theory of poetic diction—the *riti* theory—by legitimizing the influence of Prakrit on Sanskrit vocabulary. And, as the Prakrits became stronger, and as they were about to branch off as independent languages, writers like Hemachandra, Rajashekhara and Jayadeva, though scholars of Sanskrit, employed Prakrit as the language for expressing new ideas. Throughout the history of classical Indian literature, Sanskrit kept declining in its power of expression, whereas the Prakrits kept gaining greater expressive power. As such, in the linguistic texture of every work in Prakrit is inscribed the history of social tensions and conflicts in India. Thanks to its non-canonical status, it is the only literature in India in ancient times, the history of which has not been distorted by the conventions of scholarship.

Ashoka's inscriptions are among the earliest samples of recorded Prakrit. There has been no doubt about their historic value and their own historicity. But some of the Buddhist scriptures were written even before these inscriptions. The Pali *Tripitika* on the more philosophical side and the *Jataka* stories on the more popular side, have a very clearly defined historical place in Buddhist literature. The *Mahavamsa* offers a good example of versified history written by monks in Sri Lanka. The Jaina history of literature is even more properly preserved. The Jaina canons, with forty-five *agamas*, eleven *angas* and twelve *upangas*, were arranged by Devadhi Ganin in the fifth century AD, in the year 454.[21]

It was about the same time that *Setubandha,* an epic narrative of exquisite beauty was composed, in the fifth century AD to commemorate the building of a bridge by Pravarasena, a Kashmiri prince. Similarly, *Gaudavaho* was composed by Vakpatiraja, under the pseudonym Bappairaa to celebrate the conquest of Bengal by Yashovarman of Kanauj in the eighth century. So did Hemachandra write in the thirteenth century about the deeds of Kumarapala. All these narratives show a preference for historical themes. Most of the Prakrit works were forgotten quickly or neglected by literary culture dominated by Sanskrit. An anthology of lyrics, most of them composed in the Maharashtri Prakrit, and put together by Hala, usually identified with Satavahana or Salivahana, was known up to the times of Rajashekhara, who mentions it in his Prakrit play *Karpuramanjiri*. Many of the lyrics included in this anthology—it was called *Sattasai*—were lost in the following centuries. However, it is clear that some of the stylistic features of the lyrics included, particularly their extraordinary musicality, were assimilated by Sanskrit versification. This was true of Sanskrit dramatic literature too. Prakrit became, through fifteen hundred years of its coexistence with Sanskrit, an unfailing, source of linguistic and literary enrichment for Sanskrit. Thanks, however, to the social stratification, Sanskrit scholarship kept Prakrit literature out of its institutions of learning. Whether it was written in Pali, or in the regional varieties branching off from Sanskrit itself, Prakrit was left to itself to form its own canon. This canon (or canons, perhaps) was taught and preserved in the Jaina and Buddhist monasteries. As these religions began with human teachers, Mahavir and Gautama, whose historical existence was never in doubt, the literary canons in Prakrit were not anxious to deny or transcend historicity. Prakrit literature in ancient India existed in the normal past tense, the *samanya*; and the dominant tradition of scholarship felt no need to change that status till the generation of Hemachandra and Jnaneshwara.

Sangam Literature

It is difficult to speculate about the attitude of the Sanskrit scholars of Rajashekhara's generation to the ancient Tamil literature, at least some of which they would have surely known. Not only that, but even the attitude of the Tamil scholars of Rajashekhara's generation to their own past is difficult to imagine. Tamil literature itself has left few clues to its medieval historiography and to the attitude to the ancient literary past implicit in it. Perhaps, the influence of Sanskrit literary culture was all too captivating;[22] perhaps, the transition from ancient Tamil to modern Tamil involved a total historical break with tradition. In order to stress how complete the break was, let us quote from a well-researched history of Tamil literature:

> The classical bardic poetry of the literary Academies (*cankam*, Sangam) ceased to be a living literature and became part of an ‘extinct’ classical heritage sometime in the 6th–8th century AD. It gave way to the religious hymnody of the Saiva and Vaisnava *bhakti* movement. In that period, everything changed: in the evolution of language, this was the time of the transition from old Tamil to middle Tamil; in prosody, this was the period of the first strong impact of Sanskritic *aksara-matra* oriented metres on indigenous Tamil structures;

> secular, anonymous love and war poems gave way to religious, highly individual hymns; the itinerant bard moving from court to court quitted the scene and his place was taken by a Saiva or Vaisnava poet-saint, visiting shrine after shrine and singing the mercy of Siva and Visnu. The classical heritage was preserved almost exclusively by learned poets, commentators and scholiasts. After ca. 1450 AD even the scholiast ceased to be interested, and with the exception of a few anthologies which still contained ancient matter, militant brahminical Hinduism apparently branded as taboo and irreligious all secular texts of the ancient era and the study of Jaina and Buddhist literature was forbidden. Even great scholars were unaware of the existence of the earliest and greatest of Tamil literary texts.[23]

Prior to this breakdown in the cultural memory of the Tamil people, literary compositions were preserved through anthologies edited with carefully conceived thematic and metrical plans. Every anthology contained several hundred poetic compositions belonging to two or three centuries. Most of the poems included in these anthologies are ascribed to human authorship, and the names of the author were clearly known. For example, *Purananuru*, the last of the anthologies, which contained four-hundred compositions, indicated the names of one hundred and fifty-seven poets who contributed to it. Similarly, the conventions of writing were handed down from generation to generation; and the anthologies show a remarkable consistency of the 'grammar of poetry'. The conventions were all set up by the *Tolkappiyam,* the founding book of Tamil grammar, linguistics and aesthetics. The poems included in the anthologies show that a 'school' or 'schools' of poetry existed in Tamil in the pre-Christian centuries; and this school literally grew round an academy of scholars in Madurai.[24] The compositions by the poets' collective, working in and around the academy, were traditionally known as Sangam poetry; and the anthologies of these compositions received patronage from successive kings who ruled the Tamil people. Many of the compositions, therefore, are devoted to the patron princes. After the eighth century, Sangam poetry declined as the patronage to it diminished.

The chart of historiographical conventions in ancient India which classified literature into the six categories discussed above was not based exclusively on linguistic, literary or aesthetic principles. It did not classify literary works in terms of primary and secondary, simple and complex, or natural and aesthetic works. The *Mahabharata* is as complex as any works of *akshara* literature. The *prakrit* works are philosophically as competent as some of the *shastra* works. And many of the Tamil lyrics are as spontaneous as the songs in the Vedic anthologies. This classification was not based on any formal principles, for certain identical verse and prose forms of literature can be found in all six categories practiced. It was not based entirely on difference in language, for, though the *prakrit* literatures and Tamil literature were seen as different from literature in Sanskrit, there were also clear distinctions within Sanskrit—*mantra* and *suta*, *shastra* and *kavya.* Similarly, literatures were not categorized on the basis of religious difference alone.

The classification combined the differences in race, religion and social status as the three criteria for literary historiography. Thus, Tamil literature was seen as being different from Sanskrit literature on the grounds of linguistic difference, which, however, can be further traced to racial difference. The *prakrit* literatures were differentiated from the Sanskrit tradition of literature on the basis of religious differences. Prakrit languages were used for literary composition primarily by the Buddhist and Jaina writers. The *suta* literature was differentiated from the *mantra*, *shastra* and *akshara* literature on the basis of the social status of the composers, those who transmitted the works, and the audiences. The *mantra* literature was treated as the preserve of the brahmins; the *suta* literature was open to those who were considered socially 'inferior' to the brahmins.

The six categories discussed in the foregoing pages can be placed in three broad categories using contemporary critical diction: (a) Oral literature, which would include *suta* literature and *mantra* literature; (b) Textual literature, which would include *shastra* and *akshara* literature; and,(c) Para-literature, which would include Prakrit and Tamil literature. This classification had no 'aesthetic' justification; but, in the classical period of ancient Indian literature it had received a general social sanction.

The perception of the relationship between literature and society changed radically from the eleventh to the fourteenth centuries. The ideological content of the category 'literature' too underwent profound changes. The sociology of oppression sanctioned by ancient literary historiography was sought to be challenged by the writers and thinkers of the new era. And, consequently, the attitude to the literary past too changed fundamentally. The agenda for the new literary history was written all over the Bhakti poetry which flourished in all parts of India for the first half of the second millennium; but nowhere else does it find a clearer articulation than in the poetry of the Marathi saint Jnanadeva.

7

Jnanadeva's Agenda

The Bhavarthadipika, popularly called *Jnaneswari,*[1] has greatly influenced Marathi literature and the speakers of the Marathi language during the last seven centuries. Written as a popular commentary on the *Gita,* it pioneered a new literary aesthetic and founded a new literary language. The discourse of Jnanadeva in this seminal text abandons the conventional historiography of stratification and announces to the world the arrival of a new literary epoch in which the *suta, shastra* and *prakrit* registers were to melt together into one luminous *bhakta* speech. Throughout the *Bhavarthadipika,* its young revolutionary writer offers explicit comments on his literary politics. And it is this 'meta' commentary that reveals Jnanadeva's agenda for the 'new' literary history.

There had been a long and illustrious tradition of writing commentaries on the *Gita* before Jnanadeva's times and, as mentioned in passing earlier, even Abhinavagupta had composed an innovative commentary.[2] Jnanadeva was almost certainly familiar with the entire tradition, particularly since a part of his mysticism came from the Kashmir-school of Saivism, of which Abhinavagupta was the greatest exponent. But Jnanadeva's aim was to integrate the Yoga of the Nathas with the Bhakti of the Bhagwats.[3] Therefore, while working within the framework of traditional discourse of commentaries, Jnanadeva seeks to transform the tradition by adding a complex inter-textuality to the established discourse.

The *Gita,* as a text, contains two levels of communication. At one level, Sanjaya, with his envisioning capacity, narrates the happenings on the war-field to Dhritarashtra, the blind prince and the father of the Kuru warriors. Often, the impatient listener urges the commentator to hold back his sense of sheer amazement at what he sees and hears. Thus, there is one level of the *Gita's* dialogic discourse within which the other, and philosophically the more important, dialogue is set. This second dialogue is that between Arjuna, the despairing hero, and Krishna, the philosophising charioteer. To these two levels of discourse, Jnanadeva adds his own dialogues, with his guru, Nivrittinath on the one hand, and, on the other, with his raptly attentive audience, Sacchittananda, the scholiast who committed the text to writing. The Saiva commentaries on the *Gita* had interpreted it as a dialogue between *Jiva* and Shiva. To this interpretation, Jnanadeva adds another originating in his devotionalism and construes the conversation between Krishna and Arjuna as a dialogue between God and the *Bhakta*, his human lover. The *Bhavartbadipika* operates at various levels of communication; and because its composer can simultaneously play upon and control all these levels, the poem never fails to charm the reader. During the course of his narrative, Jnanadeva often identifies himself with Arjuna or Krishna, and, occasionally, he asserts that it is in fact his guru who is writing the narrative through the disciple. The simultaneity of his communication strategies is also the soul of Jnanadeva's literary historiography.

The *Bhavartbadipika* begins in the traditional manner by offering propitiating invocations to all the necessary gods and literary muses; and its author presents himself as a modest disciple to his guru: "I will say what you inspire in me, just as a puppet dances when moved by a string."[4] But, by the time he enters the third chapter, the *adbyaya* that presents the *Karmayoga,* the yoga of action, the narrator has become politically more active. Taking a cue from Arjuna's critique of Krishna's advocacy of knowledge over action in the preceding chapter, Jnanadeva introduces the question of language. Arjuna says to Krishna: "with speech that seems equivocal you confuse my intelligence." (*vyamisreneva vakyena buddhim mohayasiva me)*[5]

To this Jnanadeva's Arjuna adds, 'say it all in Marathi', and with metaphors so persuasive that they would outdo Krishna's childhood implorings to his foster mother Yashoda. Arjuna says in Jnanadeva's words, or perhaps Jnanadeva says in Arjuna's words: "Are you deceiving me, or does your teaching have hidden implications ? ... O Lord, do not speak of such deep meaning. Tell me those things in Marathi."[6] And then follows the logic:

> If a disease is to be cured, medicine must be given, but
> it should be sweet and palatable. These truths, which

> are so full of meaning, should be properly told, but in a way that will enlighten my mind. O Lord ! You are my own teacher ! Then why shouldn't you grant my desire ? Why should I stand in awe of anyone ? You are our mother ! ... If a person were to reach the ocean of nectar and then suffer from thirst, why should he have taken the trouble to reach it ?[7]

Thus, Arjuna is presented as the advocate of Marathi in quest of the ocean of nectar that is Krishna's teaching. Later in the poem, Jnanadeva repeatedly claims that the Marathi discourse he has invented far surpasses the Sanskrit nectar.

By the time Jnanadeva's commentary comes to the *atmasaiyam yoga*, the sixth *adhyaya* of the *Gita*, the advocacy of the cause of Marathi acquires a moral urgency. It is at the beginning of this chapter that Jnanadeva utters his famous pronouncement: " My language is Marathi, but I will compose this work with such beautiful words and style that it will easily surpass nectar."[8] It is worth noting that he uses the same image twice before in the preceding thirteen *ovis*, involving in the process Sanjaya in favour of his argument. In the third *ovi*, Sanjaya says to Dhritarashtra: "I cannot express how great our good fortune is. It is as though a thirsty man, when drinking water, discovered that it was nectar."[9] And, in *ovi* 11, Jnanadeva says, probably, to his guru that his commentary on the *Gita* is like the mythological churning of the ocean of milk from which arose nectar. Clearly, then, the Sanskrit *Gita* is the ocean of milk, from which the nectar of Jnanadeva's Marathi is drawn; and both Jnanadeva and his Sanjaya are delighted at this prospect. But not so Dhritarashtra, the blind king, about whom Sanjaya muses: "How can a blind person see the light of the day?"[10] From this point onward in the poem, the narrative assumes the self-conscious moral responsibility to deny the hierarchic distinction between Sanskrit and the Marathi Prakrit, and to play the Marathi nectar to the milk of the original Sanskrit.

Together with his rejection of the Sanskrit-Prakrit discrimination, Jnanadeva also starts rejecting the distinction between the spoken and the written, between the orality of literature and its graphicality. In defiance of the conventional Sanskrit segregation between the *shastra* literature and the *suta* literature, Jnanadeva asserts that in listening to his Marathi composition, "tongues will spring up in the ears."

> Although listening to speech is the function of the ears, the sense of taste will say, "This joy is mine. My words will be the fragrance enjoyed by the sense of smell." Marvelling at the flowing style, the eyes will be filled with satisfaction and exclaim, "What a wonder! The treasure house of beauty has been opened for us here!" When the sentences have been arranged, the mind will rush forward with outstretched arms to embrace the words.[11]

In defence of this integration between speech and writing in his Marathi commentary, Jnanadeva further says, "Just as crows cannot recognize the moon, ordinary people will never be able to understand this work. Just as the *chakora* bird feeds on moonbeams, similarly, this writing is meant only for the wise."[12] And, in the same chapter, Jnanadeva in fact states that this promise is fulfilled as, when he praises Krishna's love for Arjuna in some domestic images, his listeners exclaim, "Oh what good fortune! What beautiful language! Doesn't its excellence surpass even that of the *Vedas* ?"[13] Jnanadeva's response is predictably, "There is nothing strange about this. When I speak in my mother tongue, Marathi, literary excellence will appear in it like the different colours in the sky." [14]

As the poem progresses, Jnanadeva's claims for the beauty of the Marathi language increase in frequency and insistence. Marathi is not only the language which can integrate speech with writing, but, in Jnanadeva's conception, the language which will allow the audiences to perceive the deeper truths hidden in Krishna's message.

> The eye will perceive the meaning before the ears hear it. And the senses will be revived by the beauty of the words, even before the tongue of reason has tasted the inner meaning. The nose enjoys the fragrance of *malati* buds, but doesn't their beauty also please the eye? Similarly, after the senses have enjoyed the beauty of the Marathi language, they will be ready to approach the deeper truths.[15]

When Jnanadeva composed his commentary, the Marathi language had hardly had any literary past. However, there was a community of listeners and readers for Jnanadeva's poem for whom Marathi was the language of everyday life. When, in an apostrophe he claims that he was going to utter "words that will surpass all other speech,"[16] he was, in fact, thinking of the community of his listeners that would provide legitimation to his literary aesthetics:

> So listen to me, for when my power of speech is fed by attention, a wealth of exposition will come forth in my words. The meaning waits on the words, meaning calls forth further meaning, and there is a full blossoming of feeling in the mind. Therefore, when the favourable wind of dialogue begins to blow, clouds of learning gather in the sky of the heart. But if listeners are inattentive, the essence of the explanation will melt away. The moonstone melts, but it is due to the action of the moon. In the same way, a speaker cannot be a speaker without listeners.[17]

This insistence on calling the listeners' attention is much more than a rhetorical strategy of the poet's discourse. There is a clear perception in Jnanadeva's meta commentary that literature is not mere composition in language, but also a living circulation of it within the community of the speakers of the language. Therefore, his image for founding a literary canon is that of founding a city. In the twelfth chapter of the *dipika*, he makes a passionate appeal to his guru to give him the power to establish the 'city' of the Marathi language:

> I beg of you, open up in the soil of the Marathi language, a gold mine of literary composition, and cultivate in it vines of discernment. Jnaneswar says, plant in it dense gardens ever full of abundant fruit of the discussion of philosophic problems. Break up the ravines of heresy, destroy the bypaths of controversy, and slay the evil beasts of false reasoning. Make me always remain seated at the feet of Lord Krishna, and set the listeners on the throne of learning. Let the blessed day of the knowledge of the Absolute come to the city of the Marathi language....[18]

Literature was performance, in Jnanadeva's agenda. It was not just graceful language stored by scholars in obscure texts.

Literature was, for him, the simultaneity of speech and writing, Sanskrit and Prakrit, orality and textuality. Literature, and the community within which it circulates, were inseparable in Jnanadeva's conception of creativity. His programme for literature as integration and performance, so ably demonstrated in his own poetry, received immediate and spontaneous response. His spiritual companion and disciple, Namadeva, travelled in northern India and composed devotional songs in Hindi. His teaching and poetry subsequently influenced Kabir and Nanak, through the saint Ramananda. Namadeva, who wrote a biographical account of Jnanadeva, also became the leader of a community of saints, all of whom composed songs in Marathi following Jnanadeva's agenda. The community of saints that gathered round Namadeva included persons of all castes and having different social standing. In the subsequent centuries, the practice of composing and singing the kind of integrative and performable poems as envisioned by Jnanadeva came to be one of the most important cultural traditions in Maharashtra. Nearly three hundred years after the *Jnaneswari* was completed, Ekanatha, a poet with versatility in many forms of composition, undertook the first major piece of historical research in the tradition of Marathi literature by preparing a scholarly edition of the *Jnaneswari.* As a critic rightly comments, "Ekanatha produced it with such meticulous care and close study of the various manuscripts available to him that it is still regarded as the standard text."[19] Ekanatha lived during the sixteenth century. During the first half of the seventeenth century Tukarama, the greatest poet in the entire history of Marathi literature, continued the work initiated by Jnanadeva in the thirteenth century. The entire movement that grew around the *bhakti* poetry written by the four major Marathi saint-poets mentioned here, made Vitthala, the god in Pandharpur, its favourite figure for worship. Vitthala was not just an idol, he was primarily the symbol for social equality and liberation. This cult of liberation, which came to be known as the Varakari cult, continues to exist in Maharashtra as an immensely popular movement even today.

The Varakari movement was but one manifestation of the bhakti-spirit. Jnanadeva was but one of the saints to initiate it. Marathi was just one of the languages invigorated by it. What has been described in the foregoing pages as Jnanadeva's agenda, through close reading of a single text, was, in fact, the literary and cultural agenda of the entire subcontinent; and its authors were numerous ranging from the Alvars and the Lingayat poets in the south, the Saivaites and the Tantrik poets in Kashmir, Hemachandra and other Jaina writers in Gujarat, Chaitanya and the other Krishna worshippers in Bengal, Tulsidas and the followers of Rama in central India, the Sufi mystics and their exquisite poetry of symbolism in Persian, and many others. The new languages of their writing ranged from Bangla, Assamiya, Oriya, Kashmiri, Punjabi, Sindhi, Hindi, Rajasthani, and Gujarati to Marathi, Kannada, Telugu, Tamil, Malayalam, Urdu, Persian and Arabic. Various forms of creativity were invented and used in the movements: while poets like Amir Khusrau in Persian and Thyagaraja in Telugu integrated poetry with music, the Mahanubhava writers in Marathi employed history and biography; poets like Akkama in Kannada and Mira in Hindi invented an enigmatic confessional mode, and Ekanatha put the folk forms like *bharud* and *johar* to use. The variety was breathtaking; the heterogeneity was immense. In this rich harvest of great literary creativity which vehemently denied class monopoly as the basis for forming literary canons, the formation of sects became the historiographical strategy.

The dynamics of Indian society during the last ten centuries has been characterised by the process of sect-formation. Sects in India are not a matter just of theological dissension; though some theological totems are the rallying points in them, they originate in social and economic differences. It is worth noting that if there is one feature common to the hundreds of Indian sects, it is their attack on the institution of social castes. Implied in this attack is also the critique of the 'establishment', which included, among other things, the monopoly of a small minority on the institutions of learning. Sects have helped the Indian masses in seeking legitimation of diverse forms of 'knowledge' and life-experiences through collective dissension. Sects therefore always have a spiritual solace for the collectivity. Their forms of knowledge easily merge into activities of one kind or another, rather than evolving into refined theories. The process of sect formation in Indian society dates back to the eighth century, a time when sects were formed around Shiva, Shakti, Vishnu, etc. This process was then appropriated by the vast communities that were trying to give literary dignity to the languages they used in day-to-day life. That is why, invariably, every new language that emerges as a literary language in India revolves around one or more prominent sects. Thus, the modern Kannada language came into being together with the Virashaiva Lingayata sect; the modern Punjabi originated with Nanak's Sikh 'panth ; modern Hindi emerged along with Kabir's sect known as the 'Kabirpanth'. Modern Marathi dates back to the period of the emergence of the Mahanubhava and Varakari sects. In other words, sect-formation has been the most central process of maintaining the progressive dynamics of society in India.

However, the procedure of sect-formation involves a self-limiting act, for though sects are formed in order to raise new questions, they are not formed around these questions but rather some totems that symbolize these questions. Totems involve rules of exclusion and inclusion; and they tend to exert a hypnotic influence on the thinking capacity of the devotee. Through this hypnosis is released a tremendous unconscious power, anarchic, equalising and restless; but it also diminishes the ability to reason. Jnanadeva raised several radical questions for Indian society. But his text was adopted by the Varakari sect as the most sacred totem; and after that, his text ceased to appeal to the rational side of the Varakaris. Some of the later saints participating in this sect, perhaps, saw with clarity the sect's appeal to the unconscious. Their knowledge of the power of the sect's impact was effectively translated in the metres they used. The metres are necessarily easy, incantatory, soothing to the ear. The attendant diction is simple, repetitive, and full of 'non-sense' phrases which directly appeal to the primeval side of the listener. Ekanatha's bharuds, Tukarama's *abhangas,* and the *bhajanas* eclectically adopted by the Varakaris immediately acquired totemic value in their sect. Each of the millions of Varakaris knew the songs, the poems, the texts, with greater intimacy and passion than modern printing technology would enable the ordinary reader to have. Hence, for generation after generation, the Varakari literature retained its audience, kept it spellbound, and managed to remain alive and vital. In fact, the history of this literature was indistinct from the history of the sect,

These sects always flourished in the countryside and away from the cities and centres of government. During the colonial period, the sects did not undergo as much transformation as the urban communities did. The result is that the innumerable sects in India, through which and around which literature in modern

Indian languages flourished, continue to inherit and carry in themselves innumerable 'texts' and versions of literary history that the modern literary scholarship has as yet barely examined.

The 'sectarian' literary history in medieval India —and also as it continues to exist in modern India— is strikingly different from what modern scholarship would label 'oral history'. Oral history is based on memory and not on rigorous memorization. Oral history makes allowance for distortions of events remembered; and the persons who are used as the 'source' for collecting oral history are rarely aware that they are 'carriers' of any history. The followers of sects are, on the other hand, conscious about their knowledge of the literature and the past of their sects. They are encouraged to stick as close to the original texts as possible. Four hundred years after the death of Kabir, hundreds of his followers gather on a tiny island in the Narmada river in Gujarat on the anniversary of his death, and sing his poems in the same rhythm and *raga* as he would have sung them. They sing certain songs while going towards the island, and certain other songs while returning, in the same sequence year after year and century after century. This phenomenon is clearly very different from what is understood as oral history,

A unique feature of literary traditions in India, a feature entirely unknown in the literatures of the Western world, is that in India literary texts may be accorded divine status, and literally treated as being on par with God. A set of literary texts, mostly poetic but occasionally prose biographies as in the case of the Mahanubhava sect, is treated as divinely ordained; and the sect considers it a bounden duty to preserve the texts. Thus, literature and worship become overlapping: all forms of literature are worshipped and all forms of worship are literary. Owing to this feature of Indian sects, they continuously keep the texts of their worship alive. New copies of the texts are made from time to time. Poems and songs are memorized and recited with ritual discipline. Occasionally, special scripts or codes are invented to keep the texts from any defilement. Biographies of the saints—poets or writers—are composed and circulated in the communities of their followers. Sect formation thus gives rise to a strategy in literary history.

As sociological processes, sect-formation and canon-formation are analogous processes. In India, they are not only analogous but even identical. It may be said that the history of the Sikh *panth* is inextricably woven together with the history of the *Granthsaheb* or that the history of the Lingayat sect is almost the same as the history of the *Vacbanas* of the Lingayat saints. With regard to the Varakari *panth*, Ekanatha's edition of *Jnaneswari*, completed in AD 1584 (the *Shako,* year 1506), which forbade any interpolation in the text as taboo, is the high watermark of the formation of the sect. At this time several canons of literature existed in India side by side. Those who learnt Sanskrit had access to the *mantra* canon, the *shastras* and *akshara* literature. Those who did not learn Sanskrit had access to the *suta* literature and the *pantha* literature. In addition to these, there were forms of literature which exploited the performative possibility of literary arts to their utmost, forms flourishing in the centres of political authority and the military camps. These gave rise in course of time to written histories of literature.

8

Pre-Colonial Historiography

Between the *Rajatarangini* of Kalhana[1] composed in the eleventh century and the *Peshavyanchi Bakhar* composed by Krishnaji Sohoni[2] in the nineteenth century, several forms of history writing emerged in India. Some of these forms were practised widely enough to form traditions of history writing. The royal chronicles in Kashmir, the hagiography practised in all parts of India, the *burunji* in Assamiya, the *bhat*-poetry in Rajasthani, the *bakhar* and *ajnapatra* in Marathi, the diaries and autobiographies in Persian, the travelogues in Arabic, official records, gazettes and histories, and many more lines of the development of history and historiography can be traced down the span of the eight centuries. Initially the histories were composed in verse; but, after paper became available to Indian writers in the thirteenth century, histories began to be written in prose form. In the beginning, there was little distinction between literature and history. Kalhana and Amir Khusrau, whose writing is used as history, were primarily creative writers. Gradually, however, history acquired a more specific purpose and method. By the time the accounts of the 1761 battle of Panipat were written, history had become an independent science with its own methods of recording facts and examining the causes of important events.

In any society, the emergence of history as a discipline distinct from literature also brings the awareness of alterity on the part of literature, an awareness that it is not history. In the process evolves the awareness of the historicity of literature, of literary history. This process took place in Europe from the middle of the eighteenth century to the middle of the nineteenth century as convincingly argued by Linda Orr in her brilliant essay, 'The Revenge of Literature: A History of History.'[3] This process took place in India about a century before it took place in Europe; and, in the seventeenth century, India started producing 'literary histories' that would be acceptable to modern scholars as being 'proper' literary history. This is not surprising considering that the use of paper for writing, the development of the prose form used for history writing, a general discourse of history, and traditions of literature about which to write, existed in India in the seventeenth century. Besides, a native variety of modern nationalism was emerging in India at this time.

In the Mogul court of Shahjahan and Jahangir there were many poets who had migrated from far off places to gain patronage from the emperor. Abu'l-Barakat Munir Lahari (1609–1654) was one of them. He travelled extensively, and wrote copiously. One of his works, the *matnawi* on Bengal resulted from such travels. It records several literary and cultural details about seventeenth century Bengal. Munir also composed a commentary on Urfi's *Quasidas*. Such commentaries were common among the scholars of that period. A modern history of Islamic literature in India observes:

> Munir was also a man of his time in writing a *tadkira* of poets, for the 17th century was the time when *hommes-de-letters* began to collect every conceivable bit of information about classical and contemporary poets and compiled biographical dictionaries. One of those famous for their *tadkiras* is the prolific Taqu Aubadi (died in 1630) who came to India in 1606. His production includes *quasidas* and *matnawis* as well as a Persian dictionary (*Surma-yi-sulaimani*) and a *tadkira* called, *arafat al-asiqin*, 'The mountain Arafat of the Lovers', a title which gives the date of its completion, i.e. 1024/1615. The book deals with 3168 Persian poets, and one of Taqu's numerous versions of this compilation, an extract called *ka'ba-yi' irfan*, 'The ka 'ba of Gnosis' was often used by later writers…
>
> Another specialist on poets' biographies was Amin Razi, a first cousin of Shah Jihan's father-in-law, I'timad ad-daula. He had compiled, in 1594, the *haft iqlim*, 'Seven Climata', a work dealing with about 1560 poets, saints and scholars arranged according to their towns and countries, so that not only the historians of literature but the geographers as well can draw upon it.[4]

The *tawarikhs* and *tadkiras* were exercises in biographical criticism and history. They contained encyclopaediac information, made interesting through their anecdotal style, about scholars, schools, poets, saints and men of letters. These histories often had a moral and theological argument. However, the material they contained used to be reliable as history due to the extreme care taken to maintain accuracy in chronology and dates. Besides, they were generously illustrated with quotations from poems and scholarly debates. In her histories of Turkish, Arabic, Persian and Urdu literature in medieval India, Annemarie Schimmel refers to a number of literary histories written during the Islamic period in India, but most of them composed mainly during the seventeenth century. Their geographical sources ranged from Lahore, Meerut and Delhi in the North to Golconda, Aurangabad and Bijapur in the South. They were also composed in Gujarat and Bengal. The tradition was continued till the establishment of a Persian printing press at the British factory in Calcutta in the early nineteenth century. Most of the historians were able poets themselves, and most of them taught in Islamic *madrasas*. The purpose in writing these histories was, clearly, to use them as text books. Since these writers came from a variety of geographical areas in India, and since they were invariably bilingual, it can be assumed that scholars in Bengal, Gujarat, Sindh, Maharashtra, Karnataka, Andhra, Central India and Rajasthan—to use contemporary geographic labels—had a definite idea of what literary history is and what it ought to be.

Schimmel mentions the following histories of literature in her survey of medieval Islamic Indian writings: [5]

(a) Sayyid Ali wrote a biographical compendium on Arabic poets and scholars. It was called *sulafat al-'asr*, 'The Best Wine of the Century', and was a history of contemporary literature. He also wrote a biographical work describing his journey from Mecca to Golconda, *salwat al-garib*. 'Consolation of the Stranger', which is of interest from the viewpoint of literary historiography.

(b) A1 Badaoni (or Badauni) wrote in his *muntakhab ut tawarikhs* an account of native and expatriate poets and writers at the court of Akbar covering a period of half a century (1556–1605). His work was written in Persian; but it covered Muslim poets writing in various languages.

(c) Isma'il Binis wrote several 'romantic' *matnawis* depicting the literary scenes in Lahore and Kashmir.

(d) Muhammad Aslah wrote an encyclopaedic work related to literary history and criticism. It was called *tadkira-yisu'ara-yi Kasmir*.

(e) A similar work was produced a little later, that is in the mid-17th century, by Nasib. It was called *risinama*, and was mainly a biographical dictionary of Kashmiri saint-poets.

(f) This had been preceded by a comparable work in Gujarat: Gauti Sattari's *gulzar-i abrar*, a dictionary of biographies.

(g) Of interest to literary historians should be an early seventeenth century composition by Muhammad Tahir Nisyani, *ta'rih-i tahiri*, a history of Sind, complemented by Yusuf Mirak Sindi's *mazhar-i sahgihani*.

(h) Mirza Bedil, the great eighteenth century Persian poet who lived in Delhi, wrote a *Cahar 'unsur*, 'The Four Elements' completed in 1704. A mixture of prose and poetry, this work offers a wealth of biographical data.

(i) Mir Gulam Ali Azad, who spent the later part of his life in Aurangabad, wrote two books of literary history. He had complete mastery over poetry in Arabic, Turkish, Hindi and Urdu. The *ma'atir al-kiram* gives biographies of 150 scholars from his home town, and *sarw-i Azad,* 'The Free Cypress', a biographical dictionary of 143 poets from all parts of Asia.

(j) Lakshmi Narayan Safiq, a Hindu pupil of Azad, who lived in the early part of the eighteenth century composed two literary histories. *Gul-i ra'na*, 'Lovely Rose' is a widely used *tadkira* of Indian poets who wrote in Persian. On the other hand, the *Sam-i gariban*, 'The Evening of the Strangers', gives an account of Persian poets who visited India.

(k) Ali Hazin, who died in Benaras in 1766, wrote a critical account of his contemporary poets in *tadkirat al-mu'asirin*.

(1) Sher Khan Lodi's *mirat al-hayal*, Binraban Das Hosgu's *safina-yi Hosgu*, and Walih Dadistani's *riyad as-su'ara*, etc., are among the *tadkiras* written during the eighteenth century.

(m) A poet called Sirajuddin of Aurangabad (1714–1763) put together an anthology of Persian poets which contains examples from some 680 poets.

(n) Mir Taqi Mir, an eighteenth century poet and scholar, who composed a *tadkira* called *Nikat as-su-ara*, 'The Fine Points of the Poets', deals with poets in Urdu from the Deccan and Gujarat up to his times.

(o) Gulam Hamadani 'Mushafi'(1750–1824) completed his most important *tadkira*, the *Tadkira-y- Hindigoyan* in 1794. It contained information about some 350 Urdu poets.
(p) Nawab Ali Ibrahim Khan's *Gulzar-i Ibrahim* (1784) contained notices about 320 Urdu poets.
(q) Nawwab Ali Khan 'Mubtala Lakhnawi' composed *Gulsan-i suban* 'Rose Garden of the Word' in 1780.
(r) The *tadkira* by Mir Qudratullah Qadiri, *Magma' a-i nagz*, 'Elegant Collection', which brought together the poetry of 800 Urdu poets, was completed in 1806.
(s) Nawab Azimuddaula Mustafa Khan 'Sefta', more famous as a friend and patron of Ghalib, put together a biographical dictionary of 600 Urdu poets in northern India under the title *Gulsan-i be-har* (in 1845).

Not all of these biographical dictionaries, autobiographies, anthologies and histories are of equally high standard. However, the chronological data provided in them is invariably accurate. The names of the places with which the poets discussed were associated, are also generally correct. The titles of their works, wherever mentioned, are dependable. The problem of inaccuracies comes up when we start examining the verses ascribed to each poet. Since printing was not used for the production of Urdu, Persian and Arabic books until the beginning of the eighteenth century, the historians had to depend on handmade copies. This is one reason why Islamic calligraphy was so well-developed. But, often, the historians recorded the source of the verses quoted by them, whether they were from the poets themselves, or reproduced from memory. In order to examine more critically the nature of literary historiography during the pre-colonial centuries. in India as found in Islamic scholarship, let us turn to Al Badaoni's *Muntakhab ut-tawarikh*.

Badaoni who worked as a historian in the court of Akbar, is counted as being among the more important historians of medieval India. However, as Muhammad Mujeeb observes, he was more passionately interested in literary history than in political history.

> Badaoni had no taste for investigation and research, no desire to add to existing historical knowledge. He states quite ingenuously that for the period beginning with

> the establishment of the Delhi Sultanate to his own time his account is just a selection from *Tarikh-i-Mubarakshahi*.... But he has added 'something of his own'.... The 'something more' which Badaoni has added to his selection of events from his two sources includes also continuous references to *sufis* and poets.[6]

The third part of Badaoni's *Tawarikh* [7] deals with poetry, language and literature. It is divided into four chapters. The first chapter describes thirty-eight learned men "who were regularly employed in the Imperial service until their fame reached such a pitch that it was as manifest as the sun at midday." The second chapter describes seventy other scholars whom the author had met at one or the other time in his life. The third and the shortest chapter presents an account of fifteen men of medicine who had acquired the power of performing miracles through their spiritual powers. These three chapters give an account of the *sufi* movement, their leaders, and the religious establishment in Mogul India and the sociology of Islamic literature in Badaoni's days.

The fourth and the last chapter of the *Tawarikh* offers an anthology of a hundred and sixty-eight poets in combination with a biographical dictionary. Badaoni asserts that he has known most of the poets discussed; those he has not known are so famous that he has reliable knowledge about their work. Besides, he makes it clear that he has used the previously written historical material. In his introductory remarks, Badaoni states:

> A full account of the poets of the reign of the Emperor Akbar is given in the *Nafa,' isu-l-Ma' asir*, well known as the *Tazkirab* of Mir 'Ala'- ud-daula, which is the source from which the materials for this brief account are extracted. Some of these poets have composed *divans*. I have written of those with whom I was acquainted, whom I have seen, whether near or from afar, or who have acquired fame.[8]

Badaoni's method in his history is to offer the essential outline of the poet's biography followed by samples of some of his best poems. There are, then, remarks on any special features of the poet's work. For example, the use of music to accompany the recitation is mentioned in the case of some poets. In some cases,

Badaoni mentions the ideological peculiarities of the poets. And finally, he gives a critical assessment of the stylistic features of the poets he discusses. There is also plenty of information about their financial and social condition. There is a sense of proportion in Badaoni's comments. He gives far more space to the major poets, while the minor poets are given no more than a paragraph or two each. For instance, writing about a poet known as Sipahi, the historian comments:

> He was the grandson of the famous Khwaja Kalan Beg. This Quaritrain is by him: 'Alas, that the season of the rose has passed so quickly, Alas, that it has passed in the twinkling of an eye! Without thy eyes and the dawn on thy cheek the violet and the hyacinth Pass their days in blindness and in mourning.' He died in Agra in the year H. 978 (AD 1570–71).[9]

But when he discusses major poets, he offers elaborate comments on their styles, with reasons for his liking or disliking them; his meetings with them; the more important events in their lives. There are, occasionally, bits of gossip that Badaoni introduces in his narrative to make it interesting. It is because of his habit of making personal remarks that we get very valuable information about the social, sexual and cultural life of the men of letters in Badaoni's times.

The history of poetry written by Badaoni can be described as a 'contemporary history', for it does not describe the entire development of Islamic literature in India from its very beginning to Badaoni's age. But, given his method of using only personally verified material as historical material and not accepting written material as authoritative, it was not possible for the historian to go beyond his own generation and period. However, in the histories of literature written after Badaoni the span of the narrative is generally much larger. Badaoni himself was conscious of the limitation of his narrative; but he did not aim at writing any 'conclusive' history of poetry. In his opinion, history writing should be an ongoing process:

> This is the account of some of those poets, most of whom were contemporary with the author and writing during the time in which he was writing, and whose *divans* are current in this age and are circulated as

> examples. As for those who have leapt from the net of this memoir and are here neither described nor indicated by casual mention, I make them over to those who shall hereafter set foot in the plain of existence, for this series of poets is as endless as *Burhan-i-Tatbiq*, and to comprehend them all within the limits of one age, or one short space of time is beyond the limits....[10]

In other words, Badaoni does not accept the responsibility of introducing periodization in his history. This is not to say that he was not sensitive to historical changes in literary style and the function of literature. On the contrary, he was so acutely conscious of the changes taking place during the period of his narrative that he made *that* awareness his chief justification for writing the history:

> I shall now explain what it was that originally led me to collect these fragments. Since a complete revolution, both in legislation and manners, greater than any of which there is any record for the past thousand years, has taken place in these days.... [11]

The great literary change that Badaoni then points out as having taken place is that poets had moved away from the love of language to the love of political patronage, power and worldly gains. Implicit in this passion is Badaoni's main historiographical principle.

In Badaoni's opinion, the love for language is identical with the love for God and religion, in this case Islam. The criterion for judging poetry, therefore, should be the saintly quality in the life of the poet and in his verses. This, of course, is a subjective judgement. To avoid the risks implied, Badaoni avoids making a distinction between 'literature' and 'para-literature'. Thus, he assumes no responsibility towards canon-making. Similarly, he avoids the division of literature into 'written' and 'recited'. As quoted above, he considers the 'circulation' of a work as the distinguishing feature of literature. His view is, that the purpose of literature is to keep the grace and beauty of language alive as well as to enhance social morality. Hence, in his history, there is scope for discussion of the orality as well as the lexicality of poetry, of mainstream literature as well as 'para' literature, of poetry by native Indians as well as that by expatriates. But there is no scope for the poems written by non-Muslims, even if they are written in Arabic, Persian, Turkish, Urdu or Hindi. Again, there is severe criticism in Badaoni for those who had any Turkish connection, an aspect of his historiography that can be explained only in terms of his religious views.

Thus, Badaoni's history does not use 'period', 'genre', 'canon' or 'language' as principles of literary history. It uses, on the other hand, 'sect' as the central principle. In it, then, get subsumed 'oral' and 'written', 'marginal' and 'central', etc. These principles are not entirely different from the principles of historiography employed by the Hindu and other non-Muslim panths in medieval India.

An exact replica of Badaoni's biographical anthology of poetry within his contemporary Hindu cults can be found in the anthology of songs prepared by the Dadupanth saints. Thanks to German scholarship of Indian literature, this anthology, known as the Panchvani, ís now available in a critical (and computer-analysed) edition.[12] It includes songs by Dadu, Namadeva, Raidas and Hardas. The inclusion of the songs in this conventional collection avoids 'period', 'language', 'canon' and 'genre' ás the criteria. The collection attempts a total integration between the written and the spoken, for even the *ragas* to which each of the songs is ascribed are fully recorded. The historiography in medieval India follows, as was logical, the actual literary practice. In this respect the comments by W.M. Callewaert, one of the two editors of the Panchvani, are worth quoting:

> Studying the songs of a poet like Namdev or Kabir is quite different from studying Shakespeare or Kalidasa. It is the ambition of a text-critic studying Shakespeare to bring out the text 'written' by the author, by looking at the various versions available in manuscripts. The text-critic soon realizes that this is impossible in the case of a Namdev or Kabir. There is no way by which we can reach beyond the oral tradition to the poets themselves. This oral tradition, unlike that of the *Vedas*, did not shun variety and creativity... Fortunately, the manuscript tradition allows us to reach the threshold of this oral tradition, or the moment when it started to be written down, some time before 1600 AD (while the oral tradition continued).[13]

The separation between the oral and the written seems to have started occurring some time in the seventeenth century. It is significant that Badaoni too felt worried about the 'gap' between writing and speech. Literary historiography in India during the seventeenth and eighteenth centuries seems to have been guided by the anxiety about the disintegration of the literary communities created by the emergence of the new languages at the beginning of the millennium.

In recent years scholars of Indian history have suggested that the 'modern' period in Indian history begins with Akbar. Whether that is true in political history or not, in literary history that indeed seems to be the case. During the seventeenth century, literatures in modern Indian languages showed signs of becoming more literate, urbane, highbrow and to some extent institutionalized or patronized. This change introduced in Indian literature, once again, the gap that Jnanadeva had sought to bridge, the gap between the 'spoken' and the 'written'.

In tune with the emergence of new canons of literature, the sense of literary history too changed, as did the anxiety and the rhetoric of literary historiography. The split between the spoken and the written was dramatically enhanced and quickened by the introduction of printing technology in India, initially and accidentally in Goa in the seventeenth century, and in all parts of India subsequently during the nineteenth century. In its turn, the technology of printing was linked with the British colonization of India. Therefore, in order to continue our narrative of historiography we must allow other beings to step in.

9

Warton's Imaginative Savages

In the story of the rise of English literary history,[1] the publication of Thomas Warton's *History of English Poetry* in four volumes (1774–1790)[2] marks a crucial turning point. Before its publication there existed a vast body of raw material for literary history such as biographical dictionaries, reviews, genre studies, historical researches related to single authors and verse anthologies. After Warton's compilation of the available body of researches in the form of an argument, all subsequent narratives about the literary past acquired the distinctive features of literary history.

Like so much else that happened in England during the last quarter of the eighteenth century in various fields of knowledge—biology, economics, psychology and linguistics—[3], Warton's historiography was not only a pioneering achievement but it also defined, for the future, the ground rules for the discourse of literary history. As Wellek points out,

> Warton was not satisfied merely to collect materials for a history of poetry, but wanted to present them in a scheme of historical and literary values, based on 'fundamental principles... ' largely the conception of a progress from 'rudeness to elegance,' the idea of a uniform advance from barbarism to refinement.[4]

Warton's evolutionary concept of literary history was in tune with the spirit of optimism that pervaded English sciences and literature in his generation, and which was expressed in a poem like Thompson's *The Castle of Indolence*. However, this evolutionary optimism was not just the ruling sentiment in Warton's history, it was the very backbone of his argument. In employing the opposition between rudeness and elegance as a theoretical argument, Warton was no doubt following a long established controversy about the nature of the poetic imagination.

About a century before Warton, the English philosopher Thomas Hobbes had taken up the issue in his famous *Leviathan*, in which he had carefully differentiated between imagination aided by reason and imagination not so aided.[5] Similarly, John Milton had written his twin poems *L'Allegro* and *Il Penseroso* precisely to make a similar distinction. Poetic and philosophic speculation about creativity and imagination occupied an important place in all intellectual activity during the eighteenth century. Invariably, the English philosophers and poets perceived imagination in terms of an opposition between the simple, untainted and barbaric imagination and the sophisticated, urbane and 'reasonable' imagination. The culmination of this aesthetics came through Edmund Burke's distinction between the sublime and the beautiful.[6] Hence, when Warton employed this opposition as his argument in the *History*, he was drawing upon a vast fund of philosophical speculation about primitivism.

In Milton's poetry the opposition between forms of imagination was presented through myth, in the form of the opposition between the mental activity of Satan and God. Half a century later, the same opposition found expression in Pope's poetry through a pair of human characters, Belinda of *The Rape of the Lock* and Eloisa of *Eloisa and Abelard*. Less than half a century later, landscape had replaced human interest; and in Thompson's *Seasons*, geography provided the metaphors for the mind. This was not surprising considering that at this time England had explored vast geographical areas and had encountered several 'primitive' races. The in-flow of information from the colonies fed the established English epistemology and aesthetics, consequently, creating a discourse that can be termed 'Savageology'.

Orientalism was one of the branches of this Savageology. It was guided by the existing British ideas of what primitive people ought to be. At the same time it strengthened these ideas by its discoveries of ancient languages and polytheistic people. This curious interlocking of Orientalism and the British ideas of primitive imagination had a profound impact on Warton's historiography. And, in order to appreciate this relationship, which in turn has great significance for literary historiography in India, it is necessary to look closely at Warton's 'Savageology'.

While it would be a slight exaggeration to say that there was a cult of primitivism in England during the mid-eighteenth century, it would be an understatement to say that there was only a nominal interest among intellectuals in primitivism. The truth is that this interest ran very strong in a variety of intellectual areas.[7] First, there were poetical works such as the *Death Song of a Cherokee Indian* by Mrs. John Hunter and the *American Love-Ode* by Lady Winchelsea. The father of Thomas Warton, the elder Thomas Warton, attempted an imitation of this poem, and Joseph Warton, the brother of the historian, wrote *Dying Indian*. Next, there were the translations of literary works that had started pouring in through the work of the Orientalists. Sir William Jones, who later translated *Sakuntala*, had published *Poems consisting chiefly of Translations from the Asiatic Languages* as early as 1772. In this book, Jones argued that the poetry of Hafiz was 'naturally' excellent, that poets in warmer climates had a more active imagination. Then, there was a current of opinion in literary criticism which considered an opulence of imagination a natural prerogative of 'primitive' poetry. In his history of literary history, Rene Wellek offers a careful account of this element of English literary criticism:

> The most common approach was through the theory of climate, popularized by Temple... The mild climate of the South was contrasted with the rigours of the North, while extreme heat was considered detrimental to the growth of literature. Or sometimes East and West were contrasted, in which case the East was identified with the South and considered favourable to the 'warmth of imagination.'.... Addison assigned 'extravagant imagery' to the 'warmer climates'. Husbands in 1731 spoke of the 'Genius of the east' which 'soars upon stronger wings, and takes a loftier flight than the Muse of Greece or Rome.' ... Sir William Jones praised the climate of Yemen in recommending Arabian poetry and spoke of the immoderate heat of the East as disposing the Eastern people to a life of indolence, which gives them full leisure to cultivate their talents. He made the alternative suggestion that the sun has a direct, physical influence on the imagination.[8]

This crude 'climate theory' of 'warm imagination' gradually came to be transformed into a critical label that could be applied to all primitive poetry. Hugh Blair, himself a poet who composed some memorable poetry on the theme of imagination during the years of the 'Sensibility School' of English poetry, used 'primitive poetry', or as he called it the 'Oriental vein of poetry', as a descriptive critical label rather than a geographic designation. The Oriental vein was, according to Blair, "characteristic, of an age rather than a century."[9]

Implicit in the Oriental/primitive thesis about active poetic imagination was a view of the development and decay of languages. This view held that in the earlier phases of the growth of a language it has greater concrete character by virtue of the immediacy between objects and words. In later stages this immediacy is lost and replaced by a greater degree of abstraction. In other words, according to this view, the primitive languages were more spontaneous and metaphoric than the synthetic and developed languages. These considerations, first applied to the evolution of languages, later attracted the attention of literary critics. When this 'organic theory of language' with its fantasy about the great emotional force of a language in its early stage was applied to the field of poetry; it followed that a sharp distinction between the primitive and the sophisticated styles of poetry had to be made. As Wellek points out,

> This emotional theory of the origin of language explained the supposed characteristic of all primitive languages (and thus all primitive poetry), its figurativeness. 'From this deduction it is plain,' said Blackwell, 'that any language formed as described above, must be full of metaphor. We must imagine the speech of savages to be broken, unequal and boisterous.' The Turks, Arabs and Indians are described as taciturn people, who, when they open their mouths and 'give loose to a fiery imagination, are poetical and full of metaphors.'[10]

The theories about the primitive imagination, those about the early stages of languages development, and the in-flow of literary information about the Oriental and other exotic cultures combined in Thomas Warton's literary historiography to form an argument. The argument was that initially the romantic fictions, folklore and myths were imported to Europe from the Oriental nations. Gradually, however, these synthesized with reason, logic, religious wisdom and stylistic good manners to produce 'literature'.

Thomas Warton's *History* runs into more than two thousand pages, each of the four volumes of which has an impressive length of five hundred or more pages. Its aim was to tell the story of the rise and development of English poetry from its beginning towards the close of the eleventh century to the commencement of the eighteenth century. However, when the fourth volume was published, the story had not reached even up to Spenser. As it was going to be a history of poetry, and as Shakespeare was considered more a dramatist than a poet, Warton's plan had excluded Shakespeare from his narrative. Thus, in effect, the four volumes of Warton's history offer us no comments on any really major English poet except Chaucer. The section on Chaucer runs into several chapters, most of which repeatedly show that the sources of his plots and characters are in Arabic, Turkish or other Oriental poetry. For instance, alluding to Milton's praise of the *Squire's Tale* of Chaucer, Warton says: "The imagination of this story consists in Arabian fiction, engrafted on Gothic chivalry. Nor is this Arabian fiction purely the sport of arbitrary fancy: it is in great measure founded on Arabian learning."[11] And after explaining in great detail the Arabic elements of Chaucer's poetic motifs, he adds,

> To trace the matter home to its true source, these fictions have their origin in a science which professedly made a considerable part of the Arabian learning. In the twelfth century the number of magical and astrological Arabic books translated into Latin was prodigious.[12]

The last two volumes of the *History* are anthologies of obscure poems rather than a history of the poets or texts.

The first volume of the history has three lengthy 'Dissertations' forming a length of almost 300 pages. They are, respectively, (i) *Of the Origin of Romantic Fiction in Europe*, (ii) *On the Introduction of Learning into England*, and (iii) *On the Gesta Romanorum*. The first of these three dissertations is devoted to showing that romance fiction in Europe is solely of Oriental origin. At the very outset, Warton states his aim:

> That peculiar and arbitrary species of Fiction which we commonly call Romantic, was entirely unknown to the writers of Greece and Rome. It appears to have

> been imported into Europe by a people, whose modes of thinking, and habits of invention, are not natural to that country. It is generally supposed to have been borrowed from the Arabians.[13]

The second dissertation describes at length the decline in learning after the fall of the Roman empire, and the recovery of knowledge at the beginning of the present millennium. Warton considers the Arabic contribution to this recovery of the greatest importance. He writes:

> After the calamities which the state of literature sustained in consequence of the incursions of the northern nations, the first restorers of the ancient philosophical sciences in Europe, the study of which, by opening the faculties and extending the views of mankind, gradually led the way to other parts of learning were the Arabians. In the beginning of the eighth century, this wonderful people, equally famous for their conquests and their love of letters, in ravaging Asiatic provinces found many Greek books, which they read with infinite avidity: and such was the gratification they received from the fortunate acquisition, and so powerfully their curiosity was excited to make further discoveries in this new field of knowledge, that they requested their caliphs to procure from the emperor at Constantinople the best Greek writers. These they carefully translated into Arabic.[14]

Of course, Warton does not forget to add that the Arabs translated only those Greek and Latin works which 'their extravagant and romantic' imagination approved.

The third dissertation prefixed to the first volume of Warton's history is on the *Gesta Romanorum*, a form of story-telling more popularly known as the *mirror* stories, which were moralising stories for rulers and administrators. Warton traces the textual histories of such *mirror* sequences in English and French, and argues that the origin of these stories was in Arabic philosophy and literature.

The question one likes to ask is: why did Warton spend nearly three hundred pages at the very beginning of his history to show the Oriental beginnings of English literature? One starts getting some ideas of his intention when one looks at his language a little more closely. In the dissertation on the *Monks' Tales*, he describes the age that produced such prolific imagination as "the age of ignorance and imagination".[15] At the very outset of his brief 'Preface', Warton states:

> In age advanced to the highest degree of refinement, that species of curiosity commences, which is busied in contemplating the progress of social life, in displaying the gradations of science, and in tracing their translation from barbarism to civility.[16]

Again a little later, he stresses that the purpose of a literary history is to show its readers the "*progress of our national* poetry, from a *rude origin* and obscure beginnings, to its *perfection* in a *polished age*."[17] Spenser's poetry was, in Warton's opinion, that perfection and polish which the English nation had brought to the obscure imaginative tales of an ignorant age in the Orient. However, he does not lavish praise on 'progress' without simultaneously lamenting the decline in 'imagination'. Wellek points out the ambivalence in Warton's vision of history:

> This curious double point of view—acknowledgement of the progress of modern civilization and even of modern taste, and yet regret for the 'world of fine fabling'—had an interesting, logical consequence. The period of English literature which combined the advantages of both early and later poetry must have seemed to Warton the natural summit and the real ideal....
>
> Ultimately, a conception of the development of English poetry in three stages emerges: a primitive, imaginative stage; a condition of synthesis between imagination and reason, realized by the Elizabethans; and a period of judgment and correctness which seemed final to Warton and ideal from the point of view of the social advance of humanity, even though it might spell death to imagination and poetry.... To a certain extent Warton anticipates Hegel's brief that the owl of Minerva flies in the dusk of a creative civilization, or—in agreement with his own metaphors—that the bright daylight of reason has dispelled the foul mists of superstition together with the golden haze of imagination.[18]

Thus the central historiographical principle in Warton's account of English literature was the dichotomy between imagination and reason.

As stated earlier, the dichotomy between imagination and reason had been a major theme in English poetic and philosophical traditions. Warton's unique and phenomenal contribution to this theme was to provide it a space-and-time framework. Space as a metaphor for the imagination was in use in English poetry during the mid-eighteenth century. More particularly, the school of poets known as the 'Graveyard School', which included poets like Young, Gray, Akenside and Blair, had been using the dark and the bright aspects of a given landscape to depict the dark and the bright sides of the human mind, and to show the opposition between imagination and reason. The Warton brothers themselves had a part to play in this poetic movement. However, in his history, Thomas Warton extended the metaphor to include global space. In this new form, the South and the East represented imagination, the North and the West represented reason. This new reading of the problematic of imagination was further enriched by Warton by giving it a vast temporal dimension too. The primitive ages and the remote past were the times for spontaneity and imaginative outbursts. The modern periods were the times for restraint and a cultivated sensibility. In other words, in writing his history of English poetry, Warton effectively historicized what so far had been considered a conflict within an individual's consciousness.

The spatial and temporal distribution of the creative faculties of the mind in Warton's historiography had drawn substance and scholarly support from 'savageology'. There were other forms of this savage-imagery in circulation during Warton's age. There was, for instance, Shakespeare's Caliban; and there already was Defoe's Man Friday. In France, Rousseau had floated the philosophy of noble savagery. Drawing on all these, Warton transformed the savage-imagery to accommodate the historicised process of creativity in it. His achievement was that he provided English literature with a sense of selfhood defined in terms of the alterity between the primitive and the modern, imagination and reason, and the Eastern and the Western.[19] Implicit in this self-definition was the possibility of a rhetoric of literature as a civilizing force. Less than half a century after Warton proposed his historiography, this possibility found its full realisation in the works of the British Utilitarians. However, during Warton's own time and in the years that followed, it was his savageology that exerted a stronger influence among English intellectuals. One branch of savageology to flourish with abundance was Indology.

10

Jones and the 'Gentoos'

Images of India were formed in ancient Europe; and they had been handed down through isolated strands of folklore as well as through the writing of Plotinus and Pythagoras. These images were more fantasy than knowledge; and in modern Europe's intellectual discourse, India as a constituent part of the Orient, had come to represent a certain kind of impious imagination. It was for this reason that during the British renaissance the dichotomy between imagination and reason acquired importance as part of the process of Britain's cultural self-definition. And if, subsequently, Warton employed the antithesis between imagination and reason as his historiographical logic, it was also used by the early historians of India to establish India's otherness from Britian's selfhood. One of the earliest histories of India written by British historians was Alexander Dow's *The History of Hindostán* (1770).[1] It provides the context within which we can appreciate the work and contribution of Sir William Jones, who turned Indology from a hobby to an academic discipline.

The History of Hindostán, which was published as a translation of Ferishta's history of India, was, in fact, a combination of translations from several historical works. Its main bulk was from Ferishta's history; but it also drew upon Abul Fazl's *Ain-i-Akbari,* Matimad Khan's *Jehangirnama,* Mirza Kasim's *Shabhjahan-nama* and such other works available in Persian. Dow's English vision of India and the Hindus was thus coloured by the vision of India in Islamic-Persian historiography.

Dow's rendering of Indian history made no secret of his censorious attitude to Indian historiography. This attitude rejoiced in the discovery of India's antiquity but lamented the utter lack of historical sense among Indian scholars and historiographers. It asserted that India had an abundance of history (as the past) but little history (as the narrative about the past). This attitude was not peculiar to Dow's response to Indian scholarship alone; it was generally shared by other British scholars engaged in interpreting Indian culture during the last quarter of the eighteenth century.

An excellent account of the early phase of British Indological studies is presented in Bernard Cohn's essay 'The Command of Language and the Language of Command.'[2] Among the more important works of this period, Cohn lists the following: *The History of Hindostan* (1770) by Dow, *A Grammar of the Persian Language* (1771) by Sir William Jones, *The Practical and. Vulgar Dialects of the Indostan Language Commonly called Moors* (1772) by George Hadley, *A Code of Gentoo Laws* (1776) by Nathaniel Brassey Halhed, *A Dictionary of English, Persian and Arabic* (1780) by John Richardson, *Institutes Political and Military of Timour* (1783) by William Davy, *The Forms of the Herkern* (1781) by Francis Balfour, *The Bhagvet Geeta* (1785) by Charles Wilkins, *A Vocabulary, Persian, Arabic and English* (1785) by William Kirkpatric, *Ayeen-i-Akberry or the Institutes of the Emperor Akbar* (1783-6) by Francis Gladwin, and *A Dictionary of English and Hindustani, Part I* (1787) by John A. Gilchrist. Cohn comments:

> ... the production of these texts and others which followed them began the establishment of discursive formations, defined an epistemological space, created a discourse (of Orientalism), and had the effect of converting Indian forms of knowledge into European objects. The subjects of these texts were first and foremost the Indian languages themselves, represented in European terms as grammars, dictionaries and teaching aids in a project to make the acquisition of a working knowledge of the languages available to those British who were to be part of the ruling groups in India.[3]

This discourse of Indology created in Bengal during the last quarter of the eighteenth century subsequently became the preamble to the cultural relationship between Britain and India. The relationship was full of ambivalent spaces thus allowing a modern day historian like A.L. Basham to defend William Jones ("When Jones translated *Sakuntala* are we to believe that he consciously thought, I am doing this in order that my country may dominate a subject people?,"[4]), as well as a fierce tirade against him by Edward Said, ("To rule and to learn, then to compare Orient with Occident: these were Jones' goals..."[5]). The important question for us is not what William Jones's intentions were, but what effects his scholarly procedures and literary products had on literary historiography in Britain and, as a result, in India.

When Sir William Jones arrived in India, the image of the Gentoo that had been circulating in British scholarship had two main sources: the Greek legends and histories which had depicted India as an exotic and intractable culture, and the travel books written by Europeans during the seventeenth century and the early part of the eighteenth century which depicted India as a land ruled by despots. This imagery thus combined allurement with fear in the contemporary British attitudes to India. Jones's scholarly project aimed at making sense of the confused imagery and in examining if those images corresponded to the reality of India.

There is no doubt that Jones's fascination with Indian culture, religions and literature never subsided during his years in Calcutta. During these years, he went about exploring as much as he could from as many sources as were at his disposal in areas as diverse as music, law, grammar, languages, philosophy, poetry, drama, myths and religion. He did not stop there: he wanted his contemporary scholars in Britain to share his excitement about the India he had discovered; and so he kept publishing the results of his researches in British periodicals and journals. The measure of his success in communicating to the British world of learning his delight in Indian literature and culture was indicated by the continuous demand for his publications in Britain. Commenting on the extent of diffusion of Jones's work in Britain, John Drew records:

> Jones's own work and that he inspired among members of the Asiatic Society was diffused most widely in the early 1790s through the *Asiatic Researches*.... Neither Journal (that is the *Researches* and the short lived *Miscellany)* was readily available in England and the shortage of copies gave rise in the 1790s to a series of reprints, mainly of Jones's, work and mainly from *Asiatic Researches,* entitled *Dissertations and Miscellaneous Pieces relating to ... Asia.* At least partly on account of their

> scarcity, if more particularly because of their merit, periodicals like the *Monthly Review* and the *British Critic* especially, and to a lesser extent the *Critical Review*, reprinted considerable extracts from Jones's articles.[6]

Jones was a pioneer in several areas: historical linguistics, comparative etymology, comparative musicology, myth-study, the Western discourse of Sanskrit scholarship and the study of Hinduism. These aspects of his work have been discussed and evaluated by critics. But one more area of study inaugurated by Sir William Jones has not received adequate attention. He was the first British scholar to perceive India in terms of a literary culture. Prior to him, others had translated or mentioned Indian source books as 'texts' of interest in Law, Grammar, Religion, etc. But it was Jones who for the first time and firmly established in the British consciousness India's image as a country with rich literature. His 'Hymns' and the translation of *Abhijnanasakuntalam*—which attracted serious literary attention in Britain and Germany—effectively made the point that the land of Gentoos, (the term used by Halhed for Hindus) is not only the land of antiquity but also a literary nation. He likened Indian literary works to Greek works while speaking of their literary merit:

> Suppose Greek literature to be known in modern Greece only, and there to be in the hands of priests and philosophers; and suppose them to be still worshippers of Jupiter and Apollo; suppose Greece to have been conquered successively by Goths, Huns, Vandals, Tartars, and lastly by the English; then suppose a court of judicature to be established by the British Parliament at Athens, and an inquisitive Englishman to be one of the judges; suppose him to learn Greek there, which none of his countrymen know, and to read Homer, Pindar, Plato, which no other Europeans had ever heard of. Such am I in this country.[7]

Jones's discovery of India as a nation with literature, and literature extending to remote antiquity, enthused his readers in Britain to look at India for literary inspiration. Jones himself believed that his discovery of the richness of Indian literature would infuse English literature with a new and powerful imagery. He was not wrong in anticipating the change: a generation of English poets—Coleridge, Shelley, Robert Southey—and the immensely popular Irish poet, Thomas Moore, derived poetic strength from the new image of India that Jones tried to popularise. The new movement, Romanticism, while in no way entirely fuelled by Indology was nonetheless, one in which Jones's literary Gentoo was one of the motivating factors.

Romanticism in English literature was in profound disagreement with the historiographical premises underlying Warton's presentation of English poetry. For Warton, the movement from imagination to reason was the hallmark of literary progress. For the Romantics it was a literary decline. Both Wordsworth and Shelley lavished praise on the primitive and the socially unhindered poetic expression in their critical writings. Warton had acknowledged the contribution of the warmer South at the inception of England's poetic tradition, but had praised the cold reasonableness of the English genius. Byron turned against this aesthetic geography and pushed the heroes of his narrative poetry southward and eastward in search of warmer climates and a more fertile imagination. Warton, who belonged to the Sensibility school of poetry, valued moral restraint, adulthood and social order in conceptualising his history. The Romantics believed on the other hand, in the primacy of innocence, freedom, childhood and the unconscious. Sir William Jones's depiction of Indian literature as comparable to Greek literature in range and richness found its place in the historiographical reversals taking place in Britain at that time but not without a certain distortion of truth which marks all cross-cultural transactions of imagery.

Jones's enthusiasm in proving to his English contemporaries the antiquity of Indian culture and literature made him and his audience forget that Indian literature was a continuously flowing cultural current and that its development in the second millennium was as important as the developments prior to the tenth century. When he compared Indian literature with Greek literature, he did not emphasise the crucial difference between the two, namely, that while Greek culture was a thing of the past, Indian culture was still surviving. In outlining the aims of his researches, Jones had very clearly put down the eleventh century as the historical limit for his enquiries. Having shared the savageology as a component of Indology during his formative years in Britain, Jones could not bring himself to think of India after the eleventh century as a country with a living literary culture. Perhaps, the decline of Sanskrit literary traditions in the Indian bhashas failed to win Jones's approval because the library resources and oral information on bhasha literatures at his disposal were not adequate to enthuse him about them. The result was that in spite of Jones's pioneering work in establishing India as a literary culture in British literary discourse, the image of Indian literature created by him could never escape the state of being chained to antiquity, almost like Shelley's Prometheus or Blake's Albion in *Jerusalem.*

In India, Jones had a phenomenal following. Partly owing to his success in British literary circles and partly owing to the demands of the colonial situation, practically every British civil servant working in India throughout the nineteenth century took an interest in Indian learning and culture. One wrote at least travel books adding to the available information about India in Britain; but none crossed the line of historical demarcation that Jones had drawn. The result was that by the end of the nineteenth century British, German and French scholars came to believe firmly that the only literature in India fit for cross-cultural dissemination and worth comparing with Greek, Latin, English, French or German literature was the canon of texts in Sanskrit, or occasionally in Persian. The rest was all decline and degradation. This image provided the narcissistic structure of European—and in particular English—literature with an image of the ‘other’ literature. If the history of English literature was—as laid down in the historiography initiated by Warton—progress, the history of Indian literature was, as perceived by Jones's Asiatic researches, a continuous decline. Jones focused his attention on the past of Indian literature and, by the same token, diminished in great proportion the image of literature in the bhashas. There was an unintended agreement between Warton's Savageology and Jones's Indology, namely, savages may be opulent in their imagination but they do not know how to cultivate it so that it receives the blessings of reason. The two pioneers shared the view that savages rest content with their past, they need no present.

About half a century after Sir William Jones began his exploration of the Indian literary past, the British opinion of India's literary wealth had gone through a radical reversal. In Britain, the Romantic revolution had come to a dead-end, the Utilitarians had taken over the task of forming public opinion, the signs of social unrest had started gaining momentum gathering themselves towards the 'sinister' Chartist Movement, and the British Government had become politically more alert to the affairs of the expanding empire. It was in this context of social rift at home and political assertion abroad that Lord Macaulay denied the imagery of Indian literature circulated by Jones' researches. In fact, Macaulay was not alone in this distrust of Jones's imagery of India. James Mill, his contemporary, had no hesitation in raising doubts about Jones's Sanskrit scholarship. Mill was convinced that though Jones had praised the *Ramayana* so lavishly, he had never read it.[8] The Macaulay generation was doing to the past of Indian literature what Jones had done to its present, namely, attempting to wipe it out of India's cultural memory. Though Indologists following Jones kept working at their researches throughout the nineteenth century, the process of reducing the history of Indian literature went on unhindered. Occasionally, someone like Friedrich Max Muller succeeded in temporarily averting the process; but in the colonial situation the odds against such solitary attempts were heavy.

The British image of Indian literature had taken such a beating during colonial rule in the nineteenth century, and the sense of British superiority over India in the domain of artistic culture and the notion that Indians had no sense of history were so fully consolidated.that, in the first quarter of the twentieth century, a patriotic poet like Sri Aurobindo had to launch a crusade against these biases. He wrote a passionate defence of Indian culture in his *Foundations of Indian Culture*.[9] Though the immediate reason prompting Sri Aurobindo to write his monumental book, first serialised through the *Arya,* was to counter William Archer's attack on Indian culture, he was at the same time responding to the colonial imagery of Indian literature and culture.

William Archer's negative criticism had enraged even some British Indologists, one of whom, Sir John Woodroffe, wrote a rejoinder under the title 'Is India Civilised?' Sri Aurobindo entered the debate through the columns of his journal *Arya* and proposed that Archer's criticism of Indian literature and culture was nothing if not politically motivated. "But hostile criticism to be of any sound value must be criticism," retorts Aurobindo, "not slander and false witness, not vitriol-throwing."[10] He pointed out that Archer's book "had an ulterior, a political object; it started with the underlying idea that India must be proved barbarous in order to damage or destroy her case of self-government.”[11] Yet Aurobindo did not overlook the benefits of facing a rationalist critique of Indian culture. He fully examines the grounds on which such a critique could be raised. While undertaking an elaborate defence of Indian literature and culture he did not forget to offer his own critique both of Indian tradition and European modernity. In the process he offers an original historiography for Indian literature, a historiography which avoided Jones's lopsided appreciation of the past and Macaulay's thoughtless negation of the tradition of Indian literature. In this sense, Sri Aurobindo was the first original historiographer of Indian literature during the twentieth century.

Sri Aurobindo argued in his passionate defence of Indian culture that though temporarily occluded, it was not an entirely atrophied culture. “The greatness of the ideals of the past is a promise of the greater ideals of the future.” He pointed out that ‘civilization’ and ‘barbarism’ are relative terms and to ‘civilize’ India on the lines offered by European models would go against the central principle of cultural evolution in India. He added that in order to understand and fully appreciate the principle of evolution it is necessary to have an indigenous perspective:

> Certainly we must repel with vigour every disintegrating or injurious attack; but it is more important to form our own true and independent view of our own past achievement, present position and future possibilities, —what we were, what we are and what we may be. In our past we must distinguish all that was great, essential, elevating, vitalising, illuminating, victorious, effective. And in that again we must distinguish what was close to the permanent, essential spirit and the persistent law of our cultural being and separate from it what was temporary and transiently formulative. For all that was great in the past cannot be preserved as it was or repeated for ever; there are new needs, there are other vistas before us.[12]

The last sentence alludes to the pervasive debate between the advocates of ‘tradition’ *(sanatana* or *purana)* and the advocates of ‘modernity’ (*nutana* or *adbunika*) carried out in India throughout the nineteenth century. If William Jones's work gave rise to a new discourse about the literary past, the debate during the so-called Indian Renaissance gave rise to the concept of a radical break between the past and the present. Though Sri Aurobindo sought to reconcile the past and the present, the social history of India during the century preceding Aurobindo's historiography had made such a happy reconciliation almost impossible. Through a series of collaborative attempts from the times of Raja Rammohan Roy to the beginning of the twentieth century, the British administrators in India and Indians seeking Anglicisation had made the knowledge of English language and English literature synonymous with progress and modernization.

The single most important factor influencing historiography in India after the Asiatic researches of Jones was the creation of the classroom for literary appreciation. Jones had highlighted Indian literary tradition in a fragmented manner; the literary classroom further eroded the authority of that tradition by validating a new and alien canon of literature. It may be of interest to us to investigate this link between the canon and the classroom.

11

Formation and Transformation of a Canon

Conventionally, the history of a literature is viewed as the history of the formation of canon and its subsequent transformations. The process of canon formation implies acts of inclusion and exclusion of literary texts, trends and traditions. One of the prime factors motivating these acts is the dominant ideological position within a given culture. When this position changes, there is a corresponding change in the literary canon. Thus formations of literary canons reflect the formation and transformation of ideological positions and power relations. When a power relation involving the domination of one culture by another involves a collision between the respective literary canons, both canons undergo a radical change. On the one hand, even minor texts, trends and traditions within the literary canon of the dominating culture are given high aesthetic value. On the other hand, even major texts, trends and traditions within the dominated culture are given a relatively low aesthetic value. The literary history of politically dominating culture swells; the literary history of politically dominated culture shrinks. Subsequently, the 'low' value literary aesthetics starts making attempts to internalise the 'high' literary aesthetics. Thus, the 'high' value literary aesthetics starts influencing the 'low' value literary aesthetics. It is when cultural ingression follows colonial formations of literary aesthetics that literary canons of the dominating society become the literary *kanuns* for the dominated society.

The English term 'canon' has several meanings; but most of them relate to religion and legal authority. The term originates in the Greek 'kanon', where it meant 'rule', 'rod for measuring', 'standard', etc. In Latin, it came to acquire religious meaning: 'church decree', 'a church office', etc. During the Middle Ages the term was used to designate a body of religious Christian laws.

This meaning is still current. Gradually, the term came to be applied to music, to indicate a ground rule in musical composition, and to literature, to indicate a given set of ancient and modern 'classics'. There are other meanings of the term which need not interest us here. One would have thought that the term *kanun* used in most Indian languages to indicate a set of moral or legal conventions has been accepted from one of the modern European languages. However, the case seems to be different, for we find this term in other Eastern languages such as Arabic and Persian. Possibly, it has a close link with the Islamic concept of *ka* indicating spiritual purity. Or, perhaps, the Arabic and Greek *kanun/kanon* have their origin in the mysterious past of the Indo-European family of languages. However, what is important here for us is that the concept of a canon existed, as the linguistic evidence shows, in the Indian languages and in English independently from the pre-colonial times. Since the concept was already available in the Indian languages, it may not have been difficult for Indian literatures to grasp the notion of English literary canon when the colonial encounter took place. Moreover, it may not have been a difficult passage for English literary canons to become the Indian literary *kanun.* This particular process occupies a centrally important place in history and historiography of modern Indian literatures. The institutional teaching of English literature has been the chief agent in its becoming a canon. Introduction of English literature in Indian education has been the more visible consequence of the literary-historical process in England; and the impoverishment of critical sensibility in India has been its less obvious but more damaging consequence.

If the history of English literature, that is literature to which the modern reader can relate, extends back to the fourteenth century, the history of institutionalized teaching of literature, has, in contrast, had a brief run of not more than a century. Introduction of the study of English in higher education in England was a result of the pressure to keep the British hold over its Indian empire, and was historically subsequent to the introduction of English study in India. The teaching of English in British schools was a result of the social and class tensions within British society during the nineteenth century. On the whole, one sees a general neglect of literary education throughout British history. If one compares the place given to literature in British social life and in some of its former colonies such as Ireland and India, the British neglect of literature becomes strikingly evident.

For centuries in its initial history, England did not have any civilized forms of education. Children were allowed to receive rudimentary private instruction till the age of seven, and then they were handed over to a guardian for vocational apprenticeship which continued till the age of fourteen. In *Beowulf*, the hero recounts that he was sent at the age of seven to the court of king Herthel, his grandfather. In such a system there was no possibility of literary education. The vestiges of this system can be found in the general upbringing of English children even today. In comparison to an Indian child, or an African child, an average English child receives far less literary input from its parents in its upbringing in early childhood. English society depends for literary education either on self-study or institutional education. This is also reflected, perhaps, in the discourse of criticism that English society has developed. No literary critic in England—except the ostracized generation of English Romantic critics—ever displays a childlike sense of wonder towards creativity and language. The critical attitudes reflect highly institutionalized, conventional observations which can be empirically verified. This is so, perhaps because an average English literary scholar gets to know his literature at a slightly more advanced age than literary scholars in India.

Organized education, not only literary education but any education at all, is of twelfth century origin in England. The medieval world, in the Orient as well as in Christian Europe, had evolved indigenous systems of higher learning. There were well developed universities in Italy, China, Persia and India around the beginning of the present millennium; and these offered systematic education in classical literature. The concept of a university in medieval England was very different from that in contemporary Italy, China or India. Joan Simon, a historian of medieval British education who has studied the social roots of education, comments:

> ...the medieval universities were not centres of higher education as the term is now understood, or of research at the expense of teaching as is sometimes held against universities today. Their primary concerns, which shaped not only curriculum and methods but

> scholarship itself, was the teaching of intending teachers. To examine the tradition established from this point of view casts light on various problems which are still actual.[1]

In medieval English universities the least important Faculty was, we are told, the Arts Faculty. This Faculty was seen as a place for preparatory education leading to higher courses, though teaching in schools was geared towards training students to take up an Arts education. Thus the Arts Faculty was somewhat like a 'junior college'. It was concerned with the seven liberal arts: grammar, rhetoric and logic (the trivium) and arithmetic, geometry, music, astronomy (the quadrivium). The aim of this education was primarily utilitarian:

> The surest sign of a learned and wise man is his ability to teach what he knows, said Aristotle. Medieval universities inherited from the ancient world, and the fathers of the church, the idea that knowledge is for teaching. Indeed the church itself rested on the idea that, after God first taught man, it remained for a chosen body... to continue this teaching to see the world to its end....[2]

Pragmatism has been a strength of English education all through its history. However, subjects like literature and the arts do not find much favour in utilitarian educational systems. To turn back to our narrative, English education stood, at the beginning of this millennium, in sharp contrast to the more lively education on the Continent, not to mention the extremely sophisticated Oriental education. In the Continental universities it was a common practice to employ complex philosophical and poetic texts for the purpose of refining the intellectual abilities of students. The text used was known as *littera* which was analysed through dialogues between the teacher and the taught. Here is an instance:

> *Teacher:* You should know that when the ancients were about to expound a text they asked seven questions: author, the title of the work, its nature, the purpose of the author, the number and sequence of the books and then the interpretation of the text itself. Nowadays we are satisfied if four things are established about a work:

> its subject matter, its aim, its underlaying purpose and what branch of philosophy it belongs to.
>
> *Pupil*: Tell me what matter, aim and underlaying purpose are.[3]

Historians of medieval education such as Anders Piltz tell us that the *littera* was not only an item in the curriculum, but an interpretative strategy too. Contemporary English education was totally innocent of such interpretative strategies.

The Renaissance saw major and radical developments in English education. These were collectively initiated by John Foxe's *Book of Martyrs* (1563), which was a radical history of Christianity, the *Thirty-nine Articles,* and the *Oath of Supremacy* (both in 1563), which defined the relation between the Crown and the Church.[4] The Oath imposed on 'all schoolmasters and public and private teachers of children' ensured that they recognised the supremacy of the Queen in Church matters before receiving their Episcopal licences to teach. In addition, a scheme of inspection of schools was provided for, to ensure that 'lewd schoolmasters' were not 'corrupting religion'.

Sir William Cecil, Queen Elizabeth's principal Secretary of State, was appointed in 1561 Master of the Court Wards, an office he held for thirty-seven years. At Cecil House in the Strand he set up what has been called 'the best school for statesmen in Elizabethan England, perhaps in all Europe'.[5] The curriculum of this school included subjects like mathematics, geography, physics, surgery, philosophy, Greek, Latin, Hebrew, logic, rhetoric, Spanish, Italian, French and High Dutch. It did not include English as a subject. The literary education included a study of the classics, elements of style and language. The Elizabethans did not think English works fit to be included in school syllabuses. Education was firmly wedded to priorities set by the Crown and the Church. Robert Browne, who ran a school in London without licence, tried to escape this extra-academic domination, and was saved from being punished for it, thanks only to his kinship with Cecil.

In India, in any given age, literary education quickly assimilated new works of literature into established canons. This happened during the advent of Buddhism to literary texts in Pali, to Lingayata and other Bhakti texts during the early centuries of the present millennium, and more recently, to English literary texts during the so-called Renaissance. Such assimilation of new or alien literary texts into the realms of knowledge becomes possible in cultures which think of language in terms of a divine presence, *shakti* or power. The attitude to language inherited by the Elizabethans was anatomical, one which perceived language as a body to be dissected. The results of this metaphysics of language were reflected in the pedagogic rituals of the classroom, and literary education had to occupy the back benches there.

Throughout the last four centuries of English educational history, the main emphasis has been on education of materially useful subjects such as science and technology, medicine, law and economics. Until the beginning of the high Romantic cultural revolt, there was practically no spokesman for the cause of English literary education; and till the generation of I.A. Richards and F.R. Leavis the spokesmen have been either feeble or ambivalent in their persuasions regarding the need to introduce English literature in the British education system.

Many ideas relating to education developed through the institution of the coffee house in eighteenth century England. It was through coffee houses that the British Society for Encouragement of Arts originated. Among the members of this society, two chemists, William Shipley and Robert Dossie, impressed Dr. Johnson so much that he proposed to help them set up a centre for dissemination of scientific ideas. The literary study that enjoyed high reputation in the eighteenth century was that of the classics; and as a poor substitute for those who were in no position to undertake it, many writers including John Dryden and Alexander Pope produced English translations of classical works.

The Romantic Age produced a strong reaction to the advocacy of exclusively scientific learning. Growth in literary criticism and the interest in institutionalizing literary education are closely interrelated, as argued by Chris Baldick in *The Social Mission of English Criticism: 1848–1932.*[6] It is possible, therefore, to connect the growing body of literary criticism during the Romantic Age with the emergent awareness of English as a subject. However, it should not be forgotten that during the last decade of the eighteenth century and the first two decades of the nineteenth century a tremendously valuable treasure of Arabic, Persian and Sanskrit literature was being made available to the more serious reading public in England through the Indological translations. Moreover, those who started using English texts in schools were persons who had some exposure to other cultures, as in the case of Hannah More. She borrowed ideas on education from France, and started using English literary texts enthusiastically in her classroom. A certain Reverend Leigh Richmond brought out his *Dairyman's Daughter* (1809), about the same time as Mrs. Sherwood, wife of a colonial servant in the 53rd regiment in India, sent home a best-selling story called *Little Henry and His Bearer.* A historian of British education comments:

> Sold to a Shropshire publisher for £ 5, it inaugurated Mrs. Sherwood's career just as that of her old schoolfellow, Jane Austen, was closing. What Jane Austen became for Victorian adults, Mrs. Sherwood became for their children. *Little Henry* remarked the first impact of her work on a society where the nursery and governess were soon to flourish.[7]

These and other such popular texts were used for English study in British schools for the lower classes during the early part of the nineteenth century. At the same time, a few 'higher' books in this field such as Hugh Blair's *Lectures on Rhetorics and Belles Letters* (1784) started becoming influential. The first Chair of English was established in 1828 at the University College of London University. To this Chair was appointed a person who was a philologist rather than a literary scholar. These isolated facts correctly reflect the tensions within the newly emergent field: the antagonism between philology and literary study which subsequently gave two distinct models of English to Oxford and Cambridge, respectively; the class-monopoly of higher knowledge related to literature, with English as the poor man's field, and the growing need of culture-control in the colonies. These were to become the three central themes of the history of English throughout the nineteenth century. Matthew Arnold must have found himself caught in these conflicts, which in turn formed the greater conflict between 'culture' and 'anarchy'. He wrote, therefore:

> Why no effective remedy is applied to this serious evil... (is)... because the upper class amongst us do not want to be disturbed in their preponderance, or the middle class in their vulgarity. Even though these prejudices are unconscious, the result is the same.[8]

The nineteenth century had much to say about intuition, inspiration and imagination; it generated some of the most hostile critiques of science; yet, its educational philosophy was always in favour of science education. Cardinal Newman as well as Matthew Arnold felt that a knowledge of poetry was necessary to bring refinement to minds rendered unimaginative by too much science education. Poetry was to be the finishing touch. The nineteenth century English ideology of education was freely borrowed from Germany. Here again, true to its utilitarian and pragmatic grain the English mind felt more easily attracted to German education in the sciences than that in literature. England's most distinguished inspector of schools, an Oxford Professor of Poetry, and a great poet himself, said in 1872 that

> it is in science that we must need to borrow from the German universities. The French university has no liberty, and the English universities have no science; the German universities have both. [9]

The study of English, as against that of the classics, took a considerably low priority in Arnold's vision of culture.

British progress in institutionalising literary study during the nineteenth century was very slow. The Indological scholars had brought to Britain a fund of knowledge about ancient traditions of Oriental literature kept alive through their systematic transmission from generation to generation. The German philosophers had given British intellectuals a new branch of knowledge called Aesthetics. Ever since the Napoleonic wars and the unification of Italy, the growing spirit of nationalism had created a national bias in other areas of human study. And above all, there was a sufficiently large number of English literary texts which compared well with the classics. Yet, none of these reasons for initiating the study of English appealed to the English mind. The reasons that did appeal were of extreme pragmatic expediency. The two hallmarks of the nineteenth century British attitude to literary study were insularity and utilitarianism. No literary texts from the colonial world were ever accepted as being of any literary value; and no policy decisions were made unless they were impelled by economic or political considerations.

All through the century, several regulations about the kind and quality of British education were passed by the British government. It is interesting to see the more central concerns of some of those regulations. The 1839 document about the Creation of the Committee of Council for Education stated[10] that the aim of education was to save British society from the menace of crime. School children from the poorer classes are described in this document as "pauper orphans, children deserted by their parents, offspring of criminals and their associates. It is from this class that the thieves and housebreakers of society are continually recruited."[11] Naturally, literature had no place in the plans of educators whose perception of poverty was so hidebound. In fact, the Wales Education Inquiry Report of 1847[12] records that "an opulent proprietor (of a private school) had withdrawn his annual subscription of £1 because writing had, against his judgement, been added to the subjects of instruction."[13]

The standards of school education in Britain during the nineteenth century were very low. The aims of school education, reflecting the literary expectations from children, as recorded in the Minutes of 1846 Committee on Education[14] were: "To read with fluency, ease and expression; To write in a neat hand with correct spelling and punctuation, a simple prose narrative slowly read to them; To point out parts of speech in a simple sentence", and so on.[15] These objectives did not change until 1861, when the Newcastle Report was compiled. That report gave English literary texts a place in the school curriculum for the first time in the history of British education. This provision was finally consolidated in 1904 by the Regulation of Secondary Schools, which stipulated that a certain minimum number of teaching hours be given to English and allied subjects.[16] These changes were closely connected with the economic history of industrial Britain, and the political history of its colonial empire.

Britain's overseas interests were one of the primary motivations for the growth of English studies in Britain during the nineteenth century. Chris Baldick records three primary causes for it:

> ...we can isolate three factors which ensured literary study, in particular of English literature, a permanent place in higher-education. These are first, the specific needs of the British empire expressed in the regulations for admission to the Indian Civil Service; second, the various movements for adult education including Mechanics Institutes, Working Men's Colleges, and

> extension lecturing; third, within this general movement, the specific provisions made for women's education.[17]

The introduction of English literature in the syllabus for the Civil Services examination was soon followed by its introduction into other competitive examinations in Britain. Thus knowledge of English literature became a passport to easy success and affluence. Many British scholars made use of this opportunity by starting private tuition and coaching classes. One of the great pioneers of English study, and a candidate for the Oxford English chair, John Churton Collins, was involved in engaging tuitions for some time for Civil Services aspirants; and scholars took pride in their being appointed as examiners for the Civil Services. Matthew Arnold was an ICS examiner, and he was proud to be one. Walter Raleigh was another such scholar.[18]

The reasons for introducing English as a major component of Indian Civil Services examination were far from being literary. Macaulay, who institutionalized English studies in India, had expressed his fear in an address to the British House of Commons that if the British did not learn their literature, the day was not far off when the Indian subjects of the Crown would surpass Britain in literary scholarship. His own words were:

> Consider too, Sir, how rapidly the public mind of India is advancing, how much attention is already paid by the higher classes of the natives to those intellectual pursuits on the cultivation of which the superiority of the European race principally depends. Surely, in such circumstances, from motives of selfish policy, if from no higher motive, we ought to fill the magistracies of our Eastern Empire with men who may do honour to our country, with men who may present the best part of the English nation.[19]

It should be noted that the moral calibre of the Company administrators during the three-quarters of a century from 1757 to Macaulay's mission in India had been consistently low. The British government would probably not have bothered much to cure this malaise had it not been for its immediate effects on the political and public life in Britain itself. The flow of money from Bengal, through the Company administrators and investors, towards British elections, had created unprecedented corruption there. All through the first half of the nineteenth century the situation had been worsening. Besides, the signs of native resistance to colonization meant that the colonial administration had to be improved. Thus the question of colonial success got tagged on to the moral quality of the British administration. It was felt, therefore, that it would be desirable to select prospective administrators from among those who had received literary education. In recognition of this pressing need of the day, the Civil Service of the East India Company Report of 1855 stipulated that a maximum of 1000 marks be allotted to the sections on English literature and history. The Report said:

> Foremost among these subjects we place our own language and literature... to (enable them to) show the extent of the knowledge of our poets, wits and philosophers.... (In imparting) a taste for pleasures not sensual, literature would help the young administrators to resist the dangers of corruption and 'scandalous immorality' to which their power might expose them.[20]

The needs abroad—to keep literate administrators in good supply, and to keep ahead of the Indian educated class in literary scholarship—were matched at home by the need to contain the growing sections of literate women and tradesmen. The Chartist movement had given the British upper classes a taste of the social consequences of industrialisation. Therefore, a movement like Christian Socialism, which dreamt of uniting classes through common sympathies, found English literature a useful political tool to ward off social discontent. English thus became, in England and in the colonies, a civilizing subject. [21]

In Warton's historiography the genius of the English people lay in civilizing the barbarous imagination of the 'rude' nations. In the colonial institutionalization of English literature as a canon for the classroom was implicit the faith that English literature could civilize the rude nations colonized by the British. Such a perspective of literature invariably surfaces through literary criticism and literary history. Critical texts and literary histories are essentially the tools of literary pedagogy. Therefore, when literature becomes an institutionalized practice and a classroom subject there inevitably occurs a proliferation of histories and digests of literature. All histories of English written after Warton's pioneering work followed one general guiding principle, namely, they divided the course of English literature into three broad periods, the old, the middle and the modern. Where exactly to place the lines of demarcation between these periods was a matter of the individual historian's freedom and choice, but to place these lines of demarcation was the general practice. Two more subsidiary principles were used by literary historians in England. The first was to make a historical classification of literary production in terms of the political history of England by using categories such as the Elizabethan Age and the Victorian Age. The second was to categorize it in terms of style-periods or theme-periods such as Romanticism and Modernism. When 'civilizing' becomes the central purpose and concern of literature, 'periodisation' becomes the central historiographical principle. How can one prove the civilizing effects of literature if one did not divide it in terms of a dark period and a luminous period?

The impact of this historiography was profound. Jones had already spoken of a luminous ancient period of Indian literature. The advocates of *nutana* and the educated classes of colonial Indians held forth the promise of a new vibrant era in literature that India would produce by following the British models and modernizing native traditions. Naturally, therefore, the Middle Ages, the centuries from the eleventh to the eighteenth were designated the dark period. Jones had given his tacit consent to the concept of the darkness of the intervening centuries. The influence of English literature on Indian literary education strengthened the assumption. That it had no real historical support and that the so-called dark age had, in fact, given rise to several vibrant and highly experimental literary traditions in the bhashas was a matter easily overlooked and pushed into the twilight region of cultural amnesia.

After all, Jones had not only discovered Indian literature, he had also inaugurated a style of *writing about it.* The institutionalised literary education enhanced the importance of *writing about* literature. Thus history as the story of the past became more important than history as the past itself. Since Westernisation or Anglicisation was seen as a mark of progress in thought and vision, it became necessary for those with a vested interest in the literary classroom to make their writing about the literary past as similar as possible to that prevalent in England.

The influence of the notion of canon and period on the Indian sense of literary tradition resulted in the denial of literary status to all non-secular and sectarian literary works. Traditionally, the links between the canonical and the non-canonical had been intimate and strong in India. The written and the oral were not distinct in qualitative terms. The high-brow and the low-brow had been mutually interdependent, and the *marga* and the *desi* had a fascinating history of fruitful exchanges. But these relationships were ignored, suppressed and erased by historiography hedged in by the notions of progress, period and canon. Warton, Jones and the literary classroom, between them, brought about this unintended result and turned what the web of literary traditions had held as sacred into vulgar and rude. If, as Warton maintained, the rude nations of the Orient had provided imaginative sources to English literature, Warton's historiography—which was one of the products of colonialism—deprived India of its right to designate a large part of its imaginative products as 'literature'. If the image of the Orient as the barbaric Other had given English poetry a sense of its historical vitality, the view of Indian literature through the colonial British perspective deprived it of just that sense of historic vitality.

It may be appropriate to conclude this brief account of the impact of colonialism on literary historiography in India by quoting from a well-researched account of various histories of Indian literature by Sujit Mukherjee:

> English literature was a major subject in our higher education, and through it we received our most abiding concept of literary history—namely, that the history of a language ought to be studied in order to appreciate the literature in that language, from where it seemed to follow that the history of a literature is the extension or elaboration of the history of that language. As the study of modern Indian languages entered our universities, courses were designed on the pattern of English literature courses. If the English language could look back to Anglo-Saxon and Teutonic speeches for parentage, so could most Indian languages to Sanskrit. On the Grimm-given analogy of Old English/Middle English/Modern English, each regional language that earned university-level study was fitted into a similar

> sequence even if the ancestry of each language did not lend itself comfortably to such treatment. Uncertainty about dates of composition made it possible for literary works to be assigned to arbitrary chronological periods, while western terms were freely borrowed to describe forms and trends in Indian writing. By planting a 'Romantic Movement' in the virgin soil of our literary historiography, we hopefully tried to ensure the sprouting of a healthy crop of modern literature in all our languages. That this entire strategy belongs to a unilanguage literary culture like that of England's has never deterred our literary historians from applying it wholesale to our multi-lingual literary culture.[22]

Any further comment is unnecessary!

However, it is well worth recording that the 'Grimm-given' model seems to have limited the influence on literary historiography to the classroom only. It is necessary to differentiate between the histories produced as intended textbooks and the approaches to the literary past implicit in the writings of thinkers, writers and critics. It is more profitable, therefore, to examine some of the major approaches to the history of Indian literature implicit in the writings of significant thinkers and creative writers while determining the extent of the colonial influence in literary historiography. In the following two sections an attempt is made to review the dominant philosophies of literary history in the West and some contemporary approaches to literary history in India. These outlines, though by no means comprehensive, should help us to determine the extent to which the allegedly nonexistent sense of a literary past in pre-colonial India was affected by the influence of Western literary historiography.

12

Some Western Approaches to Literary History

Hans Robert Jauss, one of the chief figures, along with Wolfgang Iser in the Constanz Group,[1] has done writing of significance on the question of literary history. At the beginning of one of his celebrated essays, he writes:

> In our time literary history has increasingly fallen into disrepute, and not at all without reason. The history of this worthy discipline in the last one hundred and fifty years unmistakably describes the path of a steady decline. Its greatest achievements all belong to the nineteenth century. To write the history of national literature counted, in the times of Gervinus and Scherer, De Sanctis and Lanson, as the crowning life work of the philologist. The patriarchs of the discipline saw their highest goal therein, to represent in the history of literary works (*dichtwerke*) the idea of national individuality on its way to itself. This high point is already a distant memory. The received form of literary history scarcely scratches out a living for itself in the intellectual life of our own time.[2]

Had Jauss paused after mentioning that nationalism provided the breeding climate for literary historicism, he would have, perhaps, chanced upon the other factor responsible for its growth, namely, colonialism. Naturally, with the decline in nationalism and colonialism, there has been a corresponding decline in literary historicism in Europe. However, during the two centuries of its history, Europe has made a remarkably impressive contribution to the field. It is impossible to present even a brief outline of all major European thinkers in the field of general and literary historiography.

Almost every major European thinker from Hegel to Foucault has made some contribution to this field. Of these, we will examine some major strands by taking up three specific theoretical texts.[3] They are: R.S. Crane's *Critical and Historical Principles of Literary History* (1967); Gyorgy Lukacs's *Notes on the Theory of Literary History* (1910); and Hans Robert Jauss's *Literary History as a Challenge to Literary Theory* (1970). These texts have been widely acclaimed as major texts on literary historiography. Besides, literary historiography is the main and professed subject of these three texts. Therefore, they are less ambiguous in their historiographic attitudes than texts not primarily about historiography. The main reason for selecting these three texts is that they are representative of the historical discourses to which they belong, and taken together, cover the entire ground of Western discourse of literary historiography. Crane's aesthetic argument represents the established line of historiography; Lukacs's text, with its Marxist leanings, represents the counter discourse of European historiography; and Jauss's text, propounding the reception aesthetics represents both a cross between Crane and Lukacs, as well as the more recent theoretical trends in literary thought. Jauss's historiography is a discourse resulting from the clash between the two other discourses—a second generation and a second order discourse.

Crane's literary historiography comes from the literary and critical concerns of what is referred to by its adherents as Liberal Humanism. Though extremely ennobling, the critical concerns of this branch of literary study stem from the belief that literature is a civilizing subject. Firmly rooted in the historical necessity to create a mystique around literature, the liberal humanistic criticism culminated in the Anglo-American Formalism through various branches: Richards's practical criticism, Leavis's traditionalism, New Criticism and Neo-Aristotelianism in the USA. In all these branches of Anglo-American Formalism, a work of art is considered a kind of mystery, an aesthetic structure, the beauty of which can be explained only in its own terms. Hence all critical attention is to be focused on the construction of a literary work.

Crane's essay on the principles of literary history begins by observing that literary criticism often follows two misleading modes of interpretation, the philological or grammatical mode, and the dialectical mode. The first mode merely connects parts of a work with comparable parts of other works. The second mode employs a bipolar scheme of perception in which the form and the content are treated separately, and, worse still, are profoundly misrepresented. Crane offers minute descriptions of the formal aspects of literature, and concludes that forms, materials, techniques, and individual achievements are "the major variables which must be combined somehow in any adequate narrative history of literary forms."[4] If literary histories are expected to explain the chronological changes taking place in these elements, then histories tend to be insufficiently 'literary' or critical in orientation when the principle of change alone becomes operative. Crane names the predominantly 'historical' history of literature 'atomistic history'. To this type, Crane finds opposition in the type he calls 'organic history'. Organic history does, unlike the atomistic history, explain causation and succession of literary events. However, its drive is towards reconciling historical antitheses. A third type of history described by Crane is 'narrative causal history', which has a greater capacity to disengage the complexities of historical changes. In his own words, the differences between the organic history and narrative history are:

> In the first place, the continuity achieved in narrative history is the continuity not of a dialectical integration of historical differences in terms of a single analogy or scheme. Rather it is the continuity of a sequence of distinct events connected causally by whatever individual men or groups of men, through a period of time, happened to do with respect to the element constituting the continuum of the change. Accordingly, the degree of integration attainable in such a history depends upon the possibility of discovering causal connections, in materials, techniques, forms, or ends, among the different sequences with which it deals. The particular contrarities in a narrative history, therefore, cannot be deduced from any unified scheme of common terms....[5]

In Crane's view the difficulty in writing a literary history which offers a 'systematic' causal explanation for literary phenomena, is that causal connections between the preconstruction stage and the construction stages of literature never really explain the aesthetic form of a literary work. This difficulty has its source in Crane's literary philosophy which views literary structures as self-sufficient and autonomous entities. In other words, the formal structure of literature can be explained more effectively by using the principles of literary criticism rather than the principles of historical criticism. Thus, Crane's historiography is an attempt to establish the primacy of practical criticism over philological criticism even in the sphere of literary history. In his view, history is not all historical criticism; it is, in fact, more of a practical formal analysis of forms, techniques, and materials of art. Here is the focal statement of Crane's historiography:

> ....in any history founded on the principle of artistic synthesis the central though by no means exclusive emphasis would be on the constructional aspects of literary works considered from the point of view of the problems faced by writers in the process of making poems, dramas, or narratives of different kinds. The collective enterprise of historians in this mode would consequently have as its ultimate purpose the writing of a narrative-causal history of the various literary arts in terms of four things....[6]

These four things are: formal ends, materials, new devices and techniques, and actualisation of these formal elements in literary production.

It should be clear that Crane considers the aesthetic aspects of literary art to be of supreme importance. The events to be dealt with by the literary historian are, to follow Crane, only aesthetic events such as the invention of new techniques, art materials, devices, formal modes, and so on. This kind of literary historiography overlooks, if it does not deny altogether, the pre-constructional condition of literature. The assumption behind such a position is that there are critical standards and procedures of literary assessment that have a universal standing and validity. One can indeed think of critical standards and procedures of evalution in terms of universality within the limited sphere of Western or European literatures. But when those standards or procedures are applied to literary works outside Western or European cultures, their universality seems to shrink.

Critical standards, values, procedures originate within specific cultural and historical contexts, and are relevant and useful for those specific traditions and contexts. The European canons of criticism acquired universal currency during the coercive cultural context of colonialism.[7] If one were to use those canons for constructing the history of Indian literature, a large bulk of good Indian literature will have to be left out and a large bulk of imitative, and therefore weak, literature will have to be given an important place in the narrative. Thus the critical concepts to be used as tools of literary history need to be culture-specific. Once this argument is accepted, it will follow that the discourse of literature cannot be autonomous; it is created and acquires meaning within a culture where it is circulated as a system of meaning. And, if literature is not an autonomous system, Crane's historiography needs to be radically altered before putting it to use in post-colonial literary cultures.

The fact that history precedes criticism is accepted by the Marxist-literary historiography, of which George (Gyorgy) Lukacs is an extremely important spokesman. His *Notes on the Theory of Literary History* was first published in 1910 in Hungarian, and has become available in English through Ian Fairley's recent translation. It is a work from Lukacs's early phase, known generally as his pre-Marxist phase. This particular work forms a fine balance vis-a-vis Crane's text belonging to the post-New Criticism phase. Thus, here we are not dealing with extremes of historiographical positions, but rather more balanced and nuanced positions on it.

Any reader of Lukacs's literary history, with a pre-determined idea of Lukacs as a hardcore Marxist theorist, is likely to be surprised by his energetic advocacy of the formal elements of a literary work. Lukacs's theory does not dispense with poetics and criticism at all. On the contrary, it stresses that "without poetics, literary history would lack all perspective other than that of pure sociology." [8] It is logical then to expect in Lukacs's theory an idea of form which has some legitimacy as a 'purely aesthetic construct'. The notion of form in this theory is highly intriguing, and it is central to his argument. Lukacs considers form as a psychic reality; and art exists only through form. "Within the field of literature the concept of form has no mutually exclusive opposite; there are only ever degrees of form. That which literary history and criticism in practice call 'formless' is, at most, only badly or unsuccessfully formed."[9] However, one must carefully distinguish between the idea of form in Lukacs and that in the Formalists and New Critics. For the Formalists, form is an essential hypothesis related to the inter-relationship among constituents of art. For Lukacs, form is a means of communication, and without form there can be no aesthetic communication. "Literature is therefore the communication of lived experience, and the medium of this communication is form. Form is the truly social constituent of literature...."[10]

The sociological nature of form has two important aspects: it is sociological because it mediates between the creator and the recipient; and it is sociological also because the material (such as language) that it forms is socially determined.[11] Or to represent Lukacs's views precisely, form is aesthetic in its non-temporal aspect, and sociological in its historical aspect. To combine these two aspects in literary enquiry is the main function of literary history. That is the keynote in his theory of literary history.

> The synthesis of literary history is the combination, in a new, organic unity of sociology and aesthetics. Aesthetics pursues only what is constant within those phenomena that we are accustomed to call literary; sociology attempts to describe and account for change within these phenomena. Literary history is faced with the paradoxical task of uniting these two viewpoints, of pursuing the constant within the variable and the variable within the constant. It must seek the developmental possibilities, paths and tendencies of forms conceived within the abstractions of aesthetics, while also pursuing what is constant, regular and recurrent within the highly complex mesh of the literary work, its influence and effects.[12]

The programme proposed here is to legitimize the subjective moment within the historical flow of literature as an institution of cultural production. The legitimation of the subjective within the overall sociological flow is offered by the unity of the aesthetic and the sociological, the non-temporal and the temporal, within the form. Crane's essay, on the other hand, legitimizes the historic dimension of formal, aesthetic structures, by visualizing for history the possibilities of forming a narrative. Thus, though leaning towards opposite ends of the spectrum spanning the private and the public, present and past, aesthetic and social, the later-Crane and the early-Lukacs have a relationship of close collaboration. Within this relationship, disagreements are possible, but within a common context of argument. The *literary* history and literary *history* in the West form a connected discourse and counter-discourse. They co-exist, and continuously define each other.

Writing in 1910, sixty years before the publication of Jauss's *Literary History as a Challenge to Literary Theory*, Lukacs anticipates Jauss's position in a passing flash of vision:

> One can certainly envisage a history of psychical culture (unfortunately, none as yet exists) which endeavouring simply to establish the facts, would describe without any evaluative commentary what people—and, if possible, particular groups and classes of people—read most and liked best in different periods.... This type of study is perfectly conceivable—but it would not be literary history.[13]

It is precisely this aspect of literature, which Crane called the post-constructional aspect, that forms the heart of Jauss's literary historiography. Of course, Jauss offers elaborate critiques of Formalistic as well as Marxist concepts of literary historiography, before proposing his own alternative. The critiques offered are, however, based on the hard-line views on both sides. In fact, in his enthusiasm to found a new style of literary historiography, Jauss even picks up an argument with the Positivistic school of literary history, a school which does not have even the remotest chance of revival. In spite of the strongly articulated disagreement with the three schools of literary historiography, Jauss actually builds upon the foundation laid by them. The central argument of his theory is related to the importance of the process of 'reception' of literature, which completes the process of its becoming 'literature':

> Literature and art only obtain a history that has the character of a process when the succession of works is mediated not only through the producing subject but also through the consuming subject—through the interaction of author and public.[14]

It is in the interchange of the producing subject and the consuming subject that Jauss's theory deviates from Lukacs's. But through this vital shift, Jauss creates a whole new poetics of reception, or what he calls reception-aesthetics. Towards that end, Jauss proposes (true to his German tradition) seven theses. They are, in abridged form:

a) Literary reception should be given priority over literary production.
b) Literary works can be judged advantageously within the context of an "objectifiable system of expectations".
c) Objectively reconstructed horizons of expectations help judge the degree of literary influence and quality of reception.
d) Reference to the past and present horizons of expectations brings in view the hermeneutic difference between the past and the present understanding of a work.
e) Reception aesthetics unfolds the meaning of a single work in its historical sequence, as well as the meaning of the 'literary series'.
f) Reception aesthetics can be strengthened by help from diachronic linguistics so as to create a new reception-historiography.
g) The social function of literature manifests itself in its genuine possibility only where the literary experience of the reader enters into the horizons of expectations.

The essay, formulated in an extremely systematic way through the introductory section and the seven theses, is highly programmatic. It is philosophically sophisticated in the sense that it alludes to numerous European thinkers dealing with aesthetic and historiographic problems, and draws substance from a multitude of philosophers.[15] It is possible, of course, to question the practical viability of Jauss's project. Would it ever be possible to write a history of any literature with reception aesthetics at its centre? However it is not that question that should concern us here. What is of immediate relevance here is that Jauss follows the path of European historiography to its only open frontier. The liberal-humanistic and Formalistic notions of literary history have concentrated mainly on the idea of literature as a language put in forms, a 'play with signs'. The Marxists, Freudians, Structuralists, and others have concentrated on the notion of literature as a web of meaning, a 'represented structure of signifieds'. Reception aesthetics looks at literature as a process of reception, a 'posibility and practice of signification'. Thus the historiographic triangle is complete. It is on some point of this triangle that any given Western historiographer stands and argues; it is *this* triangle of concepts of literature which forms the basis of the European discourse of literary historiography. As indicated earlier, the discourse was initiated by the history of colonialism and nationalism, Europe produced its counter discourse in the Marxist view of history; and the two apparently antithetical positions—Liberal Humanism and Marxism—though constanly collaborating within a general area of disagreement, are reconciled by the reception theory, a second-order discourse.'[16]

The post-colonial understanding of the Western discourse of literary historiography cannot be easily abstracted from the context of the political history within which it emerged, without rendering it mere abstraction. What use is Crane's historiography to literatures that, on perfectly justifiable grounds, have not developed externalised concepts of critical evaluation and classification? Would it be possible to use Lukacs's concept of sociological form in cultures that have been forced to accept literary forms developed in alien sociological conditions as universal and ideal forms of literature? How far can Jauss's theory of reception aesthetics go in communities that have thought of literature as an expression of a supernatural agency, and therefore have not preserved any records of the creators, creations and receptions of literary works?

There are many communities in our post-colonial era that are forced to think of their own literature in terms of myth while they think of the rulers' literature in terms of history. There are other societies, as in India, whose sense of literary history has been badly fractured and amputated during the colonial cultural encounter. All these cultures have to think of literary historiography in terms of their own history and culture. The sophisticated Western discourse of literary history is well developed, indeed. But it cannot be easily extricated from its particular history. It would, however, be very useful to pose for ourselves some of the central problems that were repeatedly posed by Western literary historiography for itself. Jauss has formulated the central one: "...toward what end and with what right can one today still—or again—study literary history?" This in itself is a necessary twentieth century replication of the historiographical question raised by Schiller:

> Citations customarily call upon an authority to sanction a step in the process of scholarly reflection. But they can also remind us of a former way of posing a question, to prove that an answer that has become classic is no longer satisfactory, that it has itself become historical again and demands of us a renewal of the process of question and answer. Schiller's answer to the question of his inaugural lecture at Jena on 26 May 1789, "What is and Toward what End does one Study Universal History?", is not only representative of historical understanding of German idealism; it is also illuminating for a critical survey of the history of our discipline.[17]

In reviving that question, in posing it afresh for ourselves at this juncture in India, we may try to examine some of the contemporary Indian approaches to literary history.

13

Post-Colonial Indian Approaches

It should be stated at the very outset that these are not 'theories' of literary history. They are, rather, positions taken by historiographers, historians, critics and writers with reference to their encounter with literary culture in modern India. These positions can be placed within a broad system of classification in terms of their central concerns. The eight positions are:

1. Literature as a universal entity,
2. Literature as a strictly regional entity,
3. Literature as a web of divergent trends, styles, etc.,
4. Literature as national convergence of trends, styles, etc.,
5. Heterodox modernity as a new literary tradition,
6. Modernity as a manifestation of preconditioning tradition,
7. Literature as a perennial recurrence,
8. Literature as a specific temporal occurrence.

Position '1' differs from position '2' on the question of a single language as the basis of a given or postulated literary tradition. Position '3' differs from position '4' on the question of sociology and ideology. Position '5' is different from position '6' in terms of its vision of the native tradition. Position '7' and position '8' hold opposite views on characterization of literary periods and styles. This classification may provide us a tentative framework of historiographical themes in India during the twentieth century. It may also bring out the nature of the problems faced by the discourse of literary history in contemporary India. The discussion of these eight positions does not aim at providing an exhaustive review of literary history in contemporary India. Rather it discusses representative trends and tendencies in the field. A tabular presentation of the dominant themes in the modern Indian discourse of literary history is as follows:

Twentieth Century Indian Styles of Literary Historiography				
Dominant View	Universal	Convergence	Heterodox Modernity	Recurrence
Perspective	Language	Sociology/ Ideology	Culture	Philosophy
Counter View	Regional	Divergence	Foreclosed Tradition	Singular Occurrence

The Universal and The Regional

Our illustrations for these two historiographical arguments will be, respectively, Sri Aurobindo's *Future Poetry* [1] and a collection of essays in Marathi *Vangmayetihasaci Sankalpana*.[2]

Aurobindo's *Future Poetry* is an extremely fascinating colonial text within which many battles are fought. It is a book that battles against the coercive influence of the English sensibility on Indian literature. At the same time it defies the restrictive heritage of Sanskrit metre, style and diction. It embodies too a fierce conflict between political nationalism and aesthetic universalism. Sri Aurobindo had rehearsed the argument of *Future Poetry* several times before he actually got down to writing his critical opus: one can see several previews in fragments in his *Harmony of Virtue* (1891), 'The Source of Poetry' (1905), *The National Value of Art* (1907), and in a long letter to his poet brother, Manmohan, written in 1898.[3]

The heart of the argument in all these is that the history of poetry is not a story of its steady decline. In fact, the really great poetry has not yet been written. There have been some prefatory attempts in that direction: but great poetry, which comes from the home of Truth, can be written only by divinely inspired sages, for poetry is nothing short of the aphoristic essence of the truth of all existence, presented in rhythmic language. Perfect poetry is backed by perfect inspiration. Perfect inspiration, in its turn, is possible only for perfect yogis. Once this view of literary aesthetics is proposed, the seed of a new historiography is sown. All those poets who do not appeal to Sri Aurobindo's sensibility are then described as the poets farthest from the source of divinity. All those poets against whose influence he is fighting are described as 'yogis' — but not quite perfect. Pope and Dryden are sent by Aurobindo to the aesthetic inferno he has envisioned. Shelley, Keats and Coleridge are allowed to enter the aesthetic purgatory. So is Kalidasa, who has a largeness of soul and sweetness of rhythm. The aesthetic heaven is reserved for Vyasa, Valmiki, Homer, Virgil, Dante and Shakespeare. *Future Poetry* is essentially a statement about this aesthetic heaven which will be populated by yogi-poets in future, if they succeed in combining the genius of the English language and the genius of Sanskrit poetry, particularly that of *Vedic* poetry. It is then that poetry will become *mantra*.

This theory is fascinating for its visionary zeal. It is an adventurous theory, for it challenges the English canon during the heyday of English colonialism. Perhaps, *Future Poetry* is the only independent history of English literature written in India. It is also the first major book of criticism that thinks of the possibility of an international English literature (now called 'New Literature'). It is also a text which has a close integral relationship with the philosophy of spiritual evolution propounded by Sri Aurobindo through his *Life Divine* and the epic *Savitri*.[4] Sri Aurobindo's history of English poetry is harmoniously blended with his history of Sanskrit poetry, as well as that of 'Indian' poetry within the scope of *Future Poetry*. His book, which is a major critical statement of this century in India, was initially published as a series of essays, and later compiled in a book form. The essays were written when the First World War was just about coming to an end, and Gandhi's influence in Indian politics was to replace Aurobindo's Bangla nationalism of extreme intensity. Since Sri Aurobindo was at the centre of political events in the first decade of this century, one cannot say that he was not involved in the contemporary social and political context. However, he could not have used that context for formulating a universalist historiography. It is therefore to his philosophy of the inner world that he has to turn while discussing the past and the future of poetry.

It is quite logical that any universalist historiography must cease to refer to the specific social, political or cultural context in order to be able to build a sustained vision of literary history. While a universalist literary history is likely to leave any of its readers cold, it must be acknowledged that this kind of history can be produced only in a colonized culture, which has bottomless inner cultural resources to fall back upon as dream-world compensation. Appropriately, therefore the historiographer proposes poetry as *mantra* to be the ideal for the *future*.

*Vangmayetihasaci Sankalpan*a (edited by Dattatraya Punde, 1986) is an anthology of historiographical essays in Marathi, including some essays translated from English to Marathi. The translated essays are by Srinivas Pradhan, Motilal Raina and Sujit Mukherjee. Of the Marathi essays, some were written specially for this volume, and some reprinted. Five appendices are added to the main body, in which various plan-proposals for a history of Marathi literature are reproduced, and bibliographical information is compiled. It is a volume that students of Marathi literature should find useful as a textbook. There may be similar volumes in existence in other Indian languages. The main aim of this volume is "to create a conceptual understanding about literary history in Marathi."[5] The editorial perspective is unambiguously monolingual. The volume is prepared so as to bring together important essays on literary history, to create a field of literary historiography in Marathi, to think afresh about the existing histories of Marathi literature, and to help the students of Marathi literature. These aims are not accidental in nature; they represent a well defined line of historical thought within which Marathi culture and community operate.

When modern historiography made its initial dent in India during colonial times, British historians were greatly interested in the history of the Maratha empire. Fortunately, the documentary sources for Maratha history were in plenty. As Indian scholars of history took over historical research from the British, they found the field of Maratha history very attractive for a different reason: the Maratha history of resistance and nationalism provided modern India with some ideals to look up to. The result of this concentration on one branch of Indian history by several non-Indian and pan-Indian historians was to activate history and historiography in Marathi.

When the discourse of Marathi history was being enriched, literature too had a place of significance in the cultural life of Maharashtra. As such, occasionally, some important historians have given thought to literary historiography. Since their training in history was based on the view of Maratha history as a unit, their literary historiography is closely akin to their general historiography. The best examples of this tendency are V.K. Rajwade and T.S. Shejwalkar. The volume on Marathi literary history edited by Punde owes much to the intellectual background created by these historians, though not explicitly acknowledged by the editor.

It would be very interesting to compare the two historians and their literary perspectives. Rajwade, in his essay, 'History of Prakritic Language and Literature in Maharashtra'[6] insists that the history of literature is at once the history of its language as well as the history of its sociology. In his view, "the history of creative writings is only one aspect of literary history." Rajwade thinks of literary history in terms of a science, the purpose of which is to arrange literary works chronologically, causally, and generically. If Rajwade's views on literary history can be thought of as the mainstream discourse of Marathi literary historiography, Shejwalkar's views form the counter-discourse of Marathi literary historiography. In an essay, 'Literature, Writing and Life',[7] Shejwalkar argues that literature cannot be allowed to become an end in itself without causing damaging effects on life itself. For him praxis is more important than intellection. "At present, there is a custom of spending the whole life in reading, writing and thinking. There are many who do so. But it is a social perversion." He then presents a utopian picture of an egalitarian society, in which each will contribute as much physical labour as everyone else. Literature has its place in that society, but not at the cost of everything else. The history of literature for him is the history of its relation to labour in a given society. It is not exactly a Marxist vision. It is inspired by Marxist thinking but worked out through the local history. What is common between Rajwade and Shejwalkar is that they both look at Marathi literature as a single tradition; and, whatever their differences on the nature of historical narrative, they both envisage a single and exclusive history for Marathi literature.

The route through which other Indian languages have come to think of a single language literary identity may have been somewhat different from the one through which Marathi arrived at that position. Perhaps the historical studies of Indian languages, which subsequently culminated in Grierson's monumental *Linguistic Survey of India*,[8] have created the convention of thinking of literature in each language as a self-sufficient entity. The most common trend in literary historiography in modern

India, and also the most dominant one at present, is the trend of regionalism. The political context which sanctions legitimacy to this trend is that of the formation of linguistic states. This approach is obviously restrictive in a country where bilingualism (particularly among people along state boundaries), translation, literary eclecticism and wide-ranging influences are common traits of literary traditions. Often, the linguistic regions and literary histories are seen as identical areas, with the result that literary productions in a language outside the territorial region of that language are left out of the historical account. It needs to be stressed that literary regionalism is a recent phenomenon in India, and it coincides with the colonial and post-colonial perceptions of India's nationhood.

Convergence and Divergence

Our illustrations for these two types of historiographical models will be, respectively, Sujit Mukherjee's two valuable books on literary history, Sisir Kumar Das's *A History of Indian Literature* ,[9] and several essays by Gayatri Chakravorty Spivak, Daya Pawar, Kumkum Sangari and Salman Rushdie.

Sujit Mukherjee's two books, *Towards a Literary History of India* (1975) and *Some Positions on A Literary History of India* (1981)[10] have been among the few works on literary historiography published in English in India. In both these works, he makes an extremely systematic presentation of the concept of Indian literature as visualised by him. In the Preface to the first volume, he writes:

> What has been argued here is a concept. Its validity will be proved or disproved when the project outlined in the final section is actually put into practice. To those who may reject the concept altogether and can find no interest in the project, I should like to quote Bhavabhuti:
> *Utpasyate mama tah koapi samanadharma*
> *kalohyaya nirahadhir vipula cha prithvi*[11]

The idea in the immortal verses of Bhavabhuti is that since Time has eternity and Space has infinity, some day, somewhere a like-minded person will appreciate a good poem (or concept). Sujit Mukherjee's concept is indeed worth appreciating, especially for the form in which it is presented. His book is a kind of copybook for a future historian of Indian literature. It has a chapter each on literary criticism, institutional teaching of literature, history of literary history, and the concept of Indian literature itself. In addition there are several useful appendices compiling information about common themes in Indian literary history such as translations, renderings of national classics, etc. And to top it all, there is an elaborate plan for the writing of a common history of Indian literature. The working plan covers, with great meticulousness, various aspects of history writing such as planning, research, compilation, coordination and editorial tasks (even these are arranged in a chronological sequence). Further the plan offers a Ten-Point-Programme for those who are likely to take up the task of preparing a history of Indian literature.

The fact that such histories have appeared in the past as discussed in Mukherjee's chapter on the history of literary history in India, and are also appearing now through works like Sisir Kumar Das's recent history, shows that the position argued by Sujit Mukherjee is no mere fancy. It represents a strong strand in India's cultural life, past or present. Let us use the term conventionally employed to describe this particular strand *Marga*, the mainstream or the dominant. The *Marga* view of culture and history always highlights convergence of constituents rather than the opposite.

Mukherjee refined his historiographical position and restated it in 1981 at a seminar in Pune, as well as in *Some Positions on a Literary History of India* (Mysore, 1981).[12] His presentation at Pune was later published as a Marathi translation in 1982, and reprinted in 1986. In that presentation, the thesis of his book is neatly reduced to five points. These five points, according to him, are the basic principles of Indian literary historiography.

(a) Though India does not have, for its ancient period, a sustained historical record, there is a wealth of literary sources, (available through references and cross references to other works), which can be used to reconstruct the narrative of remote historical periods in Indian literature.

(b) Indian literary historiography demands that the concepts of literary history need to emerge from other Indian fields of knowledge and social sciences. At present there is a lack of correspondence between the conceptual framework and the surrounding reality.

(c) Literary historiography in India has to have a keen social awareness of the context which produces works of literature.

Particularly in the history of those periods of literature which are rich in contextual information, literary historiography has to have a clear social orientation.

(d) It is necessary to create a general framework of critical standards which will enable historians to evaluate any work from any given Indian literature.

(e) The principles of literary historiography for the ancient period, and the principles for the medieval and modern period, have had no mutual correspondence so far. The reason for this lack of correspondence is that literary historiography for Indian literature was developed by Western scholars. It is necessary to have a consistent historiographical strategy.

Thus, in Mukherjee's formulation of literary historiography, it is necessary to have: (i) an indigenous definition of history, (ii) an indigenous critical framework, (iii) an indigenous historiographical perspective. His view of literary history is, therefore, decidedly different from Sri Aurobindo's. But at the same time it is different from regional historiography. Mukherjee's view lies between these two views. For him, literary historiography ought to be culture-specific; but the specificity should not be narrowed to the level of a single language or region. At the same time, literary history should highlight similarities between various literatures; but the comparison should stop at the national boundary. Of course, Mukherjee looks at India as a cultural unit rather than a political unit. In his account of the history of Indian literary historiography, he presents a brief account of the origin and growth of historiography in the bhashas in India.

> Early models for such undertakings were supplied by the potted histories of regional literatures prepared by well meaning Englishmen for the *Heritage of India* series planned by J.N. Farquhar and published by the Association Press (YMCA) of Calcutta in collaboration with the Oxford University Press, London.[13]

The need for such histories had been more particularly felt ever since Indian languages were given a place of honour in Indian universities after India's independence. Inevitably, the imitative historiography created its opposite in historiography of cultural chauvinism, which treats all sacred literature in a given language as world class literature. Thus the material considered changes, but the perspective does not. Mukherjee comments:

> ... perspective is what has been steadily eroded in our literary historiography. From one extreme of trying to measure our writers and writings only in terms of English (or, at time, European) literature, our literary critics have taught our literary historians to swing to the other extreme of confining literary history only to consideration of literary evidence available in that particular language. In their anxiety to prove the authenticity of a particular regional literature, its historians tend to stress its autonomy by overlooking the stimulus received from neighbouring languages and literature.[14]

The kind of integrative national history of Indian literature that Mukherjee conceptualises is to be found in the two volumes by Sisir Kumar Das prepared for the Sahitya Akademi's proposed ten volume series. These two volumes treat India as a single and relatively unified literary field. Though the data presented in them is immensely useful for comparative literary research, these volumes treat the movements and trends covered with a minimum of critical evaluation. Almost exactly opposite in orientation and method is the work of the Subaltern Studies group.

Subaltern Studies is a new movement in political and cultural historiography launched by a group of scholars, most of whom are Bangla or are interested in Bangla history and culture. Collectively, these scholars (Shahid Amin, David Arnold, Gautam Bhadra, Dipesh Chakrabarty, Partha Chatterjee, Ranajit Guha, David Hardiman, Gyan Pandey, and Sumit Sarkar) have produced a series of volumes entitled *Subaltern Studies* during the 1980s.[15] Each of the volumes includes long and informative essays about the processes of formation of colonial historiography and its inadequacy to narrate the micro-processes of history. The ideology of subaltern historiography is derived from Antonio Gramsci, who thinks of history in terms of "multiple elements of conscious leadership".[16] Gayatri Chakravorty Spivak, who acquired fame with her translation of Jacques Derrida's *Grammatology*, has contributed to the subaltern studies two 'interventions', a long essay on a provocative Bangla long story *Stan-dayini* by Mahasvetadevi, and a review, 'Subaltern Studies: Deconstructing Historiography'. She has also co-edited with Ranajit Guha the selected subaltern works.[17] Thus, though she is not a member of the subaltern 'collective' she is closely associated with the group.

The term 'subaltern', which is a creation of the British colonial contact with India, means 'subordinate' or 'inferior', and by implication, 'inferior modes of knowledge'. The subaltern historiography seeks to re-establish the balance of knowledge by demonstrating that the 'inferior' is made so through discourses of power and politics. Bernard S. Cohn's essay[18] on British attitudes to Indian languages—Persian, Arabic, Hindi, Sanskrit, Bangla, Telugu, etc. — is a fine example of deconstruction of the power structures shaping the forms of native knowledge. In this essay, Cohn's intellectual sympathies are with Persian against English, with Sanskrit against Persian, with Hindi against Sanskrit, and finally with Bangla against Hindi. Thus, he looks at the colonial hierarchy of languages from the perspective of the oppressed and the marginalised. Subaltern historiography is thus the perspective of the marginalised, of many against the dominant one. The approach is closer to Marxist historiography; but it does not poeticize peasants, and it does not undervalue the individual consciousness.

Gayatri Chakravorty's theoretical comments make a systematic statement of the aims and methods of the subaltern historiography. According to her, "The work of the Subaltern Studies group offers a theory of change." The 'theory' of change relates to the functional changes in systems of social signs within the broader text of history. However, the change has to be defined in terms of a previously existent manner of perception of signs. Hence, subaltern studies "perceive their task as making a theory of consciousness or culture rather than specifically a theory of change."[19] The implication here is that subaltern historiography views history as a continuous chain of changing signs, the changes being continuous in times of insurgency as well as in times apparently stagnant. This historiography differs from elite historiography, and from the bourgeois nationalist perspective, in that the parameter for the change for the subaltern historiography is the consciousness of relatively small groups having marginal social importance. The studies published by Ranajit Guha and his collective of scholars show an obsessive interest in the colonial period, giving the concept of 'subaltern' a specific historic grounding. Gayatri Chakravorty records her response to *Subaltern Studies* thus:

> I am progressively inclined, then, to read the retrieval of subaltern consciousness as the charting of what in post-structuralist language would be called the subaltern subject-effect. A subject-effect can be briefly plotted as follows: that which seems to operate as a subject may be part of an immense discontinuous network ('text' in the general sense) of strands that may be termed politics, ideology, economics, history, sexuality, language, and so on. (Each of these strands, if they are isolated, can also be seen as woven of many strands.) Different knottings and configurations of these strands, dependent upon myriad circumstances, produce the effect of an operating subject.[20]

It should be clear by now that subaltern historiography fights the tendency to essentialize India. In the subaltern system of significance 'India' is a changing concept, signifying a variety of social formations, power-structures, linguistic histories to a variety of social and cultural groupings of consciousness. Therefore, when extended to cover literary history, the subaltern strategy tends to deny a common identity, and a continuous diachronic self-cognition of all literatures in India, which then can be collapsed into the larger category of 'Indian literature'. In fact, the subaltern perspective likes to look at all literature as parasitical. In any case, it looks at the question of the subaltern consciousness in terms of systems of signs, a writing of sorts, with its own phonocentrism. The metaphor reverses itself when writing is the subject of subaltern historiography. Gayatri Chakravorty writes:

> The cross-hatching of the revolutionary non-possessive possibilities in the structure of writing in general and its control by subaltern phonocentrism gives us access to the micrology or minute-scale functioning of the subaltern's philosophic world.[21]

Her own essay on Mahasvetadevi's *The Breast-giver* (*Stan-dayini*) is intended to be a reading of the system of 'writing-in-general' within which the novelist articulates the marginal, tribal consciousness as its own but authentic history.

The attitude that history, and history of literature in particular, has been a long and untold tale of deprivation has its origin in several regional, national, post-colonial and international literary movements. One may specify the following three of them here, all of which are new and progressive movements: (a) Dalit writings, (b) 'New' literatures in English, and (c) Feminist writing and criticism.

Among the most distinguished thinkers in India during the twentieth century, Ambedkar has a prominent place. Apart from his part in drafting the Constitution of free India, he played a crucial and pioneering role in organising 'lower caste' Indians into a community seeking emancipation and equality. By combining the teachings of the Buddha and Karl Marx in his message to the deprived classes in Indian society, he provided a sense of self-hood to the 'untouchables'. As a result of his teachings, and the new self-consciousness flowing so powerfully from it, a new school of creative writing has emerged in Marathi, Kannada, Gujarati, Telugu and Hindi literature in the last twenty-five years. This new writing on the assertion of self-hood is extremely appealing, disturbing and challenging. *Dalit* literature, however, is not just texts or documents. The writers, in this movement show a clear awareness of belonging to a distinct literary culture and history. The origin of *dalit* literary historiography can be traced back to Ambedkar's history of dalithood. In an extremely well-argued and well-researched history of untouchability, *Untouchables: Who Were They?*[22] he discusses the anthropological and linguistic aspects of the problem, and presents a wealth of historical evidence to prove that untouchability has its roots in internal social discrimination in India and not in racial difference as had been previously argued by the sociologist Stanley Rice.

> If anthropometry is a science which can be depended upon to determine the race of a people, then the results obtained by the application of anthropometry to the various strata of Hindu society disprove that the untouchables belong to a race different from the Aryans and the Dravidians. The measurements establish that the Brahmins and the Untouchables belong to the same race. From this it follows that if the Brahmins are

> Aryans the Untouchables are also Aryans. If the Brahmins are Dravidians the Untouchables are also Dravidians. If the Brahmins are Nagas, the Untouchables are also Nagas.[23]

The literary historiography of *dalit* literature derives from this principle of racial equality of Indian society. It focuses on the questions of otherness, difference, marginality, canon and the categories of aesthetics. In order to voice the protest of the marginalised, *dalit* literature often follows the subversive historiographic path of personalising history. It is therefore, perhaps, that autobiography is the most potent and often exercised form of fiction produced in *dalit* literature.[24] If long entrenched social discrimination separates history from its original twin, fiction, *dalit* literature seeks to revert to the primal unity between fiction and history.

One of the poignant statements of *dalit* aesthetics and literary historiography comes through the 'Preface' to *Kondwada*, the first verse collection of the Marathi poet Daya Pawar. The term *kondwada* refers to restricted cultural and social space. Its literal meaning is cattle-camp/prison. In this preface, Pawar offers us a personalised history of *dalit* literature. "No star shone in my direction when I was born. Nor did the sun appear like a red fruit to me".[25] Beginning with his birth in deprived social circumstances, Pawar graduated to various levels of social violence and discrimination. His growth as a poet was also his growth as a self-conscious *dalit*. Thus, *dalithood* is something which gets into the consciousness of writers like him along with language. Pawar is acutely aware that his poetry is a class/caste poetry:

> I have had the opportunity to read my poems to audiences at various forums. Because of that I can make some surmises. In rural areas, a new educated class is coming up. There in the high school and college setting my poems are being appreciated. There is the unforgettable experience of the poetry reading at the literary conference at Mahad (the place associated with Ambedkar's social protest). The audience took poems such as 'First Night' and 'Sabha' to their hearts. Along-side are some discouraging experiences. The Marathi academic class is turning up its nose at the poems; so also there is the cold reception at the poetry reading at

> the Indian Institute of Technology, at Powai, Bombay. It was like cutting ice with a knife.
>
> Once again I am sharply reminded of the cleavage in Indian cultural life. If my poems fall a victim in the attempt to close this divide, I shall not mind. I have come to perform that role. In my poem 'Maran'(Death) I have written:
>
> Like elephants crushed
> Against sharp spiked doorways
> One should die laughing.[26]

Women's emancipation has been as powerful and as debated a theme in recent Indian literature as the *dalit* question. Literary Feminism in India, native as well as derivative, is too vast a subject to be discussed even sketchily in the present work. However, the literary historiography proposed by gender equality activists needs to be paid special attention in our discussion of the historiography of deprivation. Most of the concerns of literary gender equality activists in India—and they do not have much use of the category 'nation'—get sharply focused in a valuable essay by Kumkum Sangari, "Of Ladies, Gentlemen, and 'the Short-Cut'," which appeared in *New Literary History*. The central argument of the essay is stated by her with characteristic clarity at the outset:

> Modes of consciousness and self-consciousness, identity and experience, personality and subjectivity are constructed in response and reaction to the pressure of a given historical moment and are neither self-sustaining nor perennially 'male' or 'female'. Femaleness is neither the 'natural' property of women, nor an eternally subversive Other, nor even, beyond a point, the product of a special experience. It is not an essential, homogenous quality at the *core* of all women waiting to be discovered once social oppression and repression are removed. Like maleness, femaleness is not a fixed inalienable quantity: it is rather a mode of *social* being and so a historically specific value which can be redistributed and reformulated.[27]

The argument about the nature of difference between femaleness and maleness presented here is comparable to Ambedkar's argument about the difference between the 'touchables' and the 'untouchables'. Similarly, both protests seek for removal of the social conditions that determine the difference; they do not seek to accentuate the difference so as to establish a doctrinaire antagonism and autonomous identity. The protests are to be seen as a corrective shift in literary history rather than as revolutions.

It is a similar assertion of equality between all writers in English that we see in Salman Rushdie's essay, " 'Commonwealth Literature' Does Not Exist". He has been grouped together with other non-British, Irish and American writers writing in English in a category called 'Commonwealth Literature'. His argument is that the differences between various units of the Commonwealth are more substantial than the similarities. Rushdie vehemently explodes the artificial historical category:

> The dangers of unleashing such a phantom into the groves of literature are, it seems to me, manifold... there is the effect of creating a ghetto, and that, in turn, leads to a ghetto mentality amongst some of its occupants. Also the creation of a false category can and does lead to excessively narrow, and sometimes misleading readings of some of the artists it is held to include; and again, the existence—or putative existence—of the best distracts attention from what is actually worth looking at, what is actually going on.[28]

It should be noted that Rushdie is not criticising merely the use of the term 'Commonwealth', or the category of Commonwealth literature. He is in fact, like the *dalit* writers and the feminist critics, challenging the patronizing attitude behind it:

> ...the term is not used simply to describe, or even misdescribe, but also to *divine*. It permits academic institutions, publishers, critics and even readers to dump a large segment of English literature into a box and then more or less ignore it. At best, what is called 'Commonwealth literature' is positioned *below* English literature... or it places Eng. lit. at the centre and the rest of the world at the periphery.[29]

The sense of outrage is caused by what Rushdie himself calls the creation of the Commonwealth 'ghetto'. This ghetto can be no less oppressive to writers who wish to relate themselves to the entire English canon and the totality of the English language than the caste ghetto created for the *dalit* writers, or the gender ghetto created for women writers.

The three forms of protest, their explicit plea for equality, their desire to reconstitute the category of the aesthetic, go into their revisions of history. Their literary historiography seeks to recast literary histories based on colonial, cultural and caste discriminations and deprivations; and in their own fashion, they emphasise the texts of such deprivations against established historical narratives.

Heterodox Modernity and Foreclosed Tradition

Our illustrations for the two antithetical views on literary traditions come from the writings of two extremely significant novelists, both profoundly similar and yet greatly dissimilar. They are U.R. Anantha Murthy and Bhalchandra Nemade. They are both known as trend-setting novelists in their respective languages, Kannada and Marathi. Both have left their respective fiction traditions significantly altered since the sixties. They have been in the forefront of the little magazine movements in their languages. Though teachers of English, both have been committed to their own languages. Both have a tremendous sympathy for medieval Indian literature. Here the similarity ends. The differences will be clear when we analyse their texts: Anantha Murthy's long essay, 'Why not Worship in the Nude?'[30] and Nemade's long essay, 'The Marathi Novel: 1950–75'.[31] Both these have by now become celebrated texts, mainly because each is a comprehensive revaluation of a major tradition of fiction.

Anantha Murthy's essay, with its anecdotal style and self-dramatization, makes delightful reading. Within the scope of this essay he presents the whole range of his response to Kannada fiction written by some major writers of this century: Shivaram Karanth, K.V. Puttappa, Masti Venkatesh Iyengar, Yashwant Chittal, Lankesh, Shantinath Desai, Poornachandra Tejaswi, Devanuru Mahadeva, and others. In reflecting on their contribution to the growth of the Kannada consciousness, Anantha Murthy examines the phenomenon of modernism in India. The central question as he raises it is: Can a novelist be progressive in his rational sphere of thought and at the same time engage sympathetically in his novelistic creation? To this question, there are unambiguous ideological answers. There are also unambiguous attitudes available in the given discourses of anthropology, journalism, politics and social work. However, these unambiguous answers prove reductive and fail to understand the complexity of Indian society and culture, as Anantha Murthy argues.

The more significant fiction in Kannada is that which tries to get to the centre of the complexity in Indian culture. It is a culture, or rather a set of cultures, which brings every rational act in confrontation with an incredibly humane transcendence, every act of escape from tradition comes face-to-face with surprising discoveries of modernity in the backwaters. Making a choice between tradition and modernity in any exclusive way is, in Anantha Murthy's view, to falsify and to deny India:

> The reality of novelists in India, I am speaking from my Kannada experience, is so complex as to disallow the comforts of either status-quoist acceptance or of revolutionary ruthlessness. R.K. Narayan can afford to say 'India will go on' only as a comic realist, in his inimitable low mimetic mode. But when his insightful Indian experience is translated into ideas in a polemical indictment of Indian reality, he can afford to speak angrily and ruthlessly and plead for a thoroughgoing modernization in India—only in a polemical context. I wonder if he can maintain his position unambiguously in a novel where his imaginative sympathies are fully engaged.[32]

From this position, Anantha Murthy then analyses the works of major Kannada novelists to show that at the heart of each of the major Kannada novels is the ambiguity about modernization. It is so, because the major writers have understood the issues involved in the transition from tradition to modernity. They cannot have clear affiliations either with tradition or with modernity. All they can have is a heterodox acceptance of things as they have been, uneasily combined with the desire to change them:

> Yes—all of us are modernisers in one way or the other, but with an uneasy conscience, if we are sensitive. The great writers among us see it as inevitable and

> search for ways to preserve what is best and unique in Indian civilization.[33]

The reflections of the novelist in his time, as Anantha Murthy calls them, are all set in the disturbing social context of a tragic struggle between the forces of modernization and a group of devotees that goes through the ritual of worshipping at a temple in the nude. The conflict between the two is, in essence, the conflict between India of the past and India of the present. Anantha Murthy understands both, and therefore cannot take any one side. His is an ambivalence which desires to preserve the past and wishes it radically changed. Translated into the terms of literary historiography, this attitude articulates an intimate enemity with the literary past as well as the literary present. And, in fact, a closer look at Anantha Murthy's responses to other Kannada novelists does reveal this sense of uneasy intimacy. He likes them, and at the same time he disapproves of them. Given such a vision of one's literary tradition, and its relation to the social reality surrounding it, the only viable attitude to literary history has to be based in a poetics of heterodoxy. For Anantha Murthy, modern Kannada fiction is a combination of traditional Indian wisdom, ignorant but faithful religious rituals, rational and scientific progress, fragmented modern emotional life, and an uneasy involvement in all these on the part of the novelists. Ultimately, the essence of being a great modern Kannada novelist lies in coping with a range of heterodoxy.

In contrast to Anantha Murthy, Bhalchandra Nemade believes in an active moral engagement in the social context on the part of the novelist. This social engagement is described by Nemade by using a pair of terms, one aesthetic and the other ethical: *kriti* and *navaniti*. *Kriti* is, in his exposition of it, the linguistic action that a novelist performs in a given novelistic context dealing with social reality. *Navaniti* is the writer's ethical commitment to his medium as a means of progressive (not in the Marxist sense) critique of the society to which he belongs, for the language which he uses is social material. Nemade's aesthetic demands on fiction writers originate in his larger critical perspective of '*desivad*'. Nemade's *desivad* believes that literature is a subsystem of culture and the society that produces it; and, therefore, it acquires serious meaning only when it reflects social reality in all aspects and areas of life. This may be a highly debatable assumption. However, what interests us here is the historiographical expectations raised by *desivad.*

The Nemade style of *desivad* combines ethics and aesthetics, in effect, to create a gradation in fiction. The fiction that depicts social reality from a progressive, ethical point of view is judged the best kind. The others which either do not reflect social reality or do not show the ethical awareness expected of fiction are thought of as inferior varieties. Thus, there is a hierarchy of fiction. In Nemade's own terminology the classification, in descending order of importance, is: (i) *Kriti*-oriented novel of social realism and linguistic action; (ii) *Riti*-oriented novel of formalistic interest and linguistic self-centredness; (iii) *Pratikriti*-oriented novel of illusions, fantasy and day-dreams.

Once this hierarchy of fiction is conceptualised as a framework for critical evaluation, it implies also a historiographical strategy. Using the three-fold classification of fiction—within which one can devise further sub-classes when necessary—one can show literary history as a continuous pattern of exchanges between the three trends. Since Nemade privileges the *kriti*-oriented forms of fiction as progressive forms, he reads the history of Marathi fiction as a clash and competition between *kriti*-fiction, on the one hand, and *riti*- and *prakriti*-fiction, on the other. In his survey of Marathi fiction since 1950, he first sets out to show the history of this conflict during the preceding century of Marathi fiction, and then presents *that* history as the pre-condition for reading the subsequent periods of history. Thus, the concept of tradition in Nemade's historiography is that of a foreclosed tradition, which can acquire further complexity but never face complete displacement. Tradition always guides any subsequent period of literary history. Again, it is tradition which provides the grounds for literary criticism, by suggesting appropriate criteria to judge new developments. In justifying his method of historical assessment, Nemade states that if one wishes to understand literary culture in a given period, it is necessary to trace the dominant trends back to their origin, that is, to the very moment of the commencement of that particular literary tradition, so as to see them in their pure form. The rest of the history is nothing but a many-stranded narrative of the interplay of these strands. He calls this historiography, the 'nativistic method of historical reconstruction'.

The literary historiography proposed by Nemade offers a challenging perspective in the context of fiction criticism, since it alters the established method of considering prose-fiction as a purely imported literary form. According to Nemade's historiography, the ground rules of literary development are established at the inception of a given literary tradition. Literary history involves the gradual unfolding of those rules, the ingrained tendencies, which pass through processes of fluctuation, interplay, occasional mutations, or cross-fertilization. These changes can be explained in terms of the material of social reality reflected in literature. Thus literary traditions are essentially foreclosed systems. They are open to manipulation by writers, but not so open as to be completely wiped out. Literary trends which seem eliminated, survive underground. All of Nemade's critical writing is suffused with this faith in the predictable creativity of traditions.

If Anantha Murthy constructs modernity as a condition of knowledgeable ambivalence, the inability to decide which of the cultural pressures demanding his novelistic attention should be privileged, Nemade implies that tradition leaves very little for the writer to choose. For Anantha Murthy, tradition is freedom, for Nemade tradition is a necessity. For Anantha Murthy, tradition in pluralistic societies is heterodox. For Nemade, tradition in post-colonial societies is a means of recovering the nativistic self-awareness so as to be able to perform linguistic *kriti*, creation which is also action.

Eternal Recurrence and Specific Occurrence

The critic whose work illustrates the view of history as a perennial recurrence is Ananda K. Coomaraswamy. To illustrate this view of history I will refer to some of his major essays.[34] The text illustrating the opposite view, history as a temporally conditioned and specific occurrence is a recent essay by Rajeev Patke[35] providing a historiographical model in the context of Indian-English poetry.

Coomaraswamy's works are far too well known to require an account of his critical contribution. Here, we are concerned with the implications of his criticism for literary historiography. Obviously, we cannot benefit in that direction from his popularly known essays on Hindu aesthetics that one encounters in *The Dance of Shiva*. It is necessary to examine some of his other major essays, particularly 'Recollection: Indian and Platonic'. 'The One and the Only Transmigrant', and '*Kha* and Other Words Denoting "Zero" in Connection with the Indian Metaphysics of Space'.[36]

In his discussion of the concept of zero in relation to space, Coomaraswamy reproduces the definition of infinity given by Bhaskara in his *Bijaganita*, with an English translation:

> *ayam ananto rasib khabara ity uchyate. Asmin vikarah khabare na rasavapi pravistesvapi nihsrtesu bahusvapi syal layasrstikale 'nante' 'cyute bhutaganesu yadvat',* that is This fraction of which the denominator is Zero, is called an infinite quantity. In this quantity consisting of that which has cipher for its divisor, there is no alteration, though many be added or substracted; just as there is no alteration in the Infinite Immovable (*anante acyute*) at the time of the emanation or resolution of worlds, though hosts of beings are emanated or withdrawn.[37]

It is interesting to note that what was used by Bhaskara, the ancient mathematician as a metaphor is treated by Coomaraswamy as literal description. The mention of 'Infinite Immovable' in the original is not as emphatic as in Coomaraswamy's translation. The reason why Coomaraswamy attempts this peculiar foregrounding of metaphysical infinity in his discussion of mathematical infinity is, perhaps, that he seeks a legitimation of his own concept of perennial philosophy in the definition he discusses. The belief in perennially present wisdom or philosophy was the most central of his persuasions.

To Coomaraswamy, the fund of wisdom to which human societies have access is *anant*, infinite. What appears as new discoveries, inventions, original contributions, revolutions in thought, are nothing but fresh manifestations of knowledge that was already in existence. Hence, in the essay 'The One and the Only Transmigrant' he tries to show that the idea of transmigration in Sankaracarya, Plato, Plotinus and a host of other Indian and Western thinkers is essentially the same idea. Of course, in pointing out these similarities, he does not intend to hint at any influence of any particular philosopher on the others. The point he makes, so eruditely, is that essentially one philosophic thought can be inspired in the minds of different philosophers in different cultures and at different times. This is his perspective of perennial philosophy.

The concept of perennial philosophy has extremely important implications for historiography. And, in fact, Coomaraswamy exploits that implication to the fullest in his distinguished body of art history and literary criticism. The implication is that the history of art and literature is nothing more than a series of recurrences of some basic thought-clusters, theme-structures and styles. For a provocative articulation of his historiographical perspective we have to turn to Coomaraswamy's essay on memory, 'Recollection: Indian and Platonic'.The preamble to 'Recollection' lays bare the very heart of the entire work of Coomaraswamy:

> In the following article, the doctrine that what we call 'learning' is really a 'remembering' and that our 'knowledge' is by participation in the Omniscience of an immanent spiritual principle will be traced in Indian and Platonic texts. This corresponds, in same Perennial Philosophy, to the doctrine that the beautiful is such by a participation in Beauty, and all being a participation of Being absolutely.[38]

By drawing on a plethora of evidence from ancient scriptural sources, Coomaraswamy does indeed build a case for the view that memory is not the storehouse of new experiences, but an outlet for knowledge belonging to an Order of existence prior or superior to human existence. Memory is from the Self, and "the Self knows everything". Thus what we remember is really what we recollect; and to remember becomes the dominant mode of Becoming. All knowledge is in this sense a mere reminding. "Memory is a kind of latent knowledge." And again, "the ultimate source on which all memory draws"[39] is the Self or Spirit.

Given Coomaraswamy's metaphysical approach to memory, history—which persists in its attempt to recollect—becomes a highly privileged subject. At the same time, the events of history become only virtual events, being reproductions of events that have happened many times in the past. Thus, Coomaraswamy's historiography undercuts the importance of history as the past, forcing it into the realm of an ever-present, at the same time inflating the importance of history as a discourse which he makes the source of all knowledge including spiritual knowledge.

The view of literary history as a pattern of recurrences is not peculiar to Coomaraswamy's philosophy alone. Some variants of this philosophy can be traced to some nineteenth century philosophers. Friedrich Nietzsche was the most important of its exponents. In a sense, works of literature, which survive their own chronological time, come into existence repeatedly in every subsequent period when new generations of readers encounter them. However, it is not in any metaphorical sense that Coomaraswamy thinks of philosophy, knowledge and literature as eternally recurrent phenomena. He thinks of history as a recurrence in the literal as well as philosophical sense.

> The providential principle, in other words, is the immanent Spirit, the Knower of the field, apart from whom, on the one hand, no birth could take place... and apart from whom, as only seer, hearer, thinker, etc. in us..., neither experience nor memory could be conceived. [40]

The historian becomes, then, a prophet who must keep looking for immanence of the Self in all recurrences seen outwardly as history.

Rajeev Patke's essay, published recently in *Kavya Bharati* is an attempt to make sense of the large crop of anthologies of Indian poetry in English, and to provide a historical perspective to the process of canon formation in this new branch of Indian literature. He rests his argument on Frank Kermode's observation about canons being trans-historical in some sense but which also have to be set within the framework of historical periods.[41] By following closely the changes in the patterns of imitation in Indian English poetry during the last hundred years, Patke splits it into periods, that match respectively with the two criteria (which Lionel Trilling devises for a different purpose) of sincerity and authenticity. Thus in his reading of the history of Indian poetry in English, there is a period of sincerity followed by another period of authenticity. What is worth appreciating in Patke's historiography is that he divides the poets into periods without any strained attempt to show them totally different from one another. Thus there is a continuity between the two periods as well as a difference. Therefore, Patke can speak of the canon as well as periods in Indian English poetry. He states this aim with clarity at the outset of his essay:

> The usual way of making sense of any such body of writing is to treat it not as a mere sequence in time but as an historical process. The notion of process recognises change as the effect of a cause which may be located in the literary sensibility of a culture. When a change in literary sensibility is shared by a number of authors, the literary historian can nominalize it as literary period. The concept of period may be open to abuse as mere convenience or as a bed of Procrustean simplification. But when properly used, it defines the recognition that literary changes of a substantive and irreversible kind have occurred in the process that is literary history. The authors and texts who reflect these changes constitute the canon for that period. Canons are necessarily plural. They are also thoroughly historical, and contingent on the values of specific periods.[42]

The need to periodize rests on the recognition that large scale changes in literary tastes call for corresponding shifts in the perception of literature. This recognition helps historians to link all literary events in a single chronological category of literature or tradition, while enabling them to link together all literary events of a specifically common character into a single synchronic category of period. Thus each literary period is *literary* but not literary in the same way as all other periods are. Each literary period, author, text, or event is an occurrence by itself and never totally *identical* with any other period, author, text or event.

The view that literature is an occurrence in itself, only marginally linked with the literature of preceding or succeeding periods, reflects the critical values and literary historiography available in the dominant Anglo-American schools of literary thought. This view can be seen at play in those literary histories which consider periodisation as an essential function of literary historiography. It can be located in the critical and philosophic perspectives dominant in the European discourse and preception of general history. The same historiographical perspective is also at the base of most of the textbook histories of literature currently produced in India.

Occasionally, a perceptive critic like Namvarsingh, who writes in Hindi, has given a brilliant exposition to a contrary view. In his *Itihasa aur Aalochana*, Namvarsingh points out the dangers of using periodization in constructing the history of Hindi literature. However, he does not mystify history as Coomaraswamy does. His is a culture-specific argument which in translation would read as follows:

> If periodization is to be seen as a 'Methodological necessity' its appropriateness must derive justification from its practical utility. Therefore, if the concept interferes with our perceiving the past as it really was, it is desirable to abandon the method.
>
> Judging by the use of the device of periodisation in the history of Hindi literature so far, it needs to be said that it does distort the historical reality. The periods conceptualized have fragmented our literary history. The periods offer only fragmented images of the past not its continuous flow. The points of time demarcating the periods become not only disjointed but, in the process, one stands to miss a lot from history.[43]

The discussion of these post-colonial Indian approaches to literary history indicate the range and variety of critical responses to India's literary past. These approaches, though not fully developed philosophies of literary history, indicate the direction in which literary historiography in India has been moving during the twentieth century. Taken together, they indicate that history is open to numerous interpretations, all of which can be 'valid' interpretations, and possesses, like a literary text itself, the quality of interminable indeterminacy. They suggest that the polemics of progress along the fixed line of transition from imagination to reason will diminish the complexity and diversity of the literary past and present in India.

Considering the vast temporal scope of Indian literary creativity and the numerous social dissensions that it has drawn upon, literary historiography demands of a historian a multiple and complex mechanism of cognition with regard to India's literary past. The differences among the approaches outlined regarding the phenomenological limits of literature—ranging from the universal (Sri Aurobindo), national (Sujit Mukherjee), regional (the *bhasha* historiography) and the sub-Iinguistic/ regional (*dalit* and subaltern historiography) — show that the concepts of selfhood operating behind them are not identical. Hence, literary historiography in India will gain by exploring the notions of *self* and *other* in Indian social practice and philosophical traditions. Besides, the question of the relationship between canon and para-literature, between literature and the non-verbal arts will have to be tackled before establishing the guiding principles of literary historiography in India. Taken together, the Indological attitude, the nationalistic attitude and the nativistic attitude suggest that any definition of tradition in Indian literature will have to take into account the micro-level cultural transactions more seriously than any history based on the concepts of progress-periods-canon has done in the past. In short, a literary history in India, if it has to be a properly ordered illumination of the literary past, will have to be a history, to allude to Rajashekhara's eloquent phrase, 'Of Many Beings'.

14

Para-Literature

"In every literary epoch there is," according to Russian Formalism, "not one but several literary schools. They exist in literature simultaneously, but one of them represents the canonized crest. The others are not canonized and exist obscurely...."[1] The Formalistic historiography allows an element of arbitrariness in canon formation, which it describes as "automatization perceptibility." Once allowance is made for the mysterious arbitrariness in how some literary trends get to become the canonised crest and others exist obscurely, the creation, existence and decline of the non-canonised other trends becomes a foreclosed question. However, the question of obscure traditions, marginal styles and non-canonised texts is of utmost importance to literatures with multilingual historical contexts. The question has a great political urgency in societies that have experienced colonial domination and gender discrimination.

Let us try to conceptualise the 'other, obscure, suppressed or sub-cultural' literary phenomena by using the epithet 'para'. [2] This prefix has travelled from its Greek origin through Latin, and Middle French to Middle English, retaining most of its original sense, and it now means: 'by the side of, beside, alongside of, by past, and beyond.' Para-literature would, therefore, include all such activities as are normally considered socially parallel, linguistically parasitical, psychologically paranoid and historically parenthetical. What is common to all forms of para-literature is that they are literatures without interlocutors, taboo to literary history.

Para-literature as creative activity is analogous to Comparative Literature as a method of literary study in one important respect. In the initial stages of its development, European scholars of Comparative Literature divided the entire field of literary study into National Literature, Comparative Literature, and General Literature.[3]

Whereas National Literature and General Literature were defined with relatively greater precision, Comparative Literature, being neither, was given the nebulous and vast middle space between the two. Similarly, Para-literature occupies the middle space between literature and non-literature. It is not literature, because it is not accepted in literary canons. It is also not non-literature, because it has the formal attributes of literature. Para-literature is, thus, the middle space literature.

The middle space is densely populated. It contains a bewildering range of forms of linguistic creativity such as science and crime fiction, magazine stories, film and television scripts, street-plays, biographies, autobiographies, memoirs, travelogues, philosophic writings, religious discourses, popular and folk songs, folklore, proverbs, mantra, tantra and liturgical verses, lullabies, oral narratives, archaic literature, works in slang and dialect, children's literature, performed poetry (as in *mushairas*), pornography, graffiti, comics, advertisements, jokes, cartoons, translations, adaptations, abuse terms and letters. Of course this is a random list of middle space literary forms. It can accommo-date other forms not listed above provided they are literary and overlooked by histories of literature.

The middle space literature can be differentiated from non-literature by virtue of its context, style and performance. For instance, abuse terms, graffiti, pornography, popular romances and love-letters have in common the theme of sex-relations; yet each of these has its proper style, context and performance. We cannot interchange the style, context and performance of any of these genres without risking disastrous consequences. In other words, the middle space literature is not without its aesthetic form, unlike non-literature. All forms of middle space literature involve a certain linguistic skill and aesthetic sensibility. They have their own distinctive discourses and conventions, standards of excellence and criteria of achievement. They all have their cultural uses. Any language would be much the poorer without these or similar forms of linguistic creativity.

It is the differentiation between literature and the middle-space literature that is the more problematic. One may hastily assume that para-literature or the middle space literature is "low-brow" literature. But that is not the case. It cuts across all social classes. Who does not require, at one time or another in their lives, abuse words, graffiti, detective or pulp fiction, oral narratives, popular poetry, love-letters and religious recitations? Can we say that liturgical verses or national anthems are low brow?

One may argue that the creative imagination called in operation by para-literature is inferior to the imagination employed by the writers of classics. This claim needs to be investigated by psychologists. However, there are countless writers who work as journalists, commercial copywriters, film and television writers. For instance, one of the most creative of India's contemporary poets, Arun Kolatkar, works in the field of advertising. He writes very good poetry in two languages: Marathi and English. Can the imagination that writes poetry in Marathi be different from the imagination that writes Kolatkar's poetry in English and the "poetic" imagination different again from the imagination that writes advertisement copy? [4] To put this in another way, not all good poets can be good prose writers, or good journalists or commercial artists. Each kind of writing requires a specific kind of linguistic orientation, and none of these orientations is superior or inferior. The notion that poetic imagination is closer to Truth, and therefore superior to other forms of imagination, is a belief left over to us by the nineteenth century European conflict between reason and imagination, which created exaggerated and romantic claims in favour of imagination. On the other hand, if poets were traditionally expected to be prophets in India, they were also expected to quieten their mental activity, including that of imagination, in order to be able to receive large visions of life. The idea that *literature* employs imagination which is superior to the kind of imagination used in para-literature reflects the equation of power between the two types of literature rather than any valid aesthetic perception.

The question of power immediately brings in the question of institutionalisation of literature. Rather than saying that para-literature is non-literature, it would be more appropriate to say that it is non-classroom literature, that as literature it is neither taught nor learnt. Para-literature is all literature which is excluded from literary history; and if seen grudgingly as a document it is never given the status of a monument. The difference between literature and para-literature has to be sought, therefore, with reference to the causes behind institutionalised literature teaching. Two questions need to be asked here: why do we teach literature? and, why do we not teach all manifestations of literary creativity?

Literature teaching is a unique invention in human history. It does not pass on knowledge in the same way as the teaching of sciences and technology do. Sciences and technology face the danger of extinction if they are not transmitted through some form of teaching. Literature faces no such danger, for literature as a creative activity does not depend on the teaching of literature. Literature teaching does not aim at shaping future writers as the classroom work in fine arts aims at shaping artists. While other human sciences deal with human reality, literature teaching deals with a level of reality *created* by human beings. Closest to it come the teaching of linguistics and philosophy which handle a secondary level of reality, namely, language and thought. But they rarely glorify the aesthetic and emotive aspect of their subject to the extent literature teaching does. To generalize, literature teaching has the following two characteristics: it is a non-useful activity, and the thought content it seeks to transmit is irrational.

Perhaps the above generalization can be restated by saying that the greatest use of literature teaching is that by using ambivalent literary signs for the construction of its pedagogic narratives, it allows the irrational elements in a culture a respectable articulation. If scientific thinking keeps a society moving forward, signs of irrational impulses keep it integrated. Literature is such a system of signs. It is, in other words, a totemic system. It is a system embodied in verbal signs which continue to persist in their meaning over long periods of time, signs which are totems that articulate for successive generations of people the irrational content of their own personalities. Literature, this system of totems, keeps successive generations bound by a sense of historic flow of time, by a sense of being a community. All communities are bound together by the literary signs they value. No literature is *objectively* beautiful or useful in itself. Literatures are vested with these qualities by the communities that are bound together by those linguistic totems. Literature is taught as a valuable discipline because it helps us to identify the most persistent and irrational images of our ancestors in the verbal icons created by them. Totems do not possess any inherent significance. They acquire it by virtue of their situation in a given community.

It may be possible to understand the universal urge to impart literary teaching to younger generations in any given society in the light of the above comments. The reason why all kinds of literature do not receive an institutional status is that totems always create, and almost inevitably depend on, a contrary system of taboos.[5] If, literature is understood as a system of totems, para-literature can be seen as a system of taboos, which is not allowed to enter the sacred portals of a classroom. In fact, collectively and irrationally agreed upon, taboos too keep communities bound together. Totems and taboos, respectively, represent a community's desires in their sublimated or repressed forms. The relationship between the two is the relationship between the sacred and the profane. This relationship depends on how a given community distributes its cultural space. In terms of the material substance of which they are composed, their structural organisations, and their expressivity, totems and taboos may be identical; but their status in terms of the sacred and the profane may vary radically. For instance, pornography and romance, or abuse terms and proverbs, may have identical substance, structure and complexity; yet the irrational needle of a community's compass mapping the range of the sacred and the profane will show the forms in these pairs as distinct as the east and the west, or the north and the south.

It may be deduced from these anthropological observations about the nature of canon formation in literary studies that the distinction between literature and para-literature, even if explained in terms of a science of literary criticism, is really guided by the systems of totems and taboos of the society that creates and preserves a given literary tradition. Exclusions of authors, texts, styles in a given history of literature, or inclusion of certain other authors, texts, forms and styles, are matters which, in the first instance, are determined by extra-literary considerations. It is not because the critical consensus about an author or a technique is initially wrong that after a time that author or technique is given legitimacy. These fluctuations occur because taboos can turn into totems in course of time. For example, travelling across the seas was taboo in India till the early part of this century. Today it has a totemic importance. Neither totems nor taboos have permanence of status. They may interchange their positions with appropriate shifts in the cultural history of a community. This exchange is an essential aspect of literary history, though unfortunately it has remained generally neglected.

When new literary traditions emerge, or branch off from an established literary tradition, the new literatures are initially treated as taboo/para-literatures. The history of literature in the modern Indian languages tells us that in the initial period of development of these new traditions, the period of transition from Sanskrit to these new languages was seen as a gradual vulgarization. A similar attitude was displayed in Europe towards the literatures and languages branching out of Latin in medieval times. In the early phases of English literary writing outside England and Scotland, in countries like Ireland, America and Australia, the British attitude to such literature was invariably patronising. On the other hand, when a literary tradition acquires substance, the preceding literary trends or traditions lose their acquired status. Though it is true that not all obsolete literature gets relegated to the category of para-literature, literary history does keep agitating against literary obsolescence.

However, not all para-literature is a product of literary history's amnesia, nor is all of it the result of hesitation on the part of literary criticism to assimilate new modes of writing. Much of para-literature is downgraded to that status due to contemporary repressions guided by the hierarchic stratification within a community. In most communities a lower "aesthetic" value is attached to literature produced by and for women and children in literary criticism and history controlled by the men and adults of those communities. Children and women form two major repressed segments of most communities. Their literary requirements, and aesthetic sensibilities are taken less seriously than they deserve. Para-literature therefore accurately reflects the patterns of social repression. In addition to these, there is one more conventional method of repression in India. The subcontinental and poly-linguistic country always has had a common mainstream literary tradition, whether in Sanskrit, Pali, Persian, Hindi or English. The regional literary traditions in India have to encounter the imperialism of the mainstream traditions. At present, this is the condition of about eighty-five tribal and minority languages and literary forms in these languages. Each of these languages is spoken by more than 10,000 people but not listed as languages of administration in the eighth Schedule of the Indian Constitution.[6] The literary aesthetics of these languages is never given even the minimum passing consideration in Indian literary discourse. Their situation is like that of literatures in Indian languages in relation to the contemporary world canon of literature. Para-literature is thus the literature of linguistic communities on the periphery of political orders.

The psychological desire to castrate one's adversary often takes linguistic expression. The linguistic creativity of politically subjugated sections is then made a victim of this desire by the dominating language groups. During the nineteenth century, European anthropologists turned perfectly normal literary activity in Africa into para-literature. Orientalism did that for the Asian nations. Para-literature, in which it is the usual practice to include oral narratives and folk forms, is perceived to be closer to the region of the unconscious. If one were to follow psychoanalytic criticism with persistence, it would seem to provide an explanation of the phenomenon. However, the unconscious itself is not a category free of political conditioning, as argued by Kumkum Sangari.[7] In a thought-provoking essay, she shows how Freud's discovery of the unconscious was an inevitable result of the political history of European colonialism during the nineteenth century:

> A significant facet of the history of designating the unconscious in Europe consists of the histories of primitivization. In the late nineteenth century the primitivization of certain categories becomes quite strident: most notably of sexuality and of women who, along with non-western societies are placed on the scale of evolution.
>
> The scientization of the primitive is carried out side by side with its aesthetization through a series of 'revaluations'. The 'primitive' ranges from the external and measurable to the internal and immeasurable... Conversely, the 'primitive' can either be equated with or contained in the unconscious.[8]

The primitive in society, the unconscious in the psyche, and the 'para' in literature may have intrinsic attributes in a given period, but these are not absolute categories. Their attributes in a given period are gradually determined over a preceding long period through processes of repression. Therefore, what is civilized can come to be considered primitive, what belongs to accessible areas of consciousness can be relegated to the territory and terror of the unconscious, and what is literature can invite description as para-literature. Movements in the opposite direction too are possible. These movements are of crucial formative importance in the history of literature, both as a system of totems and taboos and as dynamic cultural practices.

Since there is essentially no difference between literature and para-literature, the boundaries between the two are not permanently sealed, and there is a constant mutual exchange. This exchange proceeds along certain established lines. To articulate the nature of this exchange should be one of the primary objectives of literary history. As in the history of language, so too in the history of literature, the trends and styles initially developed on the margins tend to gravitate towards the centre. Removed from the original context, sometimes the para-styles change their intended performance in the changed literary context. Conventions of comic literature often originate in the not-so-comic dialects of the socially less privileged classes. Conventions of the tragic, epic and canonical originate in the well-formed registers of the socially privileged classes. Once formulated, these languages and literatures become socially usable systems. Thus, the marginal (or *desi*: regional) and the dominant (or *marga*: mainstream) literary traditions keep alternating their positions.[9] This continuous and inevitable mobility of literary conventions is what the term 'evolution' of literature should rightly imply.

Literature, as a social and cultural activity, is a continuous reordering of the total field of meaning available to a society through language, a continuous restructuring of various levels of received language. Literature, in order to be socially meaningful, has to reappropriate the sources of language so as to invest the language system with new possibilities of consciousness. Hence, the linguistic activity on the margins of a language community, the para-literary activity, has an important role to play in the literary enrichment of that language. For this reason it deserves attention as literary history.

It may be said that the distinction between literature and para-literature is not a distinction between two different fields, but a distinction within a single field, as the one between totems and taboos within a single culture, or as between the self and the non-self within a single field of consciousness. The political dispossession of linguistic and social margins is the root cause of the creation of such categories. The relationship between literature and para-literature is closely comparable to that between the psychologically masculine and the psychologically feminine other. It is a relationship in which the female other is seen as being closer to the unconscious, the primitive, the marginal, and yet indispensable. Ultimately, it is the need for this dialectics of self-cognition of literature that creates the category of para-literature.

If the dialectical relationship between the dominant trends and marginal trends is considered a process forming the backbone of the history of literature, it would still be necessary to specify the nature of this dialectics in a given culture, for it may vary from culture to culture. In other words, canon formation may be a common experience for all literatures in the world, but the processes through which canons are formed in a given literary culture are likely to be peculiar to that particular literary tradition. For instance, the canons of English literature have been shaped generally speaking by the conservative forces in British society. The canons of post-Sanskrit Indian literatures have, on the other hand, been formed by socially heterodox tendencies. It is not enough for literary history to describe the canons; it is also necessary, and even more important, to explain the culture specific processes of canon formation so as to make literature a socially integrated sub-system of culture. Therefore, if the relationship between literature and para-literature is of vital importance to the self-cognition of literary canons, it would be essential for any perspicuous literary history to take into account the nature of a society's narcissistic structure.

15

Swa and *Para*: Self and the Other

It is at this stage that we have to introduce another term to help us conceptualize the narcissistic structure of Indian society, as understood in Indian traditions. The term we can use is *para,* which is accepted by a large majority of modern Indian languages as the term for 'other'. The original Sanskrit term, replete with meanings, indicates: "distant, further, enemy, afterwards, beyond, other, far off, etc." Its superlative form, *param* however moves into a more idealistic plane by generating sacred terms such as *parameshwar and parabrahman*, terms related to the discourse of the other world. The term is shared by Dravidian languages too, with revealing deviations. Tamil uses *parai* as the term for drums played by outcaste drummers of the *paraiyan* community, which, incidentally, is also the origin of a similar English term, 'pariah'. One is not sure if the Greek *para* and the Sanskrit *para* have a forgotten common source; but it is possible to deduce from the linguistic evidence we have, that in all languages in which the Greek and the Sanskrit term *para* has been assimilated, the term is used to indicate 'otherness' as a psychological phenomenon as well as a spatial term, as if the psychological space is revealed through this term as a geographical metaphor. Thus modern English has 'parish' and 'parochial' indicating restricted psychological and geographical spaces. In Indian languages the term *paradesh* is used to indicate foreign or alien land. Such peculiar usage of the term for describing space as well as otherness, indicating unarticulated wisdom inherent in human languages, is properly theorized in Lacan's formulation:

> The notion of the role of spatial symmetry in man's narcissistic structure is essential in the establishment of the basis of a psychological analysis of space.... Let us consider that animal psychology has shown us that

> the individual's relation to a particular spatial field is, in certain species mapped socially, in a way that raises it to the category of subjective membership. I would say that it is the subjective possibility of the mirror projection of such a field into the field of the other that gives human space its originally 'geometric' structure, a structure that I would be happy to call *kaleidoscopic* .... Such, at least, is the space in which the imagery of the ego develops, and which rejoins the objective space of reality.[1]

Indian epistemology too admits the kaleidoscopic structure within the ego-space. But the kaleidoscoping it visualizes is not between the field of the self and the field of the non-self. It is rather between the field of the self and the field of the greater-self. It is a theology-bound epistemology. The *Katha Upanishad* is eloquent on this issue:

> The tree of eternity has its roots in heaven above and its branches reach down to earth. It is Brahman ... Brahman is seen in a pure soul as in a mirror clear, and also in the Creator's heaven as clear as light; but in the land of shades as reflections in trembling water. When the wise man knows that the material senses come not from the Spirit, and their waking and sleeping belong to their own nature, then he grieves no more. Beyond the senses is the Spirit of man, and beyond this is the Spirit of the universe, and evolver of all. And beyond is Purusha, all pervading, beyond definitions. [2]

Here too, as in Lacan, the key terms are 'mirror' and 'reflection' which complete the grand circle of human consciousness by inductive leaps. But the mapping of the narcissistic structure is different.

Indian texts, whether emerging from the *Vedas,* the *Upanishads*, or secular literature, see the self and the non-self as reflections of Purusha, the greater-self, as mere passing images of a reality beyond human perception. In that sense, the dichotomy between the self and non-self has not been conceptualized in radical terms. Buddhist psychology too did not visualize any such opposition between the self and the non-self. In fact, the entire spectrum of human existence is seen in Indian thought in terms of a complex continuum. To introduce concepts of polarities in it is considered by Indian thought as tantamount to a profoundly ignorant act of consciousness.

How can one reconcile this concept of the ego-space with the rational and sensory perceptions, which form the physical basis for the recognition of the non-self? Traditional Indian epistemology circumvents this difficulty by introducing a taxonomy of knowledge. Indian tradition divided knowledge into false knowledge, *avidya*, and authentic knowledge, *vidya*. The two are not radically different, but they can be recognised as such in terms of a polarity in the spectrum of knowledge. *Avidya* is the knowledge flowing from the senses to the soul. *Vidya*, on the contrary, is the knowledge flowing from the soul to the senses. The knower of *vidya* is a guru, a spiritual guide. These categories were neatly separated from those related to systematised perception of material phenomena, for which the terms *jnana* and *vijnana* (approximately corresponding to modern humanities and science, respectively) were employed. The knower of the latter was known as *acharya*, a teacher, a scholar. An experience of *para,* the foreign or alien, thus brings into play the knowledge of the other, which, when it is guided by *vidya* (spiritual knowledge) obscures the duality between the self and the non-self, leading to a recognition of the self within the non-self.

Sudhir Kakar, who has presented highly engaging theses on Indian psychoanalysis, comments on the sense of the self in Hindu tradition at length in his study, *The Inner World.* His observations as a professional scholar of psychology would be of immense use to us in defining the priorities of Indian literary history. Discussing the concepts of 'I', 'Ego' and 'Self', he writes:

> The distinction between *vidya* and *avidya*—true and false consciousness—between reality and *maya*, illustrates a fundamental difference between Hindu and Western world images, as well as a discrepancy in the modes of thought and perception, which even the best intentioned movements of cultural ecumenism cannot hope to bridge satisfactorily. The maintenance of ego boundaries, between 'inside' and 'outside', and between 'I' and 'others', and the sensory experiences of

> social relations based on these separations, is the stuff of reality in Western thought and yet *maya* to the Hindus, The optimal discrimination of this reality of separateness, expressed in terms of heightened ego functions such as reality sense, reality testing and adaptation to reality, is the stated goal of most Western psychotherapies, but of paltry importance in the Hindu ways of liberation. A good reality sense, according to psychoanalysis, shows itself in the absence of a conscious feeling of the self or the various selves. This, however, is precisely the situation which the Hindu ways of liberation would seek to reverse. And if in the course of development, the child learns to differentiate between himself and what is not a part of him, between 'me' and 'not-me'—a process in which the individual's sense of space, time, causality and individuality are formed, and ego boundaries are constituted—then in a certain sense the Hindu ways of liberation ... seek to undo this process of ego development.[3]

If, as modern psychoanalysis tells us, the tendency of the dominant Indian psychological type is towards establishing the non-duality of self and non-self in the narcissistic field, the tendency in the altruistic field must, therefore, be that of allowing a free interplay between the central and *para* cultural elements.

It would, however, be inaccurate to think that the Aryan epistemology of the self-other relationship remained unchanged in the long history of India. Hinduism has been an amorphous mass of ideas and practices, within which an amazing variety of dissenting viewpoints emerged and eventually merged. Besides, for about a thousand years India has produced a powerful and complex tradition of Indian Islam, and for two centuries created hybrid cultural practices out of the encounter with the modern West. Yet, the amazing capacity to assimilate alien cultural, linguistic, and literary elements is a unique and essential feature of Indian history. Though the Western countries too have been exposed to a very large number of alien cultures during the last two hundred years, their assimilation of alien cultural traits has been relatively restricted in correspondence with their relationship of otherness with the foreign cultures.

It is of course not true that the metaphysics of non-duality between the self and the non-self did not create social stratification in India. All the evidence in Indian history goes directly against such an assumption. No other society in the world is, has been, perhaps more fragmented, stratified and torn with strife as Indian society. It is divided linguistically, regionally, in terms of caste, income, faith, and profession. What is true, perhaps, is that the tendency of dissension is counterbalanced by the political and social organization based on consensus. It is for this reason that a careful study of the exchanges between literature and para-literature becomes all the more vital to a proper understanding of India's literary past, and through it the literary present.

16

Tradition and Transactions

European literary historiography uses the paradigm of a single dominant literary tradition. There is very little debate about the central canons of British literature. Occasional debates about particular preferences of styles and periods do take place, such as the one created by T.S. Eliot's preference for the Metaphysicals over the Romantics, but the overall range of the canon has never been in doubt. At no stage in the tradition of English literary criticism was any allowance made for the inclusion of a non-British writer in the British canon,[1] even when some very good works were produced in the language of the British isles outside, in other continents. On the other hand, in India a writer of Greek ancestry like Ashvaghosha, or of Irish nationality like Nivedita, or with Caribbean background like Naipaul or with Arabic training like Ibn Battuta, have been accepted as *Indian* writers. Languages such as Persian, Arabic, English, French, and Portuguese have been accepted in India as languages of *Indian* literature. The English canons have never thought of any translation as a *great* work of literature, the emphasis of Anglo-poetics being on the original (though perhaps aesthetically the most intricate work in English is the King James' version of the *Bible*, a translation). In India some of the most respected literary classics have originated in attempts to translate: the *Jnaneswari* in Marathi, Kamban's *Ramayana* in Tamil, Tulsi's *Ramayana* in Hindi, Tagore's *Gitanjali* in English are some examples. Again, Indian literature has in it the peculiar phenomenon of bilingual writers. The number of bilingual writers in India is so large, and the longevity of this practice is so substantial that bilingual literature is more a norm than an exception in India. Considering these major differences between literary practices in India and Western countries, it is obvious that the concept of a single dominant literary tradition, a single and fairly well-defined literary canon and historical criticism couched in a unidirectional philology will not prove adequate to interpret the history of literature in any Indian language.

This particular problem for literary historiography can get a useful lead from developments in general historiography in India in recent years. Specifically useful in this respect is Romila Thapar's important essay on tradition in *Cultural Transaction and Early India: Tradition and Patronage.*[2] In this essay Thapar discusses the Indian views of tradition, more particularly the historical reconstruction of tradition. Through several convincing examples, she makes it clear that at any given time there may be a normative code of tradition, but at the same time there exist numerous deviations from the norm. It is therefore possible, as Thapar argues, to project a variety of traditions as dominant in Indian history and culture, none of which is more or less authentic than the rest. One of the more striking examples she selects to put her view across is that of the *Mahabharata.* The story of Shakuntala used by Kalidasa existed in *Mahabharata* previous to his rendering. The two versions have different philosophical and ideological orientations. After Kalidasa's use of the story, the two versions co-existed in Indian culture. Thapar asks: Which of the two is more authentic? Her answer is that authenticity of tradition arises out of subjective reading by historians:

> For such a diverse community to create a uniform cultural tradition for itself can become an exercise in juggling with history. Traditions are not self-created: they are consciously chosen, and the choice from the past is enormous.... If we are to understand the role of religion in the Indian society of earlier times we may have to be moved away from the paradigm of Hinduism and the other religions in India as projected in the colonial period.... Complex societies have competing value systems and attempts are made by the more established to delete ideologies of protest or of divergent values...[3]

What is true of the national history of India is also, and far more pertinently, true of its literary history, given the multilingual literary context. Western historiography of literature is based on literary histories which do not have multiple parallel traditions. The term 'parallel' can be applied to popular or folk traditions in

European contexts. In India the parallel traditions are really alternative traditions rather than 'low' value traditions.

When Panini wrote his grammar in the pre-Christian centuries, he spoke of two discourses in Sanskrit, one used by the common people and another that was grammatically correct. When Bharata composed his treatise on drama, he spoke of two types of theatre, one catering to the public and the other based on dramatic conventions. Both Panini and Bharata speak of the popular and the doctrinaire as insiders, not in terms of the self and the other. Dandin, the seventh century Sanskrit theoretician, describes several competing literary styles from different regions of India. They were all styles of Sanskrit poetry; in describing these, Dandin does not arrange them in an aesthetic or sociological hierarchy. In the eleventh century, Rajashekhara could write plays in Maharashtri as well as in Sanskrit. Jayadeva in the twelfth century wrote poetry in Bengali as well as in Sanskrit. Hemachandra, in the thirteenth century, wrote in Gujarati and in Sanskrit. Namadeva wrote poems in Hindi and in Punjabi too, in addition to writing in Marathi. Thyagaraja, writing in Telugu had no hesitation in learning the diction and metre of Gujarati poetry. Ekanatha prepared a scholarly edition of Jnanadeva's *Bhavarthadipika,* using writing as the medium, and 'published' most of his own poems using the oral medium of singing. There are innumerable writers who write in Urdu and Hindi, Hindi and Punjabi, Oriya and Bangla, Gujarati and Marathi, English and some Indian language. None of them show signs of any unusual anxiety of being torn or split between traditions. An average Indian reader, if he or she is reasonably well educated, reads works in his or her own language, in one or two other Indian languages, in English translation from other languages; and yet does not feel anxiety or guilt for the loss of his linguistic, literary or cultural identity. The Indian tradition has given to every sensitive Indian the ability to internalize a multiplicity of traditions.

In India, the folk traditions can be as erudite as the dominant lexical traditions; and apparently outmoded styles and diction can find unexpected revivals. Thus it would be improper to classify the traditions either into clearly demarcated periods, or into categories with clearly demarcated class origins of literature. It would be inappropriate even to speak of literary traditions in terms of a tradition of texts in a single given language. A more appropriate approach would be to think of literary history in terms of a constant exclusion of para-literatures from the cultural centres creating a constant assimilation of *para* literatures into the centres of culture, creating a complex pattern of conflict and collaboration of many minor traditions. It may have been purely a linguistic coincidence that the term for tradition in Indian languages, *parampara*, implies the historiographic view proposed by Romila Thapar, for the term is formed by combining *param* (superlative of *para*) and *para*.[4] We may interpret the term to mean, in the light of the foregoing discussion, 'consideration of all literary margins'. Such a view of *parampara,* tradition, will not be very far from the spirit of the term *sahitya,* meaning togetherness or co-existence, employed for the literary arts.

The term *sahitya,*[5] one of the several Indian terms for literature, has implicit in it a vitally important insight for literary historiography. There are other terms in Indian languages which are synonyms for *sahitya* such as *vangmaya, saraswata*, *kavya*, *lekhan*, etc. While *vangmaya* and *saraswata* indicate the literary or poetic quality of writing, *lekhan* refers to the act of writing. None of these has superseded *sahitya* so far because it accurately reflects the historical fact that all literary traditions and movements in India resulted from a togetherness, *sahitya*, of multiple traditions.

The idea of a pure state of authentic existence at the point of origin is not appropriate to view Indian literary history; probably it is not appropriate to view any literary history at all, except that of proto-Indo-European literature, if it existed at all, for at that point of history we have with us nothing but a sense of mystery and myth. So far, Western literary historiography has not come to terms with the basic fact about literary history that all traditions of literature originate in the act of translation. An act of translation holds together two, or sometimes more, different traditions momentarily, for a cross fertilization, and in that sense all translations are *sahitya.*

17

Translation as Origin

"Translation is the wandering existence in a perpetual exile," says J. Hillis Miller.[1] The statement obviously alludes to the Christian myth of the Fall, exile and wandering. In Western metaphysics translation is an exile, a fall from the origin; and the mythical exile is a metaphorical translation—a post-Babel crisis. Given this metaphysical precondition of Western aesthetics, it is not surprising that literary translations are not accorded the same status as *original* works. Western literary criticism provides for the guilt of translations for coming into being *after* the original; the temporal subsequentiality is held as a proof of diminution of literary authenticity of translations. The strong sense of being an individual, given to Western individuals through systematic philosophy and the logic of social history makes them view translation as an intrusion of 'the other'. This intrusion is desirable to the extent it helps define one's own identity; but not beyond that point. It is, of course, natural for the monolingual European cultures to be acutely conscious of the act of translation. The philosophy of individualism and the metaphysics of guilt, however, render European literary historiography incapable of grasping the origins of literary traditions.

One of the most revolutionary events in the history of English style has been the authorized translated version of the *Bible*. It was also the literary expression of Protestant Christianity. The recovery of the original spirit of Christianity was thus sought by Protestant England through an act of translation. It is well known that Chaucer was translating the style of Boccacio into English when he created his *Canterbury Tales*. When Dryden and Pope wanted to recover a sense of order, they used the tool of translation.[2] Similar attempts were made in other European languages such as German and French.

During the last two centuries the role of translation in communicating literary movements across linguistic borders has become very important. The tradition that has given us writers like Shaw, Yeats, Joyce, Beckett, Heaney in a single century — the tradition of Anglo-Irish literature—branched out of the practice of translating Irish works into English initiated by Macpherson towards the end of the eighteenth century.[3] Indian English literature too has gathered its conventions of writing from the Indological activity of translation during the late eighteenth century and the nineteenth century. Many of the Anglo-Irish and Indian English writers have been able translators themselves. Similarly, the settler colonies such as Australia, Canada, New Zealand have impressive modern traditions of literature, which have resulted from the 'translation' of the settlers from their homeland to alien locations. Post-colonial writing in the former Spanish colonies in South America, the former colonies in Africa, and in other parts of the world have experienced the importance of translation as one of the crucial conditions for creativity. In fact modernism and post-modernism as international movements would never have come into existence without the mediation of repeated acts of translation. Those who study Theory today know that if they did not have translations of theorists from a dozen different cultures, it would be impossible to think of a revolution in literary thought at all. Thus origins of literary movements and literary traditions can be traced back to various acts of translation.

Considering the fact that most literary traditions originate in translation, and gain substance through repeated acts of translation, it would be useful for a theory of literary history to seek support from a theory of literary translation. However, since translations are conventionally perceived as *unoriginal*, not much thought has been devoted to the aesthetics of translation. Most of the primary issues too have not been settled in relation to translation: issues related to the 'form' and 'meaning' of translation. No major critic has taken any well-defined positions about the exact placement of translations in literary history. Do they belong to the history of target languages, or do they belong to the history of source languages? Or do they form an independent tradition all by themselves? This ontological uncertainty which haunts translations has rendered translation study a haphazard activity which devotes too much energy to discussing the problems of the original meaning and the meaning of the altered structure.[4]

Unfortunately for translation the various developments about the interdependence between meaning and structure in the field of linguistics have been based on monolingual data and situations. Even the sophisticated and revolutionary theoretical formulation proposed by Structural linguistics are not sufficient to unravel the intricacies of translation activity.

Structural linguistics considers language a system of signs, arbitrarily developed, that tries to cover the entire range of significance available to the culture of that language. The signs do not mean anything by or in themselves, they acquire significance by virtue of their relation to the entire system to which they belong. This theory naturally looks down upon translation which is an attempt to rescue/abstract significance from one system of signs and to wed it to another such system. But language is an open system. It keeps admitting new signs as well as new significance in its fold. It is also open, in the socio-linguistic sense that it allows an individual speaker or writer to use as much of it as he can or likes to do. If this is the case, then how 'open' is a particular system of verbal signs when a bilingual user, such as a translator, rends it open? Assuming that, for an individual, language resides within his consciousness, we can ask whether the two systems within his consciousness can be shown as materially different, whether they retain their individual identities within the sphere of his consciousness?

Or do such systems become a single, open and extended system ? If translation is defined as some kind of communication of significance, and if we accept the structuralist principle that communication becomes possible because of the nature of signs and their entire system, it follows that translation is a merger of sign systems. Such a merger is possible because systems of signs are open and vulnerable. The 'translating consciousness' exploits the potential openness of language systems; and as it shifts significance from a given verbal form to a corresponding but different verbal form it also brings closer the materially different sign systems.

If we take the lead from Phenomenology and conceptualise a whole community of 'translating consciousness', it should be possible to develop a theory of inter-lingual synonymy as well as a more perceptive literary historiography. The concept of 'translating consciousness', and of communities of people possessing it, are no mere notions. In most Third World countries, where a dominating colonial language has acquired a privileged place, such communities do exist. In India several languages are simultaneously used by language communities as if these languages formed a continuous spectrum of significance. To conceptualize this situation is beyond European linguistics, which is based mostly on a monolingual view of language. The use of two or more different languages in translation activity cannot be understood properly through studies of foreign language acquisition. Such theories work round the premise that there is inevitably a chronological gap, an order or a priority scale in language learning situations. The field is stratified in terms of value based indicators LI and L2, though in reality language learning activity may seem very natural in a country like India. In Chomsky's linguistics the concept of semantic universals plays an important role. However, his level of abstraction marks the farthest limits to which the monolingual Saussurean linguistic materialism can be stretched. In actual practice, even in Europe, the translating consciousness treats the Source Language and Target Language as parts of a larger and continuous spectrum of various intersecting systems of verbal signs.

The privileged discourse of general linguistics today is closely interlinked with developments in anthropology, particularly after Durkheim and Levi-Strauss. Colonial Europe had distributed various fields of humanistic knowledge into a three-fold hierarchy: Comparative studies for Europe, Orientalism for the Orient, and Anthropology for the rest of the world. In its various phases of development modern Western linguistics has connections with all these. After the discovery of Sanskrit by Sir William Jones, historical linguistics in Europe depended heavily on Orientalism. For a long time afterwards linguisticians followed the path of comparative philology. And after Saussure and Levi-Strauss, linguistics started treating language with an anthropological curiosity. When linguistics branched off to its monolingual structuralist path, Comparative Literature still persisted in its faith in the translatability of literary texts.

Comparative Literature accepts that between two related languages there are areas of significance that are shared just as there may be areas of significance that can never be shared. Translation can be seen as an attempt to bring a given language system in its entirety as close as possible to the areas of significance that it shares with other given language or languages. All translations operate within this shared area of significance. Such a notion may help us distinguish synonymy within one language and the shared significance between two related languages.

The translation problem is not just a linguistic problem. It is an aesthetic and ideological problem which has a significant bearing on the question of literary history. Literary translation is not just a replication of a text in another verbal system of signs. It is replication of an ordered sub-system of signs within a given language into another corresponding ordered sub-system of signs within a related language. Translation is not a transposition of significance or signs. After the act of translation is over, the original work still remains in its original position. Translation is rather an attempted revitalisation of the original in another verbal space and temporal span. Like literary texts that continue to belong to their original periods and styles *and* also continue to exist through successive chronological periods, translation at once approximates to the original and transcends it. The problems in translation study are, therefore, very much like those in literary history. They are the problems of the relationship between origins and subsequentiality. And as in translation study, so in literary history the problem of origin has not been tackled satisfactorily. The point that needs to be made is that probably the question of origins of literary traditions will have to be viewed differently by multilingual literary communities possessing a 'translating consciousness'.

18

The Course and the Discourse of History

History is a mass of facts, events and episodes, as well as a structured narrative intended for communication of attitudes, perceptions and analysis of relationships between historical events. Or more appropriately, history is not just facts, dates, events. If history is seen as being so, it will have no framework at all. The process of inclusion will be endless. If, on the other hand, history is seen merely as a narrative, a structure or framework within which all facts, dates, and events fit perfectly well, it will be unrealistic and tend to become pure fiction. History is ideally speaking, an interrelationship between facts and narratives, between the course of history and the discourse of history. It takes no great imagination to realise that not all forms of narrative are adequate for all kinds of facts. Poets use elegy when talking about death, and novelists use the stream of consciousness while revealing the working of the unconscious. Some themes find more truthful expression in some literary forms, other themes may find some other forms appropriate. Similarly, not every strategy of historical narrative may be appropriate to express the essence of each and every kind of literary culture, movement, tradition.

The relationship between the course and the discourse of history is like that between language and reality. Reality is understood, philosophically speaking, as an undistinguished and continuous stream or spectrum of existence, material as well as non-material. Language is understood as a system which imposes 'meaning' on reality through arbitrary signs and systems of signification. It is through the apparently arbitrary signs that language creates meaningful patterns out of the experience of existence. Similarly, the course of history is a continuous, inexorable flow, which the discourse of history tries to illuminate. There is another similarity between the two relationships.

This similarity is that the discourse of historiography is itself not history; the discourse is merely a series of statements about history. Due to these similarities, a philosophy of language-meaning relationship can be of interest to the study of the relationship between the course and the discourse of history.

It is again to Bhartrihari that we have to turn in order to understand the language-meaning relationship in its central form of conceptualization in Indian tradition.

The central tenet of Bhartrihari's opus on semantics, the *Vakyapadiya*,[1] is that meaning is not a property of an isolated word or phonetic unit; it is a property of complete sentences. A sentence, in his idea of meaning, is a single undivided utterance which conveys a single undivided meaning.[2] He maintains that the sentence-meaning is grasped as a unity. This aspect of his theory allowed Indian critics in the past to build a theory of poetic meaning, as John Brough points out:

> The important point is that the sentence-meaning is grasped as a unity. The situation is compared to our apprehension of a picture. This we perceive as in some sense a unity, and although we can analyse the field of vision... nonetheless, we are normally aware of the integrated whole. ...In the end the utmost that can be said of the meaning of a sentence according to Bhartrihari is that it is grasped by an instantaneous flash of insight (*pratibha*).[3]

Brough points out that it was this theory of *vakya* combined with the semantic concept of *sphota* that led to Anandavardhana's theory of *dhvani* in the ninth century.

If we think of the interdependence between the facts of history and the story of history in the light of this theory it can be proposed that literary facts, events, episodes, etc., have no historical meaning in themselves. This is not to say that they have no meaning at all (which they must have as texts, writing, etc.) but rather they will acquire a historical identity only when placed in an order, either as a canon formed by writers, or as a tradition formed by texts alluding to earlier texts.

Our sense of history gets blunted by descriptive labels which are over-used. Labels like 'Romanticism', 'Classicism', 'Gothic', 'Renaissance', 'Modernism', 'Post-structuralism', 'Bhakti period', 'Indian sensibility', 'Post-colonial literature', are without exception hopeless as indicators of any discernible literary quality or styles. The worst failure common to all labels is that they tend to be too inclusive; even if this is not intended initially so, they come to be so in the course of their career. A time comes in the life of these labels when their meanings can be clear only in opposition to some equally nebulous label: thus 'romantic' is that which is not 'classical', 'post-colonial' that which is not 'pre-colonial', and so on. Such labels defeat the very purpose of literary history, which is to impose a structure of meaning on the flow of literary history. If literature is seen as an activity in which hundreds of people belonging to a given culture take part, which makes a feeble faltering beginning before becoming a powerful trend or current, it follows that prior to History, in any given literature, there exist Orders, Discourses and Traditions. For a realistic perception of literary history, it is necessary to understand these distinctions clearly.

Every history is ultimately an exercise in criticism. All historical description, by its very nature, is also critical description. Works of literature are arranged by critics, and also by historians, in order of their merit. An ordering of writers and texts, is an extremely useful activity for writers belonging to subsequent generations. They choose their past for themselves by ordering the existing past according to their own taste. T.S. Eliot's concept of the past that is also present was of this nature. When he 'dropped' Milton and 'included' Donne and Herbert in his order, it was not an exercise in rewriting the history of literature. It was an attempt to show that multiple orders co-exist within a single tradition, with which a given writer can establish his/her relationship. An order is, therefore, an intellectual abstraction, a certain projected subjective perception within a single chronological unit, or within a given tradition, or within the consciousness of a critic or writer. Several such orders can co-exist simultaneously.

When critics and historians notice pronounced similarities, contrasts, or correspondence of some kind between various texts or authors within either a single language tradition, or a multi-lingual tradition, they can speak in terms of certain conventions of writing, style, thought, theme, treatment, and so on. When these conventions become sufficiently clear to establish relations of a certain kind among the works in question, one can speak of a discourse of literature—a new form, trend, fashion, style, wave, movement, protest, revolution, shift, and so on. The discovery of a discourse by a historian is relatively value free. That is, if locating a literary order involves great critical self-consciousness, locating a literary discourse does not involve the same degree of critical self-consciousness. A literary discourse need not be restricted to a single language. Thus if an order is predominantly a single language phenomenon, discourse need not be so. For example, one can speak of the nationalist discourse in Indian poetry, or the discourse of psychoanalysis in the short story. Every literature is made up of several concurrent discourses as well as several possible orders that co-exist simultaneously.

If orders and discourses are predominantly contemporary, that is, restricted in their temporal spans, traditions exist in an extended time span. For instance, one can speak of the Petrarchan sonnet as a tradition, or the tradition of children's writing, or the tradition of socially committed poetry. Tradition is different from discourse mainly in that tradition refers to the chronological space, discourse refers to stylistic or philosophic practices. Traditions subsume orders, and they overlap with discourses. However, traditions do not come into existence unless they are willed to come into existence. Tradition is like the command of a computer to search for a definite line of arrangement in a given data. One can speak of the tradition of saint poets in Bangla or Telugu; it is only recently that we have started speaking of the tradition of women writers in Indian languages. So far, we have not looked for a tradition of environmentally alert literature but it is possible to think of it. If and when we do so, perhaps oral poetry, which consumes no paper, will be offered a higher aesthetic position. It is possible to think of a tradition of urban or rural literature, a tradition of writers who died young, writers who were sexually liberated, writers who did not attend formal school, and so on. Within a tradition one can locate several orders of writing and several discourses of literature. The history of literature contains descriptions of literary orders, descriptions of literary discourses as well as a narration of literary traditions. It is the business of literary history to describe the emergence of various literary discourses and the decline of other discourses, the formation of new literary orders, and subsequently, over an extended temporal span, the formation of several literary traditions. The dynamic relationship between orders, discourses and traditions should be of abiding interest to literary history.

19

Nation in Narration

Literary orders, discourses and traditions are not primarily logical or ontological formations. They are phenomenological strategies which assist the celebration of a culture's self-recognition. Just as every nation with a modern state-structure likes to acquire an independent military force, every society in possession of printing technology likes to have a literary history of its own. In those societies where the creative use of language of literary merit has not been frozen in cold print, the need for a cold chronological record of literary events is not felt so strongly. In India there are about eighty-five such language communities whose literature remains non-printed, and therefore, non-historicised even now. Of course, the technology of long distance (or impersonal) literary communication is not the only condition for the emergence of literary history. There are two more, and equally important conditions: the institutionalized teaching of literature, and the emergence of a culture's self-recognition. For example, millions of people all over the world travel every day for various reasons; and often they travel through towns, territories, nations which are not their own. No one has thought of writing a history of literature by and for travellers in the world. But as soon as these people acquire a sense of sharing a common fate, the sense of being a community, there will emerge a need for the history of expatriate literature. This imaginary history, then, will appropriate the epic form of poetry which narrates long and heroic journeys, the picaresque form of fiction which depicts the moral growth of travellers, expatriate writers like James Joyce, Beckett, Conrad, Naipaul, Rushdie, and texts like *Don Quixote, Divine Comedy, The Heart of Darkness, India: A Wounded Civilisation*, etc. If some academics decide to create such a course in their university, college or polytechnic, the need for a history of this tradition of literature will be felt intensely and immediately.

Thus literary history is a phenomenological strategy the need for which is felt by communities engaged in consolidating their newly formed or perceived identities by creating systems of literary totems and taboos. On the other hand, if a community dissolves into many segments, or is swallowed up by another larger community, its need for literary history will change accordingly. The need for history will also undergo a major change when the present mode of storing knowledge, which is the printed text, changes. And, finally, it will be modified in correspondence with the changes in the courses of institutionalized literary instruction. These ideas may become clear if we examine the case of a new literary history at its very inception.

Tariq Rahman, a literary scholar from Rawalpindi, has published the first history of *Pakistani Literature in English* (1991).[1] His book is the first and the only exercise in this area and it generates several interesting questions about the nature of literary history itself. The first question is related to the antecedents of this literature: Pakistan and India were one country during the British raj, and prior to the raj from the beginning of the subcontinent's recorded history. The recorded history of the territory now called Pakistan spans about six millennia. For five out of these six millennia of its history, Islam was unknown to the people of that territory. Most of them were converted to Islam from the eleventh to the eighteenth centuries. But the people in the territory known today as Pakistan and those in the area that is now known as India had nothing to distinguish them as two very distinct units of culture. Thus there is nothing peculiarly Indian that is not in the past of Pakistan, and vice versa. In 1947, the British divided the Indian landmass in an arbitrary manner to create Pakistan, which was intended to be predominantly Islamic in culture. About twenty-five years after its creation, a part of Pakistan separated itself from the national sovereignty of the Pakistan state. Thus in effect, Pakistan has had three phases in its political history: from the earliest times to 1947 as India, then from 1947 to 1971 as East and West Pakistan; and from 1971 as Pakistan (minus East Pakistan or Bangladesh).

Tariq Rahman's problem is, how to write about the past of Pakistani English Literature. Should he include some writers in his history from the pre-Partition days? If he does, how can he explain their Pakistanness as against the Indianness which was their nationality at that time (since the two countries were not divided then)? Should he include those writers who are likely to be claimed by Bangladeshi English Literature? Should he include those writers who spent some years in Pakistan, some in India and some in an entirely different country? Should he include those Muslim writers who had left India before the Partition and settled in another country (who, had they stayed back would have, hopefully, gone over to Pakistan?) And should he include those Muslim writers who did not move over to Pakistan, but decided to stay on in India, and yet being Muslim, represent the consciousness of the pre-partition Muslim population in India which later became the population of Pakistan? These problems are not only the problems of Pakistani literary history, or of Bangladeshi literary history. They are also the problems of Indian literary history, of the history of Hindi, Urdu and English literatures in India. The problems have to be faced by Bangla, Sindhi, Punjabi, Dogri and Gujarati literatures too, for the literary community in all these languages have been distributed between India and Pakistan. The most complicated situation, however, is that of Urdu.

Given this situation, it is interesting to watch from a theoretical perspective the reasons articulated by Tariq Rahman for writing his history and the practical strategies he employs to get round the issues raised above. In the introductory chapter of his book, Rahman stresses the need for a history of Pakistani English Literature as well as the need for its institutionalized teaching: "As yet no Pakistani university offers a course in either Pakistani or even in African, West Indian and Indian literature in English."[2] He records that not much *systematic* criticism has been written in this area, and "because of this lack of criticism the history of Pakistani literature in English has yet not been written though such histories exist for other Third World literatures in English. This book is being written to fill this gap."[3] Thus the motivation is to articulate the sense of being an autonomous cultural unit, a literary community, as distinct from the community of Pakistani writers in regional languages and also, from the community of English writers in other Third World countries. This sense of community can he created by creating an order of literary taboos and totems, freshly structured:

> Some writers who have written prolifically have been given no critical attention whereas others who have produced only one slim volume of verse or collection of short stories have been commented upon. This has been done for two reasons: either the writer has not collected his separate writings in a single collection or, and here my personal judgment comes in, I have not considered the work worthy of critical attention at all.[4]

Since there is no established criticism, there cannot be any critical consensus about writers. The canon has to be created by the first historian. And it is created on the basis of aesthetic criteria as Rahman tells us. But an aesthetic cannot be defined before the tradition of literature, which is its basis, is forged. Hence, the creation of literary history, and literary canon, and institutionalized modes of its teaching, share something with the procedures for creating totems and taboos.

In the chapter devoted to the pre-Partition writers, Rahman explains the reasons for including the writers discussed in his study:

> Among the Muslims who started writing before the Partition of India in 1947, the most famous name is that of Ahmed Ali. That is why a complete chapter of this book has been devoted to his work. In this chapter I shall deal with the writings of Ahmed Ali's Muslim contemporaries, Feroze Khan Noon, Mumtaz Shahnawaz and Khwaja Ahmad Abbas. It is easy to see why the first two should have been included in history of Pakistani literature. Noon became a Prime Minister of Pakistan and Mumtaz's famous novel *The Heart Divided* is one of the few responses in English fiction to the creation of Pakistan from the Muslim Indian point of view. But Abbas did not emigrate to Pakistan nor is he in any political sense concerned with Pakistan. However, I have dealt with Abbas because he represents a neglected aspect of Muslim consciousness which found literary expression in English before the Partition. This is the response to the ideas of liberalism and socialism which were accepted by some Indian intellectuals before the Partition and have receded into the background in Pakistan now. Abbas's work is significant

> because it represents the liberal-socialist aspect of the Indian Muslim consciousness.[5]

Ahmed Ali has been claimed by histories of Indian English literature as a pioneering English fiction writer. K.A. Abbas has been claimed by the progressive movement of the 1940s, Indian Urdu writings, and Indian cinema. On the other hand, Rahman's history leaves out Salman Rushdie, though at least his *Shame* has a reason to be placed within Pakistani writing. The principle of selection and rejection is the magical formula of being an acceptable Muslim. Of course, all other methods of historical projection also stem out of this basic method. Literary history is always more of a strategy than a logically coherent order. That nation has apparently become the defining category for modern literary histories is a reflection of the fact that the European cultures show a general agreement on the identity between language, culture and nation. Otherwise the basic unit for literary history is culture which recognises itself as distinct from other cultures.

20

The Garden and the Forest

A given culture's attitude to Language has an important bearing on its concept of literary history. In Western cultures the attitude to Language is largely anatomical—one in which Language is seen as a 'body' or a 'corpus' (which also means 'a structure of a special character in the animal body'). A 'body' can be described in terms of its birth, development and demise. It can be fitted into a meaningful historical narrative. If, on the other hand, some other culture views language as an 'ever present energy' or 'a mysterious being', it becomes difficult to speak of it in terms of a sequential historical narrative. Such energy can manifest itself at different times without decline or growth because it is beyond the laws of anatomy. Indian attitudes to Language (not language) are of this nature. Correspondingly, literature too is invested in India with supernatural powers; it is traditionally considered to have the power to control Nature and as being beyond the laws of Nature. The notion of a fixed human authorship of literary texts is relatively new in Indian literary traditions. Rather, authors are seen as vehicles of the Energy that Language is.

Western literature employs the concept of 'reader'. According to the Oxford English Dictionary, 'reader' means 'an advisor, commentator, etc. The traditional Indian term *'rasika'* for 'audience' has now been replaced *by 'vachak'*. It combines the English meaning of 'commentator' as well as the conventional Indian meaning of 'someone who participates in the language act'. Thus, the perception of literary transaction in the West is different from its perception in India. Literature, whether oral, written, translated or para-literature, is seen in India as invested with an element of the sacred. The forms of worship in India are literary, and literature too is worshipped. The literary input in a person's upbringing in Indian society is relatively far greater than that in Western societies. Since Indian myths continue to circulate meaningfully and organically in Indian social practice, the distinction between myth and literature has not been established as yet in radical terms. Our most pervasive mythology, the *Mahabharata* and the *Ramayana*, are also among our greatest literary works.

In the West, literary aesthetics and literary history have been neatly separated from the aesthetics and history of the performing arts and visual arts. Many of the Indian literary practices continue till our day primarily as performances. The tribal epics and stories are never narrated without invoking gods through painting, dance and music. We cannot separate the Varakari literature in Marathi from the music and the body movements of the Varakaris. Is it possible to fully appreciate the beauty of Jayadeva's *Gitagovinda* without bringing in the innumerable sculptures and paintings inspired by the poem? Since, the arts and literature are seen as being of common origin, of a single type of imagination and aesthetic delight, the sharp and neat distinctions between them formulated by Western principles of aesthetics become inappropriate while perceiving Indian literature. In India, literature is essentially a performance, a *prayoga.*

As pointed out before, by referring to Sudhir Kakar's psychoanalysis, a dissolution in the impersonal is seen as the highest goal of a (Hindu) person's life in India. Therefore even the greatest among the artists in India resist the creation of an 'individual' or 'unique' style. Their genius lies not in initiating 'style periods' but in forging 'style communities' which defy chronological classification. Sects and not periods chapterize the Indian literary past. Sects thrive not on the rejection of the past but on a selective renewal of the past. 'Style periods' in Western literary history are distinguished by what is unique to them, but the 'style communities' in India are distinguished by their openness to influences almost to the point of self-erasure. The poetry of the medieval saints in India represents the most distinctive example of a 'style community'.

Finally, the question of imagination itself gets complicated when seen in the context of Indian literary history. The human mind has two faculties that organize the phenomenal world: the first is imagination which organizes all space through arrangements of sensory images; the second is memory which organizes Time for us. Without our ability to perceive images, we would have been incapable of interpreting the physical space. Without the ability to remember, we would not have been able to link yesterday, today and tomorrow. When a civilization emerges, its first important engagement is with the physical space surrounding it. To that extent, imagination acquires importance in that culture. However, when any civilization has long been established and has had a surfeit of history, remembering the history becomes a more urgent cultural need. At this juncture, memory becomes more important than imagination. Indian literature has faced this problem for over a thousand years now. It has spent a major part of its creative energy in keeping the remembrance of things past alive. Literary forms, sects, practices, trends and styles in India indicate how important the question of memory has been to Indian culture throughout history. Western literary historiography, quite appropriately, has emphasized the primacy of imagination over memory while classifying, arranging, evaluating and representing literary events. A similar procedure, if it is to be followed in India, will fail to do justice to the creativity in Indian literary tradition. Creations are based mainly on imagination, performances are based mainly on memory. This distinction must never be taken as an absolute distinction. But it has merit when seen in relative terms.

That the literary past in India has run the course of several millennia, has seen the rise and fall of numerous languages, has assimilated influences from all over the world, is full of exceptions to every imaginable literary principle, and is being written or recited even today in more than twenty major languages and more than eighty-five tribal languages, will make the writing of any sort of history of one (or all of) Indian literature a near impossible task. Just as too little history makes historiography unnecessary, too much of it too makes historiography helpless.

It may be possible to name every tree and count every fruit and flower in a garden. But when one is left in the nowhere of a forest without a beginning and without an end in sight, the numerals fail to assist counting and measuring. Literary historiography developed in monolingual cultures and in cultures with a relatively shorter span of existence is like a rational argument about a manageable garden. Indian literary historiography is like entering the mythical Naimisharyana. In it any story will work, but no story will be the complete story. It will give rise to a thousand 'Once Upon a Time' but will not admit a definite conclusion. Every conclusion in it must stay perpetually tentative...

Notes and References

2. History and Literary History

1. Rene Wellek, *The Rise of English Literary History* (Chapel Hill: University of North Carolina Press, 1941), together with Chris Baldick, *The Social Mission of English Criticism, 1848–1932* (Oxford: Clarendon Press and New York: Oxford University Press, 1983).

2. See Winfred P. Lehmann, ed., *A Reader in Nineteenth Century Historical Indo-European Linguistics* (Bloomington and London: University of Indian Press, 1967), pp. 99–100.

3. Thomas Warton, *The History of English Poetry from the Close of the Eleventh Century to the Commencement of the Eighteenth Century* (1774), reprinted in 4 volumes by Thomas Tegg (London, 1840).

4. For a detailed critical comment on nineteenth century literary historiography in Germany, see Hans Robert Jauss, *Towards an Aesthetic of Reception,* trans. Timothy Bahri (Minneapolis: University of Minnesota Press, 1982). See particularly, "Literary History as a Challenge to Literary Theory", pp. 3–46.

5. Rene Wellek, "Ideas On Literary History", in *The Rise of English Literary History*, pp. 47–94.

6. David Perkins, "Literary Classifications: How Have They Been Made?" in *Theoretical Issues in Literary History*, ed. David Perkins, Harvard English Studies, 16 (Cambridge, Massachusetts and London: Harvard University Press, 1992), pp. 248–268.

7. Rene Wellek and Austin Warren, "Literary Theory, Criticism and History," in *Theory of Literature* (New York: Harcourt, Brace & Co., 1949), pp. 29–37.

3. Time and Territory

1. Heinrich Zimmer, *Myths and Symbols in Indian Art and Civilization,* ed. Joseph Campbell. The Bollingen Series VI (Princeton: Princeton University Press and New York: Pantheon Books, 1946), pp. 37–38.
2. *Everyman's Encyclopaedia, Vol. IX* (London: J.M. Dent & Co., 1978). The story occurs in Apuleius's *Metamorphosis.*
3. E.H. Carr, *What is History?* (1961; reprint, London: Pelican Books, 1964), pp. 148–49.
4. This is the view that Sujit Mukherjee presents in *Towards A Literary History of India* (Simla: Indian Institute of Advanced Study, 1975).
5. Ram Vilas Sharma, *Bharatiya Sahitya ke Itihas ki Samasyaen* (New Delhi: Vani Prakashan, 1986),
6. Anindita Niyogi Balslev, *A Study of Time in Indian Philosophy* (Wiesbaden: Otto Harrassowitz, 1983).
7. Romila Thapar, *Time as a Metaphor of History: Early India* (New Delhi: Oxford University Press, 1996).

4. Two Paradigms of History

1. Ganga Sagar Rai, *The Kavya-Mimansa of Rajasekhara edited with Prakasa* (Hindi), The Vidyabhavan Sanskrit Series, 121 (Varanasi: Chowkhamba Vidyabhavan, 1964), p. 79. The relevant verses read:

   "Puranapravibheda Evetihasah": Ityeke
   Sa cha dvidha parakriya purakalpabhyam
   Yadahuh:
   "Parakriya purakalpa itihasagatidvidha.
   Syadekanayaka purva dvitiya babunayaka".
   Tatra *Ramayana, Bharatam* Chodaharane.

2. Vidyadhar Vaman Apte, *A Concise Sanskrit-English Dictionary* (New Delhi: Gian Publishing House, 1926, 1989).
3. See P.V. Kane, *History of Sanskrit Poetics* (1923), 4th edition (New Delhi: Motilal Banarsidass, 1971), pp. 208–18, and G.N. Devy, *After Amnesia: Tradition and Change in Indian Literary Criticism* (Bombay: Orient Longman, 1992), pp. 72–73.
4. V. Raghavan, *Bhoja's Srngara-Prakasa* (Madras: Punarvasu, 1963), p. 109.

5. For a well-documented commentary on the *Natyashastra,* see P.V. Kane, *History of Sanskrit Poetics*, pp. 10–63.

6. Ibid., pp. 243–248.

7. V. Raghavan, *Bhoja's Srngara-Prakasa*, p. 601:
Itihasasbrayam kathashrayam utpadyetivritam
anutpadyetivritam pratisanskaryetivritam
Iti prabandhasbarirani. Itihasashraycmityanen
Vrittadevadicharitashansitamab–yatha Kumarasambhave.

5. Bhartrihari's Metaphors

1. Peri Sarveswara Sharma, *The Kalasamuddesa of Bhartrihari's Vakyapadiya* (*together with Helaraja's commentary translated from the Sanskrit*) (New Delhi: Motilal Banarsidass, 1972).

2. Ibid., *Karika* 15, p. 51*: Pratihaddhas ca yas tena citra visvasya vrttayab tab sa evanujanati yatba tantub sakuntikah.*

3. Ibid., *Karika* 42, p. 69.

4. Ibid., *Karika* 74, p. 99.

5. Ibid., *Karika* 70–71, pp. 96–97.

6. Ibid., *Karika* 14, p. 50.

7. Ibid.

8. Ibid., *Karika* 30, p. 61.

9. Ibid., *Karika* 3, p. 45.

10. Ibid., *Karika* 6, p. 46.

11. Ibid., *Karika* 37–38, pp. 65–67.

12. *Sphotasiddhi of Mandana Misra,* translated into English from the Sanskrit by K.A. Subramania Iyer, Deccan College Building Centenary Series, No. 25, Poona, 1966.

13. Eliot Deutsch and J.A.V. van Buiten, eds., *A Source Book of Advaita Vedanta* (Honolulu: University of Hawaii Press, 1971), p. 50. For a comment on Sankara's use of the *sphota* theory, G.N. Devy, *After Amnesia* (Bombay: Orient Longman, 1992), pp. 82–83.

14. *Sphotasiddhi of Mandana Misra* (Introduction), p. 3.

15. Ibid., *Karika* 5 (Introduction), p. 14.

16. For a probing discussion of the debate between Bhartrihari and Dignaga, see Radhika Herzberger, *Bhartrhari and the Buddhists* (Dorrecht, Holland: D. Reidel Publishing Company, 1986).

17. Ibid., p. 107.

18. Ibid.

19. For a cogent discussion of concepts of Time in ancient India, see Anindita Niyogi Balslev, *A Study of Time in Indian Philosophy* (Wiesbaden: Otto Harrassowitz, 1983); and Romila Thapar, *Time as a Metaphor of History,* 1996.

20. *Patanjali's Yoga Sutra III,* 52 as quoted by Niyogi Balslev, p. 51.

21. Ibid., pp. 52–53, quoted from K.C. Bhattacharya, *Studies in Philosophy,* Vol. 1, Calcutta, 1956, pp. 234–35.

22. Reproduced from the *Pravacanasar of Kundakunda*, in *Sources of Indian Tradition,* ed. Theodore de Barry (New York and London: Columbia University Press, 1958), pp. 73–75.

23. "The Jaina understanding of the time-atoms (*kalanu*) as ultimate, absolute and real again points to its distinction from the conventional time (*vyavahara kala*). The conventional time periods, of which we find a long list in *Pancasitikayasara,* 25, range from the minutest moment called *samaya*, through *nimisa, kastha, kala, nali, to muhurta*—equal to two *nalis, divartra*—day and night, equal to thirty *muhurtas, masa*—month, *ayana*—half year—equal to three seasons, *samvastsara*—year, which is equal to two *ayanas*. These divisions and subdivisions are linked to the different units of measurement pertaining to conventional time." Niyogi Balslev, *A Study of Time,* p. 75.

24. Romila Thapar, *Time as a Metaphor of History,* p. 44.

6. The Conventions of Literary History

1. Iravati Karve, *Yuganta: The End of an Epoch* (Hyderabad: Orient Longman, 1974), 1991, pp. 2–3.

2. Ibid., pp. 2–3.

3. Ibid., p. 2.

4. C.R. Deshpande, *Transmission of the Mahabharata Tradition, Vyasa and Vyasids* (Simla: Indian Institute of Advanced Study, 1978), pp. 7–14.

5. Quoted by Ludo Rocher, *The Puranas, A History of Indian Literature,* Volume II, part 3 (Wiesbaden: Otto Harrassowitz, 1986), p. 53; original source, *When a Great Tradition Modernizes* (New York: Praeger, 1972), p. 76.

6. The *Mahabharata for tbe first time critically edited by Vishnu S. Sukbtankar and illustrated by Shrimant Balasabeh Pant Pratinidhi* (Poona: Bhandarkar Oriental Institute, 1925–43).

7. *The Valmiki-Ramayana critically edited for Belvalkar tbe first time by J.M. Mehta and others, and illustrated by tbe Faculty of Fine Arts, M.S. University of Baroda* (Baroda Oriental Institute, 1960).

8. Rocher, *The Puranas,* p. 81.

9. For details of the debate about the chronology of the *Vedas,* see C.V. Vaidya, *A Literary History of India,* Vol.1-*Sruti (Vedic) Period,* published privately (Poona, 1930), pp. 1–40.

10. Friedrich Max Muller, *A History of Ancient Sanskrit Literature* (Williams and Norgate, 1860). See, especially the introductory sections comparing the Greeks and the Hindus.

11. C.V. Vaidya, A *Literary History of India,* Vol. l, pp. 41–67.

12. For informative comments on the *Sarvanukramani,* ibid., pp. 61–67.

13. Jaideva Singh, *The Doctrine of Recognition: A Translation of Pratyabhijnabrdayam* (New York: State University of New York, 1990). This is a translation of Kshemaraja's eleventh century text composed in Sanskrit.

14. J.L. Masson and M.V. Patwardhan, *Santarasa and Abhinavagupta's Philosophy of Aesthetics,* in Bhandarkar Oriental Series, No. 9 (Poona: Bhandarkar Oriental Research Institute, 1969), p. 108.

15. Abhinavagupta, *Gitarthasangraha,* trans. Arvind Sharma (Leiden: E.J. Brill, 1983).

16. R.K. Mookherjee, *Ancient Indian Education* (London, 1947).

17. Ganga Sagar Rai, *Rajashekhara's Kavyamimansa,* Chapter X, "*Kavicbaryu Rajacbarya Ca*" pp. 129–143,

18. Ibid., pp. 14–26, in this chapter, "*Kavyapurushotpattih*", Rajashekhara narrates the story of Kavyapurusha as a widely shared myth.

19. The tendency to ascribe the awareness of all knowledge to one's ancestors is analysed by Madhav Deshpande in his essay "History, Change and

Permanence: A Classical Indian Perspective", *in Contributions to South Asian Studies*, Vol. I, ed. Gopal Krishna (Delhi, 1979), pp.1–28.

20. *"Utpasyate mama toh koapi samanadharma*
    Kalohyaya nirabadhir vipula cha prithvi"

21. A.C. Woolner, Introduction to *Prakrit* (Varanasi: R.S. Panna Lal & Co., 1917, 1966), p. 83.

22. For an exhaustive discussion of the interrelation between Sanskrit and Tamil, see George Luzerne Hart, *The Relation Between Tamil and Classical Sanskrit Literature* (Wiesbaden: Otto Harrassowitz, 1976), *A History of Indian Literature*, Vol. X, part 2.

23. Kamil Veith Zvelebil, *Tamil Literature* in Jan Gonda, ed., *A History of Indian Literature,* Vol. X, part 1 (Wiesbaden: Otto Harrassowitz, 1974), p. 7.

24. Ibid., pp. 177–79.

7. Jnanadeva's Agenda

1. The oldest printed text of *Jnaneswari* was edited in 1909 by V.K. Rajwade. It has been reprinted by the Government of Maharashtra several times. Several English translations of it have been made. The Pradhan and Lambert translation (London, 1967, 1969) is available in a revised rendering as *Jnaneswara's Gita* (A Rendering of the Jnaneswari by Swami Kripananda), (Albany: State University of New York Press, 1989). All citations used hereafter are from this edition.

2. Abhinavagupta, *Gitarthasangraha*, trans. Arvind Sharma (Leiden: E.J. Brill, 1983).

3. S.G.Tulpule, *Classical Marathi Literature* in *A History of Indian Literature*, Vol. IX, part 4 (Wiesbaden: Otto Harrassowitz, 1979), pp. 329–34. These comments are reproduced in a somewhat amended form in Tulpule's introduction to the Kripananda English translation of the *Jnaneswari.*

4. *Jnaneswara's Gita*, 1. 81, p. 3.

5. Ibid., III. 17 which corresponds to the *Gita* III. 2, p. 33.

6. Ibid.

7. Ibid., III. 19–24, pp. 33–34.

8. Ibid., VI. 14, p. 67.

9. Ibid., VI. 3, p. 67.
10. Ibid., VI. 7, p. 67.
11. Ibid., VI. 17–19, p. 67.
12. Ibid., VI. 29–30, p. 68.
13. Ibid., VI. 132, p. 72.
14. Ibid., VI. 133, p. 72.
15. Ibid., VII. 201–204, p. 97.
16. Ibid., VII. 205, p. 97.
17. Ibid., IX. 26–29, p. 111.
18. Ibid., XII. 12–16, p. 175.
19. Tulpule, *Classical Marathi Literature*, p. 359.

8. Pre-Colonial Historiography

1. For an excellent account of the *Rajatarangini* as history, Romila Thapar, "The Historical Ideal of Kalhana as Expressed in the *Rajatarangini*", in *Historians of Medieval India*, ed. Mohihbul Hasan and Muhammad Mujeeb (Meerut: Meenakshi Prakashan, 1968), pp. 1–10.
2. K.N. Sane (ed.), *Peshavyanchi Bakhar*, 5th edition (Kalyan, 1925). For succinct comments on *bakhar* literature, see Tulpule, *Classical Marathi Literature*, pp. 442–446,
3. Linda Orr, "The Revenge of Literature: A History of History", *New Literary History*, Vol. 18, No. 1, Autumn 1986, pp. 1–22.
4. Annemarie Schimmel, *Islamic Literatures of India*, in A *History of Indian Literature*, Vol. VII, no part number (Wiesbaden: Otto Harrassowitz, 1973), pp. 32–33.
5. Ibid.; and *Classical Urdu Literature from the Beginning to Iqbal*, in *A History of Indian Literature*, Vol. VIII, part 3 (Wiesbaden: Otto Harrassowitz, 1975),
6. Muhammad Mujeeb, 'Badaoni', in *Historians of Medieval India*, ed. Mohibbul Hasan and Muhammad Mujeeb, pp. 109–110.
7. *Muntakhabu-'t-Tawarikh by Abdu-'l-qadir ibn-i-mulukshah known as Al-Badaoni,* Vol. III, translated from the Persian and edited by Sir Wolseley

Haig, (Calcutta: The Asiatic Society of Bengal, 1925; reprint, Karachi: Karimsons, 1978).

8. Ibid., p. 239.
9. Ibid., p. 340.
10. Ibid., p. 526.
11. Ibid., p. 529.
12. *Nirguna Bhakti Sagar: Devotional Hindi Literature: A Critical edition of the Panc-Vanior Five Works of Dadu, Kabir, Namdev, Raidas, Hardas with the Hindi Songs of Gorkhanath and Sundardas, and a Complete Word-Index* (2 volumes), ed. W.M. Callewaert and Bart Op de Beeck, (New Delhi: Manohar, 1991).
13. Ibid., Vol. I, p. 9.

9. Warton's Imaginative Savages

1. For an extremely well-documented account of the emergence of literary history in England, see Rene Wellek, *The Rise of English Literary History* (Chapel Hill: University of North Carolina Press, 1941).
2. Thomas Warton, *The History of English Poetry from the Close of the Eleventh Century to the Commencement of the Eighteenth Century (1774–1790)*, cd. Richard Price (1824, reprint, London; Thomas Tegg Printers, 1840).
3. For an illuminating analysis of this period in Western European history, Michel Foucault, *The Order of Things* (London: Tavistock, 1970).
4. Wellek, *The Rise of English Literary History*, p. 180.
5. Thomas Hobbes, *Leviathan* (1651), ed. Michael Oakshott, (Oxford: Oxford University Press, 1946).
6. Edmund Burke, *A Philosophical Enquiry into the Sublime and Beautiful* (1757), ed. J.T. Boulton (Notre Dame: University of Notre Dame Press, 1958).
7. Wellek, *The Rise of English Literary History*, p. 180.
8. Ibid., pp. 55–56.
9. Ibid., p. 67.
10. Ibid., p. 87.
11. Warton, *The History of English Poetry*, Vol. II, p. 233.

12. Ibid., Vol. 11, p. 238.
13. Ibid., Vol. I, p. i.
14. Ibid., Vol. I, p. xci.
15. Ibid., Vol. I, p. cxlii,
16. Ibid., Vol I, p. a2.
17. Ibid., Vol. 1, p. a3 (Emphases mine).
18. Wellek, *The Rise of English Literary History,* pp. 192–194.
19. For an excellent account of the development of the sense of duality between Britain and India, see Sara Suleri, *The Rhetoric of English India* (Chicago and London: University of Chicago Press, 1992).

10. Jones and the 'Gentoos'

1. Alexander Dow, *The History of Hindustan,* 3 volumes (London, 1768–72).
2. Bernard S. Cohn, "The Command of Language and the Language of Command", in *Subaltern Studies* (New Delhi: Oxford University Press, 1985), pp. 276–329.
3. Ibid., pp. 282–83.
4. Kate Teltscher, "Sir William and the Pandits: The Legal Research, Poetry and Translation of William Jones", in *India Inscribed,* pp. 192–228. As quoted by Teltscher from O.P. Kejatiwal, *The Asiatic Society of Bengal and the Discovery of India's Past, 1784–1838* (New Delhi: 1988), 'Foreword', p. x.
5. Edward Said, *Orientalism* (New York: Pantheon, 1978), p. 78.
6. John Drew, *India and the Romantic Imagination* (New Delhi: Oxford University Press, 1987), pp. 70–71.
7. Garland Cannon, ed., *The Lectures of Sir William Jones,* 2 volumes (Oxford: Oxford University Press, 1970), pp. 755–56, cited by Teltscher in *India Inscribed,* p. 206.
8. James Mill, *The History of British India,* 6 volumes (London: 1826), Vol. II, pp. 46–47.
9. Sri Aurobindo, *The Foundations of Indian Culture,* Birth Centenary Library Vol. XIV, Pondicherry, 1972.

10. Ibid., p. 44.

11. Ibid.

12. Ibid., p. 33.

11. Formation and Transformation of a Canon

1. Joan Simon, *The Social Origins of English Education* (London: Routledge & Kegan Paul, 1970), pp. 88–89.

2. Ibid., p. 96.

3. Anders Piltz, *The World of Medieval Learnings* trans. David Jones (Oxford: Basil Blackwell, 1978), p. 85. Piltz has done extensive research in medieval teaching methods and has reproduced the earliest classnotes used in universities. *Littera,* any text used, helped the teacher to initiate the *lectio* or *lectura*. Ibid., p. 86.

4. The book popularly known as *Foxe's Book of Martyrs* was *The Acts and Monuments of Matters Happening in the Church.* W.H.G. Armytage comments: "This anecdotal treasury was bought by many clergymen for their churches where it was chained to the lectern and sifted for sermons. Almost all Puritan households turned to it as the standard authority for church history." *Four Hundred Years of English Education* (Cambridge: Cambridge University Press, 1964, 1970), p. 2.

5. Ibid., p. 2. Quoted by Armytage from Joel Hurstfield, *The Queen's Wards* (1958), p. 255.

6. Chris Baldick, *The Social Mission of English Criticism: 1848–1932* (Oxford: Clarendon Press, 1983).

7. Ibid., p. 70.

8. Ibid., pp. 71–72.

9. Ibid., p. 140.

10. Ibid., pp. 168–69.

11. J. Stuart Maelure, ed., *Education Documents—England and Wales: 1816 to the Present Day* (London: Methuen, 1965, 1986), pp. 42–45.

12. Ibid., p. 41.

13. Ibid., pp. 56–57.

14. Ibid., p. 57.
15. Ibid., pp. 52–55.
16. Ibid., pp. 53–54.
17. Baldick, *The Social Mission of English Criticism: 1848–1932*, p. 61.
18. Ibid.
19. Ibid., pp. 71–72.
20. Ibid., p. 70.
21. For a full discussion of the three factors leading to the establishment of English studies in Britain, see the chapter "A Civilizing Subject" in Baldick. Also see Bernard Bergonzi, *Exploding English: Criticism, Theory, Culture* (Oxford: Clarendon Press, 1990), p. 40. Bergonzi offers an extremely readable and illuminating survey of the development of English studies at Oxford and Cambridge. His account is full of nostalgia. However, as historical document it is extremely useful.
22. Sujit Mukherjee, *Towards a Literary History of India* (Simla: Indian Institute of Advanced Study, 1975), pp. 17–18.

12. Some Western Approaches to Literary History

1. For an initial introduction to the ideas of the Constanz Group, see Robert C. Holub, *Reception Theory: A Critical Introduction* (London and New York: Methuen, New Accent Series, 1984), pp. 53–106.
2. Hans Robert Jauss, *Toward an Aesthetic of Reception,* translated from the German by Timothy Bahti, Introduction by Paul de Man (Brighton: The Harvester Press, 1982); p. 1.
3. Important works in the area of literary history are listed in the Bibliography. The three works discussed in the present chapter are respectively: R.S. Crane, *Critical and Historical Principles of Literary History*, first published as a chapter in *The Idea of the Humanities and other Essays, Critical and Historical*, ed. R.S. Crane (Chicago: University of Chicago Press, 1967, reprinted as a single volume, with a Foreword by Sheldon Sacks in 1971), Gyorgy Lukacs, *Notes on the Literary History,* translated from the Hungarian and introduced by Ian Fairley, in *Comparative Criticism* (Cambridge: Cambridge University Press, Vol. 13, 1991), pp. 195–245. Hans Robert Jauss, *Literary History as a Challenge to Literary Theory* (Brighton: The Harvester Press, 1982).

4. R.S. Crane, *Critical and Historical Principles of Literary History*, p. 50.
5. Ibid., p. 35.
6. Ibid., p. 37.
7. Sec Baldick, *The Social Mission,* and Terry Eagleton, *The Ideology of the Aesthetic* (Oxford: Basil Blackwell, 1990).
8. Gyorgy Lukacs, *Notes on the Theory of Literary History*, p. 215.
9. Ibid., p. 215.
10. Ibid., p. 218.
11. Ibid., p. 219.
12. Ibid., p. 211.
13. Ibid., p. 212.
14. Jauss, *Literary History as a Challenge to Literary Theory,* p. 15. On Jauss's own admission his theory rests mainly on the hermeneutics of Hans-Georg Gadamer, who in turn bases it on Kant's critique of aesthetic experience.
15. For a commentary on Jauss's debts to other theories see Robert C. Holub, *Reception Theory* (London: Methuen, 1984), pp. 63–69. The most obvious debt, however, is the use of the expression 'ideological horizon' used by Bakhtin in P.N. Medvedev and M.M. Bakhtin, *The Formal Method in Literary Scholarship: A Critical Introduction to Sociological Poetics,* translated from the Russian by Albert J. Wehrle, The Goucher College Series (Baltimore and London: The Johns Hopkins University Press, 1978), pp. 159–60.
16. *Jauss, Literary History as a Challenge to Literary Theory*, p. 15.
17. Ibid., pp. 5–6.

13. Post-Colonial Indian Approaches

1. Sri Aurobindo, *Future Poetry,* first issued as a series of essays in *Arya* (1917–1919), reprinted as a single volume in 1950. Several reprints have been made, all through Sri Aurobindo Ashram Press, Pondicherry, including an authoritative edition, *Works*, Vol. 8, 1972.
2. Dattatraya Punde, ed., *Vangmayetihasaci Sunkalpana* (in Marathi), (Pune: Pratima Prakashan, no date). Also important is G.M. Kulkarni and Dattatraya

Punde, *Vangamayetihasa: Sadyasthiti ani Apeksha* (in Marathi), (Pune: Mehta Publishing House, 1995).

3. All writings of Sri Aurobindo are available in *Works*, Birth Centenary Publication, Pondicherry, 1972. "Source of Poetry", in *Harmony of Virtue,* Vol. V, pp.105–8. "National Value of Art", *in The Hour of God,* Vol. XVII, p. 231. "Letter to Manmohan", *Supplement,* Vol. XXVII, p. 148.
4. Sri Aurobindo, *Life Divine,* in *Works,* Vols. XVII, XVIII. *Savitri,* in *Works,* Vols. XXVIII and XXIX.
5. Punde, *Vangmuyetihasaci Sankalpana*, 'Preface', p. 7.
6. V.K. Rajwade, "Maharashtratil Prakritik Bhashancha va Vangmayacha *Itihas",* in *Rajwade Lekh-Sangrah,* ed. Laxmanshastri Joshi (New Delhi: Sahitya Akademi, 1958), cited by Punde, 'Appendix 43'.
7. Tryambak Shankar Shejwalkar, *Nivadak Lekhasangrah*, ed., H.V. Mote, Introduction by G.D. Khanolkar (Bombay: H.V. Mote Publication, 1977), pp. 437–39.
8. George Grierson, *Linguistic Survey of India* (Calcutta, 1902–1928).
9. Sisir Kumar Das, *A History of Indian Literature, 1911–1956* (New Delhi: Sahitya Akademi, 1995), and *A History of Indian Literature, 1800–1910,* (1991). The two volumes form a part of the proposed series of 10 volumes.
10. Sujit Mukherjee, *Towards a Literary History of India* (Simla: Indian Institute of Advanced Studies, 1975); *Some Positions on a Literary History of India* (Mysore: Central Institute of Indian Languages, 1981).
11. Mukherjee (1975), "Preface", p. vi.
12. Sujit Mukherjee, *Some Positions on a Literary History of India, "Bharatiya Vangmayetibasakhanachi Panch Adhartatve*" (*Five Principles of Indian Literary History*), translated from English by S.G. Malshe, *Alochana* (April 1982), reprinted in Punde, pp. 70–85.
13. Mukherjee, *Towards a Literary History of India,* p. 18.
14. Ibid., p. 20.
15. Ranajit Guha, ed., *Subaltern Studies* (New Delhi: Oxford University Press, 1984–87), 5 volumes.
16. Antonio Gramsci, "The Modern Prince", in *Prison Notebooks* (New York, 1973), p. 196, cited by Gautam Bhadra, in "Four Rebels of Eighteen Fifty-Seven", *Subaltern Studies:* IV (1985), pp. 229–275 (pp. 273–74).

17. For Gayatri Spivak's views on history expressed in works other than the *Subaltern Studies*, see her *The Post-Colonial Critic*, ed. Sarah Harasym (New York and London: Routledge, 1990).
18. Bernard S. Cohn, "The Command of Language and the Language of Command", in *Subaltern Studies*, Vol. IV, pp. 276–329.
19. Gayatri Chakravorty Spivak, *Subaltern Studies,* Vol. IV, p. 330.
20. Ibid., p. 341.
21. Ibid., p. 354.
22. B.R. Ambedkar, *The Untouchables: Who Were They?* (New Delhi: Amrit Book Co., 1948).
23. Ibid., p. 62.
24. Among the more important autobiographies in Marathi *Dalit* writings: 1978, Daya Pawar, *Balut;* 1980, Laxman Mane, *Upara;* 1981, Shankarrao Kharat, *Taral-Antaral;* 1987, Bebi Kamble, *Jina Amuche;* 1987, Laxman Gaikwad, *Uchalya.* For a perceptive account of *Dalit* autobiography, see R.V. Dhongade, *Dalit Atmacharitre, Sahitya Ani Samaj* (Pune: Dilipraj Prakashan, 1992).
25. Daya Pawar, *Bombay Literary Review,* No. 2, 1990, p. 5.
26. Ibid., p. 17.
27. Kumkum Sangari, *New Literary History,* Vol. XIX, No.3, 1988, p. 713.
28. Salman Rushdie, *Imaginary Homelands* (London: Granta Books, 1991), pp. 63–64.
29. Ibid., p. 66.
30. U.R. Anantha Murthy, "Why Not Worship in the Nude ? Reflections of a Novelist in His Time", in *Bahuvachan; An Occasional of the Arts and Ideas* (Bhopal: Bharat Bhavan February, 1988), pp. 95–117. This paper was initially presented at the Conference on Indian Literature, Festival of India, University of Chicago, 17–20 April, 1986.
31. Bhalchandra Nemade, "The Marathi Novel: 1950–75", translated from the Marathi by G.N. Devy, *Setu,* Vol. II, No. l, 1986, pp. 29–72. The essay was initially presented at the Seminar on Marathi Literature: 1950–75, Shivaji University (August 1980), and included in the proceedings, *Marathi Sahitya: Prerana va Swarup: 1950–75,* edited by G.M. Pawar and M.D. Hatkananglekar (Bombay: Popular Prakashan, 1986), pp. 13–56.
32. Anantha Murthy, "Why Not Worship in the Nude?", p. 95.

33. Ibid., p. 111
34. Ananda K. Coomaraswamy, *Works*, 3 volumes, ed. Roger Lipsey, Bolingen Series LXXXIX, 1977, Vol. 2, *Selected Papers: Metaphysics,* pp. 49–264.
35. Rajeev Patke, "Canon and Canon-making in Indian Poetry in English", *Kavya Bharati*: *A Review of Indian Poetry,* No. 3, 1991, pp. 13–37.
36. Coomaraswamy, *Works*, Vol. II, pp. 49–65.
37. Ibid., p. 226.
38. Ibid., p. 49.
39. Ibid., pp. 56–7.
40. Ibid., p. 58.
41. See Frank Kermode, "Canon and Period" in *History and Value,* Clarendon Paperbacks (Oxford, 1989), pp. 108–127.
42. Patke, "Canon and Canon-Making in Indian Poetry in English", pp. 13–14.
43. Namvarsingh, *Itihas aur Aalochana* (New Delhi: Rajkamal, 1957 and 1986), pp. 164–65. Translation mine.

14. Para-Literature

1. Bhaktin and Medvedev, *The Formal Method in Literary Scholarship: A Critical Introduction to Sociological Poetics*, trans. Albert J. Wehrle, The Goucher College Series (Baltimore and London: The Johns Hopkins University Press, 1978), p.160.
2. G.N. Devy, "Para-Literature" in *Approaches to Para-Literature,* ed. Amiya Dev (Calcutta: Jadavpur University, 1992), pp. 50–57.
3. See Rene Wellek, "The Name and Nature of Comparative Literature", in *Discriminations: Further Concept of Criticism* (New Haven and London: Yale University Press, 1970); Henry H.H. Remak, "Comparative Literature at the Crossroads: Diagnosis, Theory and Prognosis", in *Yearbook of Comparative and General Literature,* Vol. I, IX, 1960; S.S. Prawer, *Comparative Literary Studies* (London: Duckworth, 1973).
4. For a provocative discussion of Kolatkar's bilingualism, see B.V. Nemade, "Arun Kolatkar and Bilingual Poetry" in *Indian Readings in Commonwealth Literature,* ed. G.S. Amur, V.R.N. Prasad, B.V. Nemade and N.K. Nihalani (Delhi: Sterling, 1985) pp. 71–86.

5. See Claude Levi-Strauss, "Social Structure", in *Structural Anthropology*, translated from the French by Claire Jacobson and Brooke Grundfest Schoepf (Harmondsworth: Penguin, 1963 and 1979), pp. 277–323.

6. The 8th Schedule lists the following languages; Assamiya, Bangla, Dogri, Gujarati, Hindi, Kashmiri, Kannada, Konkani, Manipuri, Maithili, Malayalam, Marathi, Nepali, Oriya, Punjabi, Tamil, Telugu, Sindhi, Urdu.

7. Kumkum Sangari, "Figures for the Unconscious", *Journal of Arts and Ideas,* March 1991, Nos. 20–21, pp. 67–84.

8. Ibid., p. 75.

9. For a historical account of the two categories, *desi* and *marga* see G.N. Devy, *After Amnesia: Tradition and Change in Indian Literary Criticism* (Bombay: Orient Longman, 1992), pp. 78–82.

15. Swa and Para: Self and the Other

1. Jacques Lacan, *Ecrits* (London: Tavistock, 1977), p. 27.

2. *Upanishads,* Penguin Classics, 1965, p. 65.

3. Sudhir Kakar, *The Inner World: A Psychoanalytic Study of Childhood and Society in India* (New Delhi: Oxford University Press, 1981), pp. 20–21. See the critique of Kakar by D. Venkata Rao, "The Stunting Lebensraum: Sudhir Kakar and the Subject of Psycho-coloniality", *Journal of Contemporary Thought,* No. 1, 1991, pp. 111–124.

16. Tradition and Transactions

1. Examples of writers of non-British origin in the history of English literature that can be cited as exceptions are Henry James, T.S. Eliot, Joseph Conrad, Arthur Koestler, etc. However, each of these had to make efforts to project himself as a conformist to English cultural values in order to be accepted. W.B. Yeats, who did not follow the trend, continued to be treated as Irish.

2. Romila Thapar, *Cultural Transaction and Early India: Tradition and Patronage* (New Delhi: Oxford University Press, 1987), pp. 7–22.

3. Ibid., p. 23.

4. For a discussion of the difference between-'tradition' and 'parampara' see G.N. Devy, *After Amnesia*, pp. 16–20.

5. Though the term 'Sahitya' was highlighted by Viswanatha in the fourteenth century, it was in use in the discourse of Sanskrit poetics for many centuries preceding him. For a discussion of the concept see K. Krishnamoorthy's introduction to Sanskrit Literary Criticism in *Comparative Indian Literature,* ed. K.M. George (Madras: Macmillan, 1984–86).

17. Translation as Origin

1. I have quoted from my notes of a lecture given by Prof. J. Hillis Miller at the ninth centenary celebration symposium at the University of Bologna, Italy, in October 1988.
2. Susan Bassnett-McGuire, *Translation Studies* (London: Methuen, 1980), pp. 58–64.
3. Robert Welch, "Language and Tradition", in *Changing States: Transformation in Modern Irish Writing* (London and New York: Routledge, 1993), pp. 11–34.
4. J.C. Catford, *A Linguistic Theory of Translation* (London: Oxford University Press, 1965).

18. The Course and the Discourse of History

1. J.H. Shukla, *Bhartrihari's Vakyapadiya with Gujarati Translation and Notes* (Ahmedabad: L.D. Institute of Indology), 1984.
2. Ibid., p. 34. The verses quoted are from the *Pratbama Kanda:* 49–51.
3. John Brough, in *A Reader in Nineteenth Century Historical Indo-European Linguistics*, ed. Winfred P. Lehmann.

19. Nation in Narration

1. Tariq Rahman, *Pakistani Literature in English* (Rawalpindi, 1990).
2. Ibid., p. 10.
3. Ibid., p. 11.
4. Ibid.
5. Ibid., p. 15.

Bibliography

The following publications will be of interest to scholars engaged in research and teaching of literary history. It may be noted, however, that the list of publications given here is by no means a comprehensive bibliography.

AHMAD, Aijaz. *In Theory: Classes, Nations, Literatures*. London and New York: Verso, 1992.

Perhaps, the most significant critical text produced in India since Coomaraswamy's *The Dance of Shiva*. Ahmad takes up a classical Marxist position *vis-a-vis* Edward Said's *Orientalism*. The most useful part of the volume is the chapter on the concept of Indian Literature (pp. 243–85), which is written from the perspective of Commonwealth Literature.

ALPERS, Svetlana and Paul. "Ut Pictura Noesis ? Criticism in Literary Studies and Art History". *New Literary History*, Vol.3, No.1, Autumn 1971, p. 437 ff.

ALTIERI, Charles. "An Idea and Ideal of a Literary Canon". *Critical Inquiry,* Vol. 10, No. 1, September 1983, pp. 37–60.

Altieri argues that "the past that canons preserve is best understood as a permanent theatre helping us shape and judge personal and social values, that our self-interest in the present consists primarily in establishing ways of employing that theatre to gain distance from our ideological commitments, and that the most plausible hope for the influence of literary study in the future lies in our ability to transmit the past as a set of challenges and models." (p.40).

ARCHIBALD, Douglas, N. "Yeats's Encounters: Observations on Literary Influence and Literary History". *New Literary History*, Vol. 1, No. 3, Spring 1970, p.439 ff.

ASHCROFT, Bill, GRIFFITHS, Gareth, and TIFFIN, Helen. *The Empire Writes Back: Theory and Practice in Post-colonial Literatures.* London and New York: New Accents, Routledge, 1989.

The authors discuss issues related to aesthetics, canon and theory in the context of Anglophone Commonwealth Literature with a passionate anti-colonial bias.

BALDICK, Chris. *The Social Mission of English Criticism.* Oxford: Clarendon Press, 1983.

Well-documented discussion of the contribution of colonialism to the development of literary criticism in Victorian England.

BANFIELD, Ann. "Where Epistemology, Style, and Grammar Meet Literary History". *New Literary History*, Vol. 9, No. 3, Spring 1978, p.415 ff.

BARTHES, Roland. "History or Literature", in *On Racine*, translated by Richard Howard. New York: Octagon Books, 1964 and 1977, pp. 151–72.

Barthes explores the tension between the perception of an individual author as an author and his image and place in the institutional existence of literature, that is an author as part of a tradition of writing. The comments are made in the context of Racine-scholarship in France, particularly the trends issuing from Lanson's historical criticism.

BASSNETT-MCGUIRE, Susan. *Translation Studies.* London & New York: New Accent, Methuen, 1980, pp. 145–152.

Presents an excellent beginner's bibliography on history and theory of translation studies.

BATESON, F.W. "Literary History Non-subject Par Excellence". *New Literary History*, Vol. 2, No. l, Autumn 1970, p. 115 ff.

BAXANDALL, Michael. "The Language of Art History". *New Literary History*, Vol. 10, No. 3, Spring 1979, pp. 453–66.

A distinction is established between the articulation of history of arts and the articulation of history of verbal arts.

BENJAMIN, Walter. "Theses on the Philosophy of History", in *Illuminations*, edited by Hannah Arendt and translated by Harry Zohn. New York, 1986.

BENNETT, Tony. *Outside Literature.* London and New York: Routledge, 1990.

Bennett looks at literature as an institution with its power-structure and power-politics. A work not as original as Terry Eagleton's, but more useful for classroom discussion.

BERCOVITCH, Sacvan. "The Problem of Ideology in American Literary History". *Critical Inquiry*, Vol. 12, No. 4, June 1986, pp. 631–53.

Discusses the place of ideology in the writing of literary history with reference to the author's multi-volume undertaking on American literary history. Bercovitch advocates a 'flexible, open-ended, and self-reflexive' approach to literary history.

BERGONZI, Bernard. *Exploding English: Criticism, Theory, Culture.* Oxford: Clarendon Press, 1990.

Bergonzi presents a personal history of the formation of the English literary canon through institutionalized teaching of literature at Oxford and Cambridge.

BHABHA, Homi K. *Nation & Narration.* London and New York: Routledge 1990.

The volume includes essays by Ernest Renan, Martin Thom, Timothy Brennan, Doris Sommer, Sneja Gunew, Geoffrey Bennington, Simon During, John Barrelf, David Simpson, Rachel Bowlby, Bruce Robbins, James Snead, Francis Mulhern, Gillian Beer, Homi K. Bhabha. Of particular interest is Bennington's "Postal Politics and the Institutions of the Nation" (pp. 121–137). The volume tries to bring together a variety of case studies to form a perspective on the question of nationality and the literary identity of writers/critics.

BRUNS, Gerald L. "What is Tradition?". *New Literary History,* Vol. 22, No. 1, Winter 1991, pp. 1–22.

"I can't produce a clear idea of what tradition is. Possibly it will be enough if I can just make it harder for people to speak of tradition in the usual way, which is to say without a second thought." (p. 1) Bruns demonstrates the inner contradictions in European tradition: Ancients vs Moderns, Petrarch vs Descartes, Allegory vs Satire, Judaism vs Christianity, Authority of the Claim vs Authority of Rule.

BUCK, Gunther. "The Structure of Hermeneutic Experience and the Problem of Tradition". *New Literary History,* Vol. 10, No.1, Autumn 1978, pp. 31–48.

Presents the German tradition of hermeneutics and its use in grasping the complex nature of historical understanding.

CAMEROON, J.M., "Problems of Literary History". *New Literary History,* Vol. l, No. l, Autumn 1969, p.7 ff.

CARROLL, David. *Paraesthetics: Foucault, Lyotard, Derrida.* New York and London: Methuen, 1987.

This book discusses the contributions made by Lyotard, Foucault and Derrida to pushing the question of the aesthetic beyond the usual limits of literary enquiry. Carroll uses the term *paraesthetics,* to indicate the common elements in these three thinkers. "Paraesthetics indicates something like an aesthetics turned against itself or pushed beyond or beside itself, a faulty, irregular, disordered, improper aesthetics, one not content to remain within the area defined by the aesthetic. Paraesthetics describes a critical approach to aesthetics for which art is a question not a given, an aesthetics in which art does not have a determined place or fixed definition." (p. xiv)

CHAKRAVORTY SPIVAK, Gayatri. "Subaltern Studies: Deconstructing Historiography". *Subaltern Studies*, Vol. 4, New Delhi: Oxford University Press, 1985, pp. 330–63.

Other essays of interest by Spivak are: "The Rani of Sirmur: An Essay in Reading the Archives", in *History and Theory*, Vol. 24, 1985, pp. 247–72 and "Can the Subaltern Speak?", in Larry Grossberg and Cary Nelson (eds.) *Marxist Interpretations of Literature and Culture: Limits, Frontiers, Boundaries.* Urbana: University of Illinois Press, 1987, pp. 271–313.

CHANDRA MOHAN. *Aspects of Comparative Literature: Current Approaches*. New Delhi: India Publishers & Distributors, 1989.

This volume contains essays by various Indian and non-Indian scholars, some of which present surveys of developments in Comparative Literature in various parts of the world.

CHAPPELL, Fred. "Six Positions about Literature and History". *New Literary History*, Vol. 1, No. 3, Spring 1970, p. 513.

COHEN, Ralph, ed. *New Directions in Literary History.* Baltimore and London: The Johns Hopkins University Press and Routledge and Kegan Paul, 1974.

In this pivotal volume edited by Cohen there are essays by Hans Robert Jauss, Robert Weimann, D.W. Robertson, Jr., Alastair Fowler, Geoffrey Hartman, Louis O. Mink, Wolfgang Iser, Michael Riffaterre, Barbara Harrnstein Smith' Henry Markicwicz, Svetlana and Paul Alpers, Francis R. Hart, George Garrett, and an introduction by Ralph Cohen. Cohen is also the founder and editor of *New Literary History: A Journal of Theory and Interpretation since 1969.* It is published three times a year by the Johns Hopkins University Press, Baltimore, Maryland.

Cohen's essay "History and Genre", *New Literary History*, Vol. 17, No. 2, 1986, pp. 203–218, shows that 'genre' is a historical category and that it changes continuously in the course of time, at the same time literary history is influenced by thc catcgory of genre. His essay should be read together with two comments in the same issue by Dominick Lacapra (pp. 219–22) and Richard Harvey Brown (pp. 223–28).

COHN, Bernard. "The Command of Language and the Language of Command". *Subaltern Studies,* Vol. 4, New Delhi: Oxford University Press, 1985, pp. 276–329.

Cohn offers an interesting account of the initial interaction between the English language and Indian literary tradition.

COOMARASWAMY, Ananda K. *Selected Works,* 3 volumes, edited by Roger Lipsey. Bolingen Series L. XXXIX, Princeton: Princeton University Press, 1977.

The three volume edition by Lipsey includes 56 of Coomaraswamy's more important essays, besides a detailed biographical sketch and a comprehensive bibliography of Coomaraswamy's publications.

CORSTIUS, Jan Brandt. *Introduction to the Comparative Study of Literature.* New York: Random House, 1968.

This volume is written to help students who "have had some training in the study of literary history and are interested in comparative literature." Chapter IV, "Conventions and Literary History" (pp. 103–28) is of particular interest. Corstius takes up the issues related to the institutionalization of literary education and literary history in his essay, "Literary History and the Study of Literature", *New Literary History,* Vol. 2, No. 1, Winter 1971, pp. 65 ff.

COSTA-LIMA, Luiz. "Erich Auerbach: History and Metahistory". *New Literary History,* Vol. 19, No. 3, Spring 1988, pp. 467–500.

An extremely readable account of Auerbach's vision of language, literature and history in comparison with that of Vico, who is presented here as the greatest influence on Auerbach. A profitable reading for students of Comparative Literature, which shows Auerbach's interest in realism as an influence on his interest in history.

CRANE, R.S. *Critical and Historical Principles of Literary History,* first published as a chapter in *The Idea of the Humanities and Other Essays, Critical and Historical,* 2 volumes edited by R.S. Crane. Chicago and London: University of Chicago Press, 1971.

CULLER, Jonathan. "Structure of Ideology and Ideology of Structure", *New Literary History,* Vol. 4, No. 3, Spring 1973, pp. 147–82.

An argument towards establishing a theoretical meeting point between Deconstruction and Marxism.

DAS, Sisir Kumar. *A History of Indian Literature: 1800–1910 Western Impact: Indian Response,* Volume 8, New Delhi: Sahitya Akademi, 1991.

———. *A History of Indian Literature: 1911–1956: Struggle for Freedom: Triumph and Tragedy.* New Delhi: Sahitya Akademi, 1995.

Includes a comprehensive bibliography of literary history in India during rhe modern period. Titles cited are from English as well as Indian languages. These volumes should be read together with Das's *Integrated History of Indian Literature: A Draft Working Paper.* New Delhi: Sahitya Akademi, 1986. Also of interest are; *Comparative Literature: Theory and Practice* (co-edited with Amiya Dev), New Delhi and Shimla: Allied Publishers and Indian Institute of Advanced Study, 1989; "Comparative Literature in India: A Historical Perspective", *in Aspects of Comparative Literature: Current Approaches,* edited by

Chandra Mohan. New Delhi: India Publishers & Distributors, 1989, pp. 1–16. In the last mentioned essay, Das offers a survey of the development of Comparative Literature as an academic discipline in India.

DASGUPTA, R.K. "Literary Historiography", in *Indian Literature,* edited by Arbinda Poddar. Simla: Indian Institute of Advanced Study, 1972, pp. 426–35.*

DAVIDSON, Arnold I. "How to do the History of Psychoanalysis: A Reading of Freud's Three Essays in the Theory of Sexuality". *Critical Inquiry*, Vol. 13, No. 2, Winter 1987, pp. 252–277.

Strategies for the history of psychoanalysis.

DE BARY, Theodore. *Sources of Indian Tradition.* New York: Columbia University Press, 1958.

For students who have no access to medieval Indian thought through an Indian language, the following sections of this reference volume edited by De Bary will be instructive—Chapter XIX: "The Importance of the Study of History," pp. 519–28.

DE MAN, Paul. "Literary History and Literary Modernity", in *Blindness & Insight: Essays in the Rhetoric of Contemporary Criticism*, 2nd edition. London: Methuen, 1983, pp. 142–65.

De Man establishes the 'historicity'[1] of 'modernity' in literature, and explores the paradoxical relationship between the two concepts.

DEV, Amiya. *The Idea of Comparative Literature in India.* Calcutta: Papyrus, 1984.

This volume traces the main themes of Comparative Literature in the context of modern Indian literatures with particular attention paid to the question of influence. The essay, "Literary History and Comparative Literature" forms the most essential text for Indian literary historiography. The argument is that literary history is best understood when seen in terms of influence-impact-effect. "Comparative Indian Literature", *in Yearbook of Comparative and General Literature*, Vol. 34, 1985, pp. 114–17. "The Concept of 'Influence' in the Indian Context", in *Sensus Communis: Contemporary Trends in Comparative Literature*, edited by Janos Riesz, Peter Ilorner, Bernard Scholz and Gunter Narr. Tubingen: Verlag 1986, pp. 227–35. In these articles Dev seeks to decolonize the study of literary influence. "Literary History From Below" in *Comparative Literature: Theory and Practices*, edited by Amiya Dev and Sisir Kumar Das. Delhi and Shimla: Allied Publishers & Indian Institute of Advanced Study, 1989, pp. 319–28. "Towards Comparative Indian Literature", in *Aspects of Comparative Literature: Current Approaches* edited by Chandra Mohan, Delhi: Indian Publishers & Distributors, 1989, pp. 35–46. Discusses the identity of Indian Literature.

EAGLETON, Terry. *The Ideology of the Aesthetic.* London: Basil Blackwell, 1990.

Discusses from a post-Communism Marxist point of view the formation of the aesthetic canon in Europe by selective and provocative comments on Shaftesburry, Hume, Burke, Schiller, Fichte, Schelling, Hegel, Schopenhauer, Kierkegaard, Marx, Nietzsche, Freud, Heidegger, Walter Benjamin, Theodor Adorno, and some recent post-structuralists. Very interesting analysis of the processes of canon formation and canon-privileging.

EDEL, Leon, ed. *Literary History and Literary Criticism.* New York: New York University Press, 1964, 2nd impression 1966.

A collection of papers and abstracts of papers presented at the ninth Congress of the International Federation for Modern Languages and Literatures held at New York University, August 1963. This collection contains nine plenary papers, five East-West symposium papers and seventy-nine abstracts.*

ELLMANN, Richard and FEIDELSON, Charles, Jr. *The Modern Tradition: Background of Modern Literature.* Oxford and New York: Oxford University Press, 1965.

Of particular interest are pp. 453–533 forming Part IV of the volume, which includes selections from Hegel, Croce, Vico, Nietzsche, Spengler, Yeats, Malraux, Berdyaev and Darwin. Each selection is prefaced by well-informed comments by the editors.

FOGLE, Richard Harter. "Literary History Romanticized". *New Literary History,* Vol. l, No. 2, Winter 1970, p. 237 ff.

FOWLER, Alastair. "Genre and the Literary Canon". *New Literary History,* Vol. 11, No. l, Autumn 1979, pp. 97–120.

Should be read together with "Periodization and Literary Analogies", *New Literary History,* Vol. 3, Spring 1972, p. 487 ff. A systematic and sympathetic presentation of para-literature and para-canon, of the processes of formation of genres and periods. Also discusses the formation of the hierarchy of genres within a given literary period.

FOKKEMA, Douwe W. *Issues in General & Comparative Literature: Selected Essays.* Calcutta: Papyrus, 1987.

This selection contains essays on reception, literary history, cultural relativism, canon and aesthetics. Of particular interest are the following essays: "Literary History: A Comment on some Problems in Literary Historiography", pp. 24–42; "A Semiotic Definition of Aesthetic Experience and the Period Code of Modernism", pp. 87–117; "Canon as an Instrument of Problem Solving", pp. 157–74. Most of the discussion concerns itself with the methodology of literary history. One of the important works in the field of Comparative Literature published in India.

FROW, John. *Marxism and Literary History.* Oxford: Basil Blackwell, 1986.

This volume has a purely theoretical orientation. It employs Marxism, Foucault, discourse analysis and such other high-profile theories to discuss the nature of literature as a system. But the volume shows commitment neither to literature nor to philosophy, neither to Marxism nor to Post-Structuralism, and in its non-affiliations, it becomes an exercise in itself.

FRYE, Northrop. "Literary History". *New Literary History*, Vol. 12, No. 2, Winter 1981 (special number on 'Interpretation and Literary History').

Frye suggests that literary history as it exists in current practice has been unsatisfactory. By taking up the *Bible* as his example, and Vico as his philosopher, Frye designates three phases of language development— Hieroglyphic, Hieratic, Demotic—as the taxonomy that will provide the backbone to literary history.

GARRETT, George. "Dreaming with Adam: Notes on Imaginary History", *New Literary History,* Vol. l, No.3, Spring 1970, p. 407 ff.

GEERTZ, Clifford. "History and Anthropology". *New Literary History,* Vol. 21, No.2, Winter 1990, pp. 321–36.

An energetic discussion of the convergences and divergences between history and anthropology. Following this essay, there is a response to it by Renato Rosaldo, pp. 337–42.

GENETTE, Gerard. "Introduction to Paratext". *New Literary History,* Vol. 22, No. 2, Spring 1991, pp. 261–72.

Genette's definition of 'paratext' is: "the means by which a text makes a book of itself and proposes itself as such to its readers, and more generally to the public." (p. 261); he also quotes another definition, by Philippe Lejeune, *Le Pacte Autobiographique*, Paris, 1975, p. 45; "...the fringe of the printed text which, in reality, controls the whole reading."

GOLDBERG, Jonathan. "Making Sense". *New Literary History,* Vol. 21, No.3, Spring 1990, pp. 457–62.

This is a defence of New Historicism, against Levin's attack. Goldberg, an important New Historicist II is rone is t, problematics the term'Sense' invoked by Levin in his attack.

GOLDMANN, Lucien. *Towards a Sociology of the Novel*, translated by Alan Sheridan. London: Tavistock Publications, 1975. In the chapter "The Genetic-Structuralist Method in the History of Literature", Goldmann argues that the relationship between literary works and social groups is the true subject of creation in literature.

GOLDSTEIN, Leon. "Literary History as History". *New Literary History,* Vol. 8, No. 2, Winter 1977, p. 3–19.

GONDA, Jan, ed. *A History of Indian Literature.* Wiesbaden: Otto Harrassowitz (10 Volumes in 30 parts published between 1973 and 1987).

The distribution of the theme, chronology, geographical areas and language groupings are innovative. Many scholars from Holland, including the editor, contribute to the series. Each volume is very well-annotated, and is written with a considerable freedom from the general conventions of histories of Indian literatures.

Vol. 1, *Veda and Upanisbads.*
i) Jan Gonda, *Vedic Literature*, 1975,
ii) Jan Gonda, *The Ritual Sutras*, 1977.

Vol. 2, *Epics and Sanskrit Religious Literature.*
i) Jan Gonda, *Medieval Religious Literature in Sanskrit,* 1977,
ii) Jean Goudriaan and Sanjukta Gupta, *Hindu Tantric and Sukta Literature,* 1981,
iii) Ludo Rocher, *The Puranas,* 1986.

Vol. 3, *Classical Sanskrit Literature.*
i) Siegfried Lienhard, *A History of Classical Poetry: Sanskrit, Pali-Prakrit,* 1984.

Vol. 4, *Scientific and Technical Literature*, Part I.
i) Ludwik Sternback, *Subhasita, Gnomic and Didactic Literature*, 1974.

Vol. 5, *Scientific and Technical Literature*, Part II.
i) J.D.M. Derrett, *Dharmasastra and Juridical Literature,* 1973,
ii) Hartmut Scharfe, *Grammatical Literature,* 1977,
iii) Edwin Gerow, *Indian Poetics,* 1977,
iv) Claus Vogel, *Indian Lexicography*, 1979.

Vol. 6, *Scientific and Technical Literature*, Part III.
i) E. te Nijenhuis, *Musicological Literature*, 1977,
ii) B.K. Matilal, *Nyaya-Vaisesika,* 1977,
iii) Michel Hulin, *Samkhya Literature,* 1978,
iv) David Pingeree, *Jyotisasastra, Astral and Mathematical Literature,* 1981,
v) Jean-Marie Verpoorten, *Mimansa Literature,* 1987.

Vol. 7, *Buddhist and Jaina Literature.*
i) David Seyfort Ruegg, *The Literature of the Madhyamaka School of Philosophy in India*, 1981,
ii) K.R. Norman, *Pali Literature, including the Canonical Literature in Prakrit and Sanskrit of all Hinayana Schools of Buddhism*, 1983.

Vol. 8, *Modern Indo-Aryan Literature*, Part I.
i) A. Schimmel, *Islamic Literatures of India*, 1973,
ii) Ronald Stuart-McGregor, *Hindi Literature of the Nineteenth and Early Twentieth Centuries*, 1974,
iii) A. Schimmel, *Classical Urdu Literature from the Beginning to Iqbal*, 1975,
iv) Braj B. Kachru, *Kashmiri Literature*, 1981,
v) Peter Gaeffke, *Hindi Literature in the Twentieth Century*, 1978,
vi) Ronald Stuart-McGregor, *Hindi Literature, from its Beginnings to the Nineteenth Century*, 1984.

Vol. 9, *Modern Indo-Aryan Literature*, Part II.
i) A. Schimmel, *Sindhi Literature*, 1974,
ii) Satyendra Nath Sarma, *Assamese Literature*, 1976,
iii) Dusan Zbavitel, *Bengali Literature*, 1976,
iv) Shankar Gopal Tulpule, *Classical Marathi Literature from the Beginning to A.D. 1818*, 1979.

Vol. 10, *Dravidian Literatures*.
i) Kamil Veith Zvelebil, *Tamil Literature*, 1974,
ii) George Luzerne Hart, *The Relation Between Tamil and Classical Sanskrit Literature*, 1976.

GOSSMAN, Lionel. "History as Decipherment: Romantic Historiography and the Discovery of the Other". *New Literary History*, Vol. 18, No. 1, Autumn 1986, pp. 23–58.

Offers a well-documented account of the rise of Romantic historiography in France and Germany as a project of modernizing the sense of self, process of individuation, which entailed the creation of the Other (the Orient). "Romantic historiography seems to have been no less deeply implicated (than anthropology) in the nineteenth century ideology of progress and the white man's burden," (p. 51), Essential reading for Indian students of literary history.

GRABAR, Oleg "History of Art and History of Literature: Some Random Thoughts". *New Literary History*, Vol. 3, No. 3, Spring 1972, p. 559 ff.

GREEN, Geoffrey. *Literary Criticism and the Structure of History*. Lincoln and Nebraska: Nebraska University Press, 1983.

A conventional and polemical account of the relationship between criticism and history.

GREENLAW, Edwin, *The Province of Literary History*. New York: Kennikat Press, 1931 and 1968.

A general, conventional view that "Literary history is learning, having its own method, its own right to exist among the learning, and having, also, important reaction to the history of culture on the one hand and to literary criticism on the other. ...while no history worth the name has any value except as it is based on exact research into the facts, the mere collecting of facts and arrangements of them in book form does not constitute history." ('Preface', pp. ix–x).

GUGELBERGER, George M. "Decolonizing the Canon: Considerations of Third World Literature". *New Literary History*, Vol. 22, No.3, Summer 1991, pp. 505–24.

A passionately sympathetic discussion of the expression *Third World Literature* in a historical perspective. The argument proposed is that no study of 'literature' is complete without the knowledge of 'third world literature'. The essay alludes to Frederic Jameson's "Third World Literature in the Era of Multicultural Capitalism", *Social Text*, 15 (1986), pp. 65–88.

GUHA, Ranajit, *Subaltern Studies: Writings on South Asian History and Society*, (5 volumes). New Delhi: Oxford University Press, 1984-87.

These volumes initiate the 'subaltern' movement in Indian historiography.

GUILLEN, Claudio. "Second Thought on Currents and Periods" in *The Disciplines of Criticism: Essays in Literary Theory, Interpretation and History*, edited by Peter Demetz, Thomas Green and Lowry Nelson, Jr. New Haven and London: Yale University Press, 1968, pp. 477–510.

"In this essay (I have) discussed some of the difficulties raised by periodization, especially with regard to diachrony and the organization of historical time ... I have tried to single out those forms of periodization that provide us not only an access to styles and values, but with a sensitive and genuine vision of history, and hence can serve as foundations for an idea of literary history" (p.507). Guillen favours "a multi-level characterization that would accommodate the realization that men apparently live in more than one 'period' at once". Also of interest is Guillen's book, *Literature as System: Essays Towards the Theory of Literary History*. Princeton: Princeton University Press, 1971.

GUILLORY, John. "The Ideology of Canon-Formation: T.S. Eliot and Cleanth Brooks". *Critical Inquiry*, Vol. 10, No. 1, September 1983, pp. 173–98.

Presents the idea that canon-formation is a production motivated by ideology.

HACKING, Ian. "Two Kinds of 'New Historicism' for Philosophers". *New Literary History,* Vol. 21, No.2, Winter 1990, pp. 343–64.

The essay has a specific philosophical orientation, being a discussion of the tradition of analytical philosophy in the USA and European linguistic philosophy.

HARTMAN, Geoffrey H. "History-writing as Answerable Style", in *New Directions in Literary History*, edited by Ralph Cohen, 1974, pp. 95–105.

Problematizes the difficulties in creating a verbal discourse about art by separating the epistemological from the ontological in art: focuses attention on the nature of the discourse of historical narratives. The essay is reproduced from *New Literary History*, Vol. 2, No. 1, 1970.

HARTT, Julian. "Theology as a Hermeneutical Salvaging of History". *New Literary History*, Vol. 17, No.2, Winter 1986, pp. 183–94.

Followed by comments from Arthur C. Danto (pp. 195–98), and also by Hartt's rejoinder (pp. 199–202). Hartt's primary interest is in giving an account of theological attempts to salvage Christianity from the framework of history.

HASSAN, Ihab: "Making Sense: The Trials of Postmodern Discourse". *New Literary History*, Vol. 18, No. 2, Winter 1987, pp. 437–59.

The essay offers a fine example of an exercise in writing the history of contemporary literature; coheres with Hassan's writings on post-modernism elsewhere.

HATZFELD, Helmut. "Comparative Literature as a Necessary Method", in *The Disciplines of Criticism*: *Essays in Literary Theory, Interpretation and History*, edited by Demetz, Green and Nelson. New Haven and London: Yale University Press, 1968, pp. 79–92.

Hatzfeld's argument is that it is necessary to study "epoch-styles" before thinking of literature or art in terms of "style-epochs"; in the light of this view he attempts a redefinition of Baroque, Classicism and Romanticism.

HERNADI, Paul. "The Erotics of Retrospection: History Telling, Audience Response, and the Strategies of Desire". *New Literary History*, Vol. 12, No. 2, Winter 1981, pp. 243–52.

An attempt to employ the generic scheme proposed by Frye in his *Anatomy of Criticism.*

HOLUB, Robert C. *Reception Theory: A Critical Introduction.* London and New York: New Accent, Methuen, 1984.

Chapter III, "The Major Theorists" has the following two subsections: "Hans Robert Jauss" and "Textuality and the Reader's Response: Wolfgang Iser", pp. 53–106. The book offers a lucid introduction to Jauss.

HUBERT, Judd, D. "Random Reflections on Literary History and Textual Criticism". *New Literary History,* Vol. 2, No. 1, Autumn 1970, p. 163 ff.

ISER, Wolfgang. "The Reading Process: A Phenomenological Approach", in *New Directions in Literary History*, edited by Ralph Cohen, 1974, pp. 125–46.

This essay presents an early version of the Reader-Response Theory developed by the Constanz Group (Jauss, Iser, etc.) At the base of the formation of history, is the reading process which is not only the discovery of the unformulated meaning, but also the discovery of the capacity to formulate it within ourselves.

JAKOBSON, Roman. "On Realism in Art", in *Readings in Russian Poetics: Formalist and Structuralist Views,* edited by Ladislav Matejka and Krystyna Pomorska. Cambridge, Mass: Harvard University Press, 1971.

JAMESON, Frederic. "From Criticism to History". *New Literary History,* Vol. 12, No. 2, 1981, pp. 367-75. It is a critical review of the essays published in the same issue of the journal, which is a special issue on "Interpretation and Literary History".

The argument of Jameson is that literature is a historical process, and to write history of literature is to come full circle after forgetting that literature was history in the beginning. He suggests that we (should) "forget about history as some reified phenomenon, and (should) think rather in terms of the conceptual and dialectical operations whereby we *historicize* our materials. If we see our critical mission in terms of a process rather than of an inert 'interdisciplinary' linkage, it will become clear that any kind of criticism is grist to the mill of history and that any critical insights of whatever variety (stylistic, psychoanalytical, archetypal, typological, generic, semiotic) can always be historicized." p. 375.

Also of interest are Jameson's other essays in *New Literary History*: "Demystifying Literary History," Vol. 5, No. 3, 1974, p. 605; "Marxism and Historicism", Vol. II, No. I, p. 41.

JAUSS, Hans Robert. *Towards an Aesthetics of Reception*, translated by Timothy Bahti, Introduction by Paul de Man. Brighton: The Harvester Press, 1982.

This collection of essays is one of the source texts for the critical theory known as 'Reception-Aesthetics' or 'Reader-Response Theory'; it includes the essays "Literary History as a Challenge to Literary Theory", "History of Arts and Pragmatic Theory", "Theory of Genres and Medieval Literature", etc. The first of these essays appeared in an abridged version in *New Directions in*

Literary History edited by Ralph Cohen, 1974, pp. 11–42, The abridgement is effected by the exclusion of some initial sections of the essay.

JAY, Gregory S. *T.S. Eliot and the Poetics of Literary History.* Baton Rouge: Louisiana State University Press, 1983.

KELKAR, Ashok R. "Making and Writing Literary History: The Critic's Role." *New Quest,* No. 80, March–April 1990, pp. 89–95.

Any literary history has to be a critical history.*

KERMAN, Joseph. "A Few Canonic Variations". *Critical Inquiry,* Vol. 10, No. 1, September 1983, pp. 107–26.

Offers a study of the concept of canon in music. Essential reading for students of literary canon.

KIERKEGAARD, Soren. *Concluding Unscientific Postscript,* (1844), translated from the Danish by Dorothy Swenson and Walter Lowrie. Princeton: Princeton University Press, 1941, pp. 286–88.

KRIEGER, Murray. "Literary Invention and the Impulse to Theoretical Change: Or Whether Revolution be the Same". *New Literary History,* Vol. 18, No. 1, Autumn 1986, pp. 191–208.

Discusses in a philosophical vein the gap between the tendency to theorize and the historical inconsistency of reality. Thus Krieger explores the phenomenon of change in relation to theory.

KULKARNI, G.M. and PUNDE, Dattatraya. *Vangmayetihasa: Sadyasthiti Ani Apeksha* (in Marathi,). Pune: Mehta Publishing House, 1995.

The volume is divided into three sections; the first section includes essays by Kulkarni, the second, essays by Punde and the third records a free dialogue between Kulkarni and Punde. The volume covers several areas of conceptual value as well as methods of historical research.

LACAPRA, Dominick. "History and Psychoanalysis". *Critical Inquiry,* Vol. 13, No.2, Winter 1987, pp. 222–51.

Exploration of the theoretical basis for history writing in Freud's work.

LEFEVERE, Andre. *Essays in Comparative Literature: A Systemic Approach.* Calcutta: Papyrus, 1988.

The volume proposes, as the title indicates, a systemic approach to the study of literature and literary history. The essays, "Power and the Canon, or: How to Rewrite an Author into a Classic", and "The Dynamics of the System: Convention and Innovation in Literary History" (pp. 57–74 and 95–114, respectively) deal directly with literary history. However, the volume is even more useful in its discussion of literary translation.

LEHAN, Richard. "The Theoretical Limits of the New Historicism". *New Literary History.* Vol. 21, No.3, pp. 533–53.

A thought-provoking essay which argues that ideology is built into modes of time. Further, "Postmodern history has been most energetic in suppressing this view, has been trying to break down the belief that history involves a 'flow' of time by substituting paradigms for process. But the use of paradigm itself... involves forms of the presentation which contain a sense of time as having direction or, equally revealing as in the case of Foucault, of history as being static, a matter of representation that is equally ideological." (p. 535)

LEVIN, Harry. "Reflections on the Final Volume of *The Oxford History of English Literature*", in *Refractions: Essays in Comparative Literature.* New York: Oxford University Press, 1966, pp. 151–70.

Illustrated discussion of how literary history needs to combine artistic monuments with historic documents.

LEVIN, Richard. "Unthinkable Thoughts in the New Historicizing of English Renaissance Drama". *New Literary History*, Vol. 21, No. 3, Spring 1990, pp. 434–47.

Attacks 'New Historicism' on five grounds, the chief among which is that New Historicism denies the historical existence of ideas, as, previously, historicism asserted the existencc of ideas. The result is that New Historicism is nothing more than a history of non-ideas. Richard Levin has been one of the most prominent critics of New Historicism.

LODGE, David. "Historicism and Literary History Mapping the Modern Period". *New Literary History,* Vol. 10, No. 3, Spring 1979, pp. 547–55.

Not very original or stimulating, but very lucid; useful for students as an introduction to the debates relating Modernism.

LUKACS, Gyorgy. *Notes on the Theory of Literary History,* first published in Hungarian in *Papers in Modern Philosophy* (1910), a festschrift for Bernat Alexander, Budapest. Later translated into English by Ian Fairley, with a critical introduction, *Comparative Criticism* (Cambridge), Volume 13, 1991.

This long essay belongs to Lukacs's pre-Marxist period. It discusses the concept of literary form as an aesthetic as well as a social construct.

MACLEAN, Marie. "Pretexts and Paratexts: The Art of the Peripheral". *New Literary History,* Vol. 22, No. 2, Spring 1991, pp. 273–80.

"Paratext and text may be most clearly observed by applying the speech act theory. There are, as Genette observes, completely different illocutionary acts involved in the paratext and in the text of a work of fiction. Indeed, it is here that we see most clearly the working of the two "rules of law" which Serres posits as standing on either side of the textual threshold.The Paratext involves a series of first order illocutionary acts in which the author, the editor, or the preface are frequently using direct performatives." (p. 274)

MAJUMDAR, Swapan. *Comparative Literature: Indian Dimensions.* Calcutta: Papyrus, 1987.

This volume of essays is essential reading for Indian students of Comparative Literature. It considers the concepts of the aesthetic, influence and reception in the context of the colonial experience. "Periodization in Indian Literature" is by far the most sensible critical statement on the question of periodization in India. This volume addresses itself to specific issues of evaluation and historical description in the context of Indian literatures.

MAKKREEL, Rudolph A. "Traditional Historicism, Contemporary Interpretations of Historicity, and the History of Philosophy". *New Literary History*, Vol. 21, No. 4, Autumn 1991, pp. 977–91.

Particularly useful for students, being an account of the philosophical interpretation of history by Ranke, Kant and Heidegger.

McDONALD, Christie V. "Literary History: Interpretation Inside Out ?" *New Literary History*, Vol. 12, No. 2, Winter 1981, pp. 381–90.

This is a response to the articles in the special number. McDonald suggests that literary history and literary criticism are intricately interwoven; the response matches with Jameson's, but the point of view here is not Marxist.

McGANN, Jerome J. "The Text, the Poem, and the Problem of Historical Method". *New Literary History*, Vol. 12, No. 2, Winter 1981, pp. 269–88.

Discussion of the gap between extrinsic and intrinsic literary scholarship, between theory and history, and the inter-relations between these opposites.

MEDVEDEV, P.N. and BAKHTIN, M.M. *The Formal Method in Literary Scholarship: A Critical Introduction to Sociological Poetics*, translated from the Russian by Albert J. Wehrle. The Goucher College Series, Baltimore and London: The Johns Hopkins University Press, 1978.

Extremely important sourcebook for Russian Formalism; Part One—*The Object and Tasks of Marxist Literary Scholarship;* Part Two—*The Contribution to the History of the Formal Method*; Part Three—*The Formal Method in Poetics*; Part Four—*The Formal Method in Literary History.*

Part Four includes the following two chapters; "The Work of Art as a Datum External to Consciousness" and "The Formalist Theory of the Historical Development of Literature".

The second chapter deals with the following topics; the Formalist conception of literary-historical change; the psychological preconditions of literary development; the scheme of literary evolution; the absence of real evolution in Formalist theory of literary history; the Law of Automatization-Perceptibility as the basis of Formalism; Ideological material in Literary History; the logical and analytical extremes in the Formalist conception of artistic perception; the absence of the category of "historical time" in Formalist Literary History; History as the illustration of theory; Formalism and literary criticism.

Essential reading for the students of literary history.

MILLER, Christopher L. "Theories of Africans: The Question of Literary Anthropology", in *Race, Writing and Difference,* edited by Henry Louis Gates, Jr. Chicago and London: The University of Chicago Press, 1986, pp. 281–300.

History is a narrative which is inevitably restricted by the racial perspective of the historian.

MINK, Louis O. "History and Fiction as Modes of Comprehension". *New Literary History,* Vol. 1, No. 3, Spring 1970, p. 541ff. Reproduced in *New Directions in Literary History,* edited by Ralph Cohen, 1974, pp. 107–24.

An introductory account of the difference between the two modes of narration. Useful text for initiating classroom discussion on the topic.

MUKHERJEE, Sujit. "Towards a Literary History of India". *New Literary History,* Vol. 8, No. 2, Winter 1977, p. 225 ff. *Towards a Literary History of India,* Occasional Papers Series, Simla: Indian Institute of Advanced Study, 1975. *Some Positions on a Literary History of India.* Mysore: Central Institute of Indian Languages, 1981.

———. "Five Principles of Indian Literary History", translated into Marathi by S.G. Malshe, "*Bharatiya Vangmayetihas lekhanachi pach adbartatve". Alochana,* April 1982, reprinted in *Vangmayetihasachi Sankalpana,* edited by Dattatraya Punde. Pune: Pratima Prakashana, pp. 70–85.

Mukherjee is one of the very few Indian scholars who have explored the area of Comparative Literature systematically. His bibliographies are comprehensive, systematic and extremely useful for future research in the area of literary history.

NAGENDRA. "A History of Indian Literature: Basic Concept and Approaches", in *Emotive Basis of Literature and Other Essays,* New Delhi: B.R. Publishing, 1986.

NGUGI, wa Thiong'o. *Decolonizing the Mind: The Politics of Language in African Literature.* James Currey: London, 1986.

A passionately presented appeal for post-colonial writers to use their own languages for creative writing; reads the English canon as an agent of colonization in the context of African literature.

NIETZSCHE, Friedrich. *The Birth of Tragedy*, translated from the German by Francis Golffing. New York, 1956, pp. 19–36.

ORR, Linda. "The Revenge of Literature: A History of History". *New Literary History,* Vol. 18, No. 1, Autumn 1986, pp. 1–22.

An extremely illuminating and absorbing presentation about the breakdown of the initial togetherness between history and literature, and a succinct graph of the rise of self-consciousness in the two disciplines.

PASSMORE, John. "History of Art and History of Literature —A Commentary." *New Literary History*, Vol.3, No.3, Spring 1972, p. 575 ff.

PATKE, Rajeev, "Canons and Canon-Making in Indian Poetry in English". *Kavya Bharati: A Review of Indian Poetry*, No. 3, 1991, pp. 13–37.

The essay discusses the process and the politics of canon formation in Indian English literature during the last thirty years.

PERKIN, David, ed. *Theoretical Issues in Literary History.* Harvard English Studies, 16, Cambridge, Mass.: Harvard University Press, 1991.

Includes contributions specially written for this volume by Ernst Behler, Ronald Hush, Paul Cantor, Ralph Cohen, Alastair Fowler, John Frow, Ulker Gokberk, Jon Klancher, Jerome McGann, Michael Valdez, Moses, Mark Perker, David Perkin and John Paul Russo.

Particularly important are "Literary Classification" by David Perkin, "Genre Theory" by Ralph Cohen, "Problem of Origin" by Ernst Behler, and "The Two Histories" by Alastair Fowler.

PORTER, Carolyn. "History and Literature: After the New Historicism". *New Literary History*, Vol. 21, No. 2, Winter 1990, pp. 253–72.

The essay explores the potentials of New Historicism and explicates the present clash between Formalism and Historicism in critical practice. The essay is followed by a response from Rena Fraden, and a counter-response from Porter,

PRADHAN, S.V. "The Concept of Literary History: A Marxist Critique". *Journal of Arts and Ideas*, No. 6, January–March 1984, pp. 67–74.

A general Marxist approach.[1]

PRAWER, S.S. *Comparative Literary Studies: An Introduction.* London: Gerald Duckworth and Co, 1973.

Useful classroom material. The volume has the following chapters: What is Comparative Literature; National Character and National Literature; Reception and Communication; Influence, Analogy and Tradition; Translation and Adaptation; Themes and Prefiguration; Genres, Movements, Periods; Structures and Ideas, 'Placing'; Theory and Criticism.

PUNDE, Dattatraya, ed. *Vangmayetibhasacbi Sankalpana* (in Marathi). Pune: Pratima Prakashan, no-date.

Useful introductory bibliography of material on literary historiography in Marathi; various plans on history of Marathi literature are appended. The volume contains edited essays written in Marathi, or translated into Marathi.

RAJAN, B. "Literary History and Historical Criticism". *The Indian Journal of English Studies,* Vol. l, 1962, pp. 106–111.

Discusses the role of literary history *vis-a-vis* criticism.*

RAND, Nicholas and TOROK, Maria. "The Secret of Psychoanalysis; History Reads Theory". *Critical Inquiry,* Vol. 13, No. 2, Winter 1987, pp. 278–86.

A psychoanalysis of Psychoanalysis from a historical perspective.

RANDALL, Marilyn. "Appropriate Discourse: Plagiarism and Decolonization". *New Literary History,* Vol. 22, No. 3, 1991, pp. 525–41.

Discusses the concepts of authorship, propriety and individuality and their deviance in the context of post-colonial literatures to investigate the aesthetics of originality. Uses as epigraph a quotation from Jean Cocteau, "The original artist is incapable of copying. Therefore, in order to be original, he only has to copy".

RIEMENSCHNEIDER, Dieter. "The 'New' English Literatures in Historical and Political Perspective: Attempts towards a Comparative View of North/South Relationships in Commonwealth Literature". *New Literary History,* Vol. 18, No. 2, Winter 1987, pp. 425–35.

Introduces 'Commonwealth Literature' to Western audiences and discusses the role of comparative strategies in historicizing it.

__________. *The History and Historiography of Commonwealth Literature.* Tubingen: Gunter Narr Verlag, 1983.

In this volume edited by Riemenschneider, there are essays dealing with the question of historiography of post-colonial literatures in various regions of the British commonwealth. This volume still continues to be the only serious work on the history of Commonwealth Literature.

RIFFATERRE, Michael, "The Stylistic Approach to Literary History". *New Literary History,* Vol. 2, No. 1, Autumn 1970, p. 39 ff. Reprinted in *New Directions in Literary History,* edited by Ralph Cohen, 1974, pp. 147–64.

Discusses the complementarity of the extrinsic (historical) and the intrinsic (stylistic) approach to literature.

———.“Interpretation and Undecidability”. *New Literary History,* Vol. 12, No. 2, Winter 1981, pp. 227–42.

“History hopes to prove its validity by recovering the intention of the author. However, what the reader has in a text is a reflection of his own intentions, which stabilizes the moveable feast. Interpretation, therefore antagonizes the past while it purports to present it”.

Riffaterre discusses the referential fallacy in use of language for historical narratives. His writings belong to the structuralist-stylistics school.

ROBERTSON, D.W., Jr. “Some Observations on Method in Literary Studies”. *New Literary History,* Vol. 1, No. 1, Autumn 1969, p. 2. Reprinted in *New Directions in Literary History,* edited by Ralph Cohen, 1974, pp. 63–76.

Robertson’s essay is an excellent classroom text for fresh postgraduate students. It makes a case for the dynamics of semantic structures, which change the language functions from time to tirne as well as literary aesthetics, to be considered as the primary problem of historiography.

RUECKERT, William. “Literary Criticism and History: The Endless Dialectic ”. *New Literary History,* Vol. 6, No. 3, Spring 1975, p. 491 ff.

SANDERS, Wilbur. *The Dramatist and the Received Idea.* Cambridge: Cambridge University Press, 1968. Particularly useful is the chapter, “Literature as History”.

SCHEUB, Harold. “Oral Poetry and History”. *New Literary History,* Vol. 18, No. 3, Spring 1987, pp. 477–496.

Exposition of historical methods in oral poetry. Useful in making sense of the past in Indian literary traditions. “Like the poet, the oral historian fashions a number of unique images in the process of recounting events in the social and historical life of his people. These result from a combination of significant cultural feelings linked to important historical events. The convergence of the two results in historical motifs that are as useful to the historian as they are to the artist. In history as in poetry, they valued for their own sake and are frequently removed from their linear contexts, transcending the moment of history.” (p. 494)

SCHMIDT, Siegfried. “Problems of Empirical Research in Literary History”. *New Literary History,* Vol. 8, No. 2, Winter 1977, p. 213 ff.

SCHORSKE, Carl E. “History and the Study of Culture”. *New Literary History,* Vol. 21, No. 2, Winter 1991, pp. 407–20.

A survey of the role history has played from Herodotus to the glasnost in analysing culture. Reading for the specialist.

SHAFFER, E.S. *Comparative Criticism: An Annual Journal* (Cambridge), Vol. 6. Special number on "Translation Theory and Practice". Pp. 347–59 provide an excellent annotated bibliography on translation studies.

SHARMA, Ram Vilas. *Bharatiya Sahitya ke Itihas ki Samasyaen* (in Hindi). New Delhi: Vani Prakashan, 1986.

An extremely well-informed critique of notions of national history from a Marxist perspective. This is useful for its research value in the area of Indian socio-linguistics.

SLAWINS KI, Janusz. "Reading and Reader in the Literary Historical Process". *New Literary History*, Vol. 19, No. 3, Spring 1988, pp. 521–40.

Written in Warsaw, this informative essay is a sympathetic critique of the Jauss school of literary history. Of interest for advanced students of literary history.

SPILLER, Robert E. "Literary History", in *The Aims and Methods of Scholarship in Modern Languages and Literatures*, edited by James Thorpe (2nd edition). Hyderabad: American Studies Research Center, 1970, pp. 55–68.

The article contains explanations on Province of Literary History; Theory of Literary History; Sources of Literature; Shaping of Literary History and Methods of Literary History.*

SPITZER, Leo. *Linguistics and Literary History: Essays in Stylistics.* New York: Princeton University Press and Russell & Russell, 1948.

The introductory chapter, "Linguistics and Literary History", offers an illustrated defence of the use of linguistics in defining style-epochs, and therefore, the use of style-study in literary history. This is one of the earliest essays on literary stylistics. For that reason it is historically important. It is important also as an essay by a major comparatist. But, apart from these considerations, the title of the volume is grossly misleading.

STIMPSON, Catherine R. "Reading for Love: Canons, Paracanons, and Whistling Jo March". *New Literary History*, Vol. 21, No. 4, Autumn 1990, pp. 957–76.

Introduces the concept of 'paracanon': "A paracanon recognizes our need for some cultural shelter, a tidy site. Simultaneously, a paracanon finds 'the canon' both a house of orthodoxy and a house of cards. To mediate between these two perceptions, the paracanon is a tenet that neither ranks cultural works nor travels a compromised *via media* among them. Instead, it negotiates a particular lease on the life of their commonalities and differences. How can a text join the paracanon? Texts are canonical if some people have loved and do love them." (p. 958)

STOCK, Brian. "Language and Cultural History". *New Literary History*, Vol. 18, No. 3, Spring 1987, pp. 657–70.

Presents a version of the Reader Response theory, whose central assertions are close to Jauss's but also invokes the linguistic structuralism of Saussure together with the phenomenological hermeneutics of Paul Recour. "In my view it is an error to focus on the written text alone. The essential element is the community, the living people whose minds are peopled and shared by thoughts, intentions, and potential actions. The normal hermeneutic activity is the experience of the text along with individual interpretations...." (p. 669)

STONE, Donald R. "Role of Literary History". *Journal of Medieval and Renaissance Studies,* 15, 1985, pp. 115–24.

Views about the past and pastness, "how and why a literary historian might have approached the same text." *

STURROCK, John. "Writing Between the Lines: The Language of Translation". *New Literary History*, Vol.4, Autumn 1990, pp. 994–1013.

TAINE, Hippolyte. 'Introduction' in *History of English Literature*, (1864), translated from the French by Henry von Laun. London, 1900, Vol. I, pp. 1–2, 5–9, 13–19.

TOMPKINS, Jane. " 'Indians': Textualism, Morality, and the Problem of History". *Critical Inquiry,* Vol. 13, No. 1, Autumn 1986, pp. 101–19.

Through a case study, this article discusses the post-structuralist perspective on historical narration.

VALDES, Mario J. "Heuristic Models of Inquiry". *New Literary History,* Vol. 12, No. 2, Winter 1981, pp. 253–67.

"A theory of literal classification that accepts phenomenological literary theory and the necessity of classification. In such a theory any concept of forms must be considered a heuristic device established for purposes of understanding the nature of literary expression. The main question for this theory is form change." (p. 265)

VIPPER, Yuri B. "National Literary History in History of World Literature: Theoretical Principles of Treatment". *New Literary History,* Vol. 16, No. 3, Spring 1985, p. 545 ff.

WASWO, Richard, "The History that Literature Makes". *New Literary History,* Vol. 19, No. 3, Spring 1988, pp. 541–64.

Argues that literature changes history by shaping the forces behind history: a history of the contribution of literature in shaping the general history should form an important feature of literary history.

WEIMANN, Robert. "Past Significance and Present Meaning in Literary History", in *New Directions in Literary History,* edited by Ralph Cohen, 1974, pp. 43–62.

An extremely valuable critique of the attitude of New Criticism to Literary History. Argument in favour of the dialectical approach in which literature itself is history.

———. *Structure and Society in Literary History: Studies in the History and Theory of Historical Criticism.* London: The University Press of Virginia (1976) & Lawrence and Wishart, 1977.

The central thesis of this important book is that "the structure of literature is corelated with its function in society and that this corelation deserves to be studied in terms of both 'genesis' (or *Entstebungsgeschichte*) and 'impact' (*Wirkungsgcschichte*)". (p. 273)

———."History and the Issue of Authority in Representation: The Elizabethan Theatre and the Reformation". *New Literary History*, Vol. 17, No. 3, Spring 1986, pp. 449–76.

Views "representation in terms of its changeful uses in literary history, as a function of social and textual identification, limitation, extension, affirmation, and even...disruption" (p. 449). Offers a theory of Authority in terms of history of literature.

WELLEK, Rene. *Concepts of Criticism*, edited by Stephen G. Nicholas, Jr. New Haven and London: Yale University Press, 1963.

This collection has several very useful and lucid essays, the more important among them being: "Literary Theory, Criticism and History" (pp. 1–21); "The Concept of Evolution in Literary History" (pp. 37–53); "The Crisis of Comparative Literature" (pp. 282–95).

Also important is: *The Rise of English Literary History.* Chapel Hill: The University of North Carolina Press, 1947. So far the only account of literary history in England during the eighteenth century and the first half of the nineteenth century.

WHITE, Hayden. "The Politics of Historical Interpretation: Discipline and De-sublimination". *Critical Inquiry,* Vol. 9, No. 1, September 1982, pp. 113–38.

Politics is seen as a condition of the possibility of interpretation as a social activity.

———. "Literary History: The Point of It All". *New Literary History,* Vol. 2, No. 1, Winter 1971, pp. 173–85.

Comments on the essays included in the same volume of *New Literary History.*

———. "Interpretation in History". *New Literary History*, Vol. 4, No. 2, Winter 1973, pp. 281–314.

A comprehensive discussion of the status of 'interpretation' and the place of' narration' in history.

———. "The Problem of Change in Literary History". *New Literary History,* Vol. 7, No. 1, Autumn 1975, pp. 97–111.

A structuralist argument about historical changes taking place in language and literature.

WOELFFLIN, Heinrich. *Principles of Art History: The Problem of the Development of Style in Later Art,* translated by M.D. Hottinger. New York: Dover Publications, 1950.

(Entries marked with an asterisk have been supplied by Dr. D.D. Punde.)

Index

Abhinavagupta, 35, 37, 46
Akenside, 73
Akkama, 52
Ali, Sayyid, 58
Ambedkar, B.R., 119, 121
Amin, Shahid, 116
Anandavardhana, 36, 37, 158
Anantha Murthy, U.R., 123, 124, 125, 127
Apte, V.V., 17
Archer, William, 81, 82
Arnold, David, 116
Arnold, Mathew, 90, 91, 93
Ashoka, 41
Ashvagosha, 37, 148
Aslah, Muhammad, 59
Aubadi, Taqu, 57
Aurobindo, Sri, 81, 82, 83, 109, 110, 115,132
Azad, Mir Gulam Ali, 59

Badaoni, Al, 58, 60–65
Baldick, Chris, 89, 92
Balfour, Francis, 76
Bana, 40
Banabhatta, 38
Basham, A.L., 76
Battuta, Ibn, 148
Beckett, 153, 161
Bedii, Mirza, 59
Bhadra, Gautam, 116
Bhamah, 36
Bharata, 19, 37, 39, 40, 150
Bharavi, 38
Bhartrihari, 21–28, 32, 38, 158
Bhaskara, 128
Bhatta, Jayanta, 26
Bhatta, Kumarila, 24, 25, 26
Bhatta, Narayana, 26
Bhattacharya, K.C., 26
Bhattanayaka, 37, 38
Bhattatauta, 37
Bhattenduraja, 37
Bhavabhuti, 38, 40, 113
Bhoja, 19, 20, 37
Bhutiraja, 37
Binis, Isma'il, 58
Blair, Hugh, 68, 69, 90
Boccacio, 152
Bonaparte, Napoleon, 5
Brough, John, 158
Browne, Robert, 88
Buddha, 119
Burke, Edmund, 67
Byron, Lord, 79

Callewaert, W.M., 64
Carr, E.H., 15
Cecil, William, 88
Chaitanya, 52
Chakrabarty, Dipesh, 116
Chakravorty Spivak, Gayatri, 113, 116, 117, 118
Chanakya, 39
Chatterjee, Partha, 116
Chaucer, 70, 152
Chittal, Yashwant, 123

Cohn, Bernard, 76, 117
Coleridge, 79, 110
Collingwood, 15
Collins, John Churton, 93
Coomaraswamy, A.K., 127–130
Crane, R.S., 9, 99, 100, 101, 103, 104, 106

Dadu, 64
Dandin, 36, 38, 40, 150
Das, Sisir Kumar, 113, 114, 116
Davy, William, 76
Defoe, 73
Derrida, Jacq*ues*, 116
Desai, Shantinath, 123
Devanuru, Mahadeva, 123
Dhananjaya, 19
Dignaga, 24, 25, 26
Dossie, Robert, 89
Dow, Alexander, 75, 76
Dryden, John, 89, 110, 152
Durkheim, 155

Ekanatha, 51, 52, 53, 55, 150
Eliot, T.S., 148, 159

Fairley, Ian, 102
Farquhar, J.N., 115
Fazl, Abul, 75
Ferishta, 75
Foucault, 99
Foxe, John, 88
Freud, 13, 140

Gandhi, 110
Ganin, Devadhi, 41
Gervinus, 6, 98
Gilchrist, John A., 76
Gladwin, Francis, 76
Gramsci, Antonio, 116
Gray, 73
Grierson, 112
Guha, Ranajit, 116, 117

Hadley, George, 76
Hafiz, 68
Halhed, Nathaniel Brassey, 76, 78
Hamadani, Gulam, 60
Hardiman, David, 116
Harsha, 38
Hazin, Ali, 59
Heaney, 153
Hegel, 15, 72, 99
Hemachandra, 41, 42, 52, 150
Hobbes, Thomas, 67
Homer, 78, 110
Humboldt, Wilhelm Von, 6
Hunter, John, Mrs., 68

Iser, Wolfgang, 98

Jauss, 98, 99, 104, 105
Jayadeva, 41,150, 167
Jnanadeva, 45, 46–55, 65, 150
Johnson, Dr., 89
Jones, William, Sir, 68, 75–83, 95, 96, 155
Joyce, 153, 161

Kabir, 51, 53, 54, 64
Kakar, Sudhir, 145, 167
Kalhana, 56
Kalidasa, 38, 40, 64, 110, 149
Kallata, 37
Kamban, 148
Karanth, Shivaram, 123
Karve, Iravati, 29
Kasim, Mirza, 75
Katyayana, 25, 33, 34, 37
Keats, John, 110
Kermode, Frank, 130
Ketkar, S.V., 29
Khan, Matimad, 75
Khan, Nawwab Ali Ibrahim, 60
Khan, Nawwab Azimuddaula, 60
Khushrau, Amir, 52, 56
Kirkpatric, William, 76
Kolatkar, Arun, 136
Kshemaraja, 35
Kumaradasa, 38
Kumarapala, 41
Kundakunda, 27

Lacan, Jacques, 143, 144
Lahari, Abu'l-Barakat Munir, 57

Lakshamanagupta, 37
Lankesh, P., 123
Leavis, F.R., 89, 99
Levi-Strauss, 155
Lodi, Sher Khan, 59
Lomharshana, 30, 33
Lukacs, Gyorgy, 99, 102, 103, 104, 106

Macaulay, Lord, 81, 82, 93
Macpherson, 153
Magha, 38
Mahasvetadevi, 117, 118
Marx, Karl, 15, 119
Masti, (Venkatesh Iyengar), 123
Max Muller, F., 34, 81
Mill, James, 81
Miller, J. Hillis, 152
Milton, John, 67, 70, 159
Mir, Taqi Mir, 59
Mira, 52
Misra, Mandana, 24–25
Misra, Parthasarathi, 26
More, Hannah, 90
Moore, Thomas, 79
Mujeeb, Muhammad, 60
Mukherjee, Sujit, 15, 96, 111, 113, 114, 115, 116, 132
Mukula, 37

Naipaul, V.S., 148, 161
Namadeva, 51, 64, 150
Namvarsingh, 131–132
Nanak, 51, 53
Nasib, 59
Nemade, Bhalchandra, 123, 125, 126, 127
Nietzsche, Friedrich, 15, 130
Nisyani, Muhammad Tahir, 59
Nivedita, Sister, 148
Niyogi Balslev, Anindita, 16

Orr, Linda, 56

Pandey, Gyan, 116
Panini, 5, 24, 32, 33, 39, 150
Patanjali, 26, 33, 39
Patke, Rajeev, 127, 130,
Pawar, Daya, 113, 120,
Piltz, Anders, 88
Pindar, 78
Plato, 78, 128
Plotinus, 75, 128
Pope, Alexander, 67, 89, 110, 152
Pradhan, Srinivas, 111
Pravarasena, 41
Punde, Dattatraya, 111,112
Putappa, K.V., 123

Quadiri, Mir Qudratullah, 60

Raghavan, V., 32
Rahman, Tariq, 162–165
Raina, Motilal, 111
Rajasekhara, 17, 18, 19, 20, 38, 41, 42, 133, 150
Rajwade, V.K., 112
Raleigh, Walter, 93
Ramananda, 51
Ranke, 15
Razi, Amin, 57
Rice, Stanley, 119
Richards, I.A., 89, 99
Richardson, John, 76
Rocher, Ludo, 32
Rousseau, 73
Rushdie, Salman, 113, 122, 161, 165

Safiq, Lakshmi Narayan, 59
Said, Edward, 77
Sangari, Kumkum, 113, 121, 140
Sankara, 25, 39
Sarkar, Sumit, 116
Satavahana, 41
Sattari, Gauti, 59
Saussure, Ferdinand, 155
Saushuka, 37
Schiller, 106, 107
Schimmel, Annemarie, 58
Shakespeare, William, 64, 70, 73, 110
Sharma, Ram Vilas, 16
Shaw, George Bernard, 153
Shejwalkar, T.S., 112

Shelley, 79, 80, 110
Shipley, William, 89
Simon, Joan, 86
Sindi, Mirak, 59
Singer, Milton, 31
Sipahi, 62
Sirajuddin, 59
Sohoni, Krishnaji, 56
Somananda, 37
Southey, Robert, 79
Spenser, 70, 72
Sridhara, 26
Subandhu, 38
Sudraka, 38
Sukhtankar, V.S., 29

Tejasvi, Poomachandra, 123
Thapar, Romila, 16, 28, 149, 151
Thompson, 66, 67
Trilling, Lionel, 130
Tilak, B.G., 33
Tukarama, 51, 53
Tulsidas, 52, 148
Thyagaraja, 52, 150

Urfi, 57
Utpaldeva, 37

Vakpatiraja, 41
Valmiki, 110
Virgil, 12, 110
Vishakhadatta, 38, 40
Vyasa, 30, 32, 110

Warton, Joseph, 68
Warton, Thomas, 6, 66–74, 79, 94, 95, 96
Warton, Thomas, (elder), 68
Wellek, Rene, 66, 68, 69, 72
Wilkins, Charles, 76
Wordsworth,William, 79

Yashovarman, 41
Yeats, W.B., 153
Young, 73

Zimmer, Heinrich, 11